GOVERNMENT RELATIONS IN THE HEALTH CARE INDUSTRY

GOVERNMENT RELATIONS IN THE HEALTH CARE INDUSTRY

Edited by
Peggy Leatt and Joseph Mapa

Westport, Connecticut
London

Library of Congress Cataloging-in-Publication Data

Government relations in the health care industry / edited by Peggy Leatt, Joseph Mapa.
　　p. cm.
　Includes bibliographical references and index.
　ISBN 1–56720–513–5 (alk. paper)
　1. Medical policy—United States.　2. Medical policy—Canada.　3. Health planning—United States.　4. Health planning—Canada.　5. Health services administration—United States.　6. Health services administration—Canada.
　I. Leatt, Peggy.　II. Mapa, Joseph, 1950–
RA395.A3 G684　2003
362.1'0973—dc21　　　　2002073912

British Library Cataloguing in Publication Data is available.

Library of Congress Catalog Card Number: 2002073912
ISBN: 1-56720-513-5

First published in 2003

Praeger Publishers, 88 Post Road West, Westport, CT 06881
An imprint of Greenwood Publishing Group, Inc.
www.praeger.com

Printed in the United States of America

🔁™

The paper used in this book complies with the Permanent Paper Standard issued by the National Information Standards Organization (Z39.48–1984).

10　9　8　7　6　5　4　3　2　1

To George and Sarah Pink
Peggy Leatt

To Sheryl, Janet, Michelle, and Ryan Mapa
Joseph Mapa

Contents

Introduction and Commentary

Peggy Leatt and Joseph Mapa

Effective relationships with governments are important dynamics for health care organizations around the world. The complex array of health care organizations that make up a country's health system is an important factor that influences the health and well-being of communities and their citizens. In most modern societies, government decisions play a major role in determining how many and what type of resources are allocated to the health system. At the macro level, governments influence the way systems are organized, financed, and managed. As a consequence, health care organizations are affected significantly by government legislation, policies, programs and resource allocations, and by the myriad decisions taken at a micro level that affect how health services are governed and operated.

Relationships between governments, providers, and citizens are paramount in determining the extent to which citizens are provided with acceptable levels of health services to meet their needs. Governments, as representatives of the public, are accountable to their citizens for ensuring appropriate levels of service. Governments, therefore, are an important component of the multifaceted environments of health care organizations when they are developing corporate strategies and, indeed, can drastically affect their performance or survival. In Canada, for example, health care organizations for whom relationships with governments are a struggle, may be missing the full potential of the care and services they can provide. In turn, health care organizations are essential components of these governments' environments if they are to develop and implement appropriate health care policies. In short, harmonious relationships among governments and health care organizations are necessary if all parties are to meet their objectives of maintaining and improving the health of the population. We propose that the development of a sound government relations strategy is vital for health services organizations in today's society.

The focus of this book is on the dynamics of effective government relations for health care organizations in Canada and the United States. Our goals are that readers will:

- understand how the external environment of governments and health care organizations impact on health policy decisions;
- understand accountability relationships, that is, who is accountable to whom for what aspects of health policy;
- examine the usefulness of principles of strategic planning and management for developing effective government relations;
- understand the value and limitations of advocacy and negotiation processes in achieving desired effects on health policies and government relations;
- be aware of different strategies and tools for enhancing government relationships so that they can be sustained over time; and
- recognize the need for continuous monitoring of government relations and their effectiveness.

APPROACH

The approach in this book is to present background information on government relationships with health care organizations that reflects the complexities of health policy processes in both the United States and Canada. First, an overview of key legislative- and policy-related factors is provided to set the stage for in-depth discussions. We introduce the idea of strategic planning and management as essential, but sometimes neglected, tasks for establishing and maintaining effective government relationships. A detailed perspective is provided on issues of accountability—a topic fraught with complexities that defy simple definition and interpretation. Illustrations are also given of processes of advocacy and negotiation, two essential steps in interactions among governments, providers, and the public. A series of case examples from both Canada and the United States illustrate the variety of strategies that are used to create structure and processes for effective government relations. In the final chapter we synthesize the lessons learned and offer suggestions for the continuation of effective government relationships and the monitoring of performance.

We are fortunate to have contributions from a diverse set of leaders in health services management and policy. All the authors have distinguished track records in working with governments and health care organizations. They have been forthright in elaborating on their experiences and have generously provided insights that we can all benefit from. We have included perspectives from both public and private sectors, as well as from inside and outside the health system.

Governments and Health Policy Processes

At least three levels of government exist in both the United States and Canada: the national or federal level; the state or provincial level; and the county, local, or municipal level. Each level of government has the authority to make decisions and is entrusted by society to define public policies in keeping with the wishes of the public they serve. The "government" is often used as a general term to include politicians, legislators, and bureaucrats—all individuals with the authority and mandate to take action on behalf of citizens.

Health Policy

Health policy refers to the set of decisions made by governments that pertain to individuals' health and the delivery of health services. The state of "health" is used broadly to refer to the mental and physical state associated with the sense of well-being of individuals who may or may not be associated with the utilization of health services. Determinants of health are known to include a broad but complex array of environmental factors including levels of poverty, social, cultural, and economic circumstances, lifestyles and behaviors, education, nutrition, employment, genetic propensity, and other environmental factors less well understood.

Health policies can take on several different forms. The more formalized policies are laws that authorize the government to act in specific ways on behalf of the public. Rules and regulations are delineated that specify how laws are to be implemented. In turn, rules and regulations set the framework for the development of programs and priorities.

Policy Making

Policy-making processes tend to operate as open systems working in reiterative cycles. This means that policies are in a continuous state of fluctuation which can be changed or modified by external influences (Longest, 2002). The process begins with inputs from the external environment or from the general context in which the policy is being made. Inputs can include a broad range of information factors that are thought to impact on health and health care and which act as cues to stimulate or precipitate discussion. Inputs can include biological, cultural, demographic, ecological, economical, ethical, legal, psychological, social, and technical inputs. Other aspects of the environment can be presented that express preferences of individuals, organizations, and interest groups such as providers of health services, or of consumers and citizens who often have well-defined positions on how to improve the provision of services. A second phase is that of policy formation where the agenda for discussion is set. These policies are derived from those inputs received that define problems to be solved as well as possible solutions. At this stage, background work is completed to assess the political circumstances, to judge the extent to which the policy is likely to be approved, and to draft potential legislation. Once policy is approved, rules and regulations for implementation of policy can be drafted and decisions about specific programs and resource allocation can be made. While this process appears straightforward, it may be fraught with challenges. At any stage, there may be feedback suggesting policy modifications by persons assessing the impact of the policies as they are being formulated. Individuals, organizations, or interest groups who may be experiencing the consequences of new policies or policy modifications can present feedback. Politicians, members of the government bureaucracy, and representatives of provider and consumer groups are constantly on the lookout for a "window of opportunity" to make their views known. Stimuli for policy changes can come "top down" from politicians, cabinet, and other decision-making bodies made up of political representatives; other sources include members of government bureaucracies or briefs from nongovernment entities such as hospitals, physician groups, or special-interest consumer groups.

Effective Government Relations

Governments are an important component of the external environment of all health care organizations, whether public or private, because they set laws and regulations in which health care organizations must operate to survive. Conversely, health care organizations are essential components of the external environment of governments. Governments need providers in order to implement policies and they need consumers for their approval of the strategies they have undertaken as governors on behalf of all citizens. It is, therefore, in both governments' and health care organizations' interests for their relationships to be effective. Historically, these relationships have tended to be haphazard, with both parties assuming reactive positions to the other parties' perspectives and demands. Clearly, as health services become more complex, and pressures mount to meet the public's needs for quality health services, this ad hoc approach is no longer appropriate.

For government relationships to work, formulation and implementation of proactive strategies are necessary. These strategies involve multiple considerations—positioning your government relations initiatives in concordance with government policy goals; building political coalitions; enlisting public influence; defining stakeholder interests; building, managing, and developing relationships at all levels; cultivating and lobbying the right people; timing interventions for maximum effectiveness; adopting the appropriate style; undertaking policy research; and negotiating win-win solutions. Both governments and health care organizations must take active steps to understand the other side of the story—the other parties' perspectives. Health care organizations need to incorporate government relationships into their strategic planning processes with the goals of building and maintaining effective relationships. Effective relationships require sheer hard work to build momentum over time. Simply knowing whom to talk to about what in government structures and understanding their goals provides opportunities for health care organizations to have input into the decisions. This kind of interaction opens doors for health care organizations to reinforce government decisions that are important to them.

There are three broad strategies that both governments and health care organizations need to adopt to set the stage for effective government relationships:

- *Understanding the external environments* in which governments and health care organizations exist and operate. For example, what are the prevalent social, political, and economic circumstances that facilitate or inhibit effective government relationships?

- *Understanding the roles and responsibilities* of governments at different levels as well as those of the critical provider and consumer organizations. For example, knowing who is accountable to whom for which decisions inside and outside government.

- *Developing a strategic plan* to outline a vision for government relationships including how such relationships should be managed. For example, finding out what goals and objectives each organization has in common with the other and exploring how joint strategies can be developed to benefit both organizations.

The Contexts of Canadian and U.S. Health Care

Canada and the United States share many characteristics and have a great deal in common, not the least important being a geographical border stretching the breadth of both countries. For both trade and pleasure activities, Canadians and Americans can move from one country to the other with relative freedom. Both countries have populations with similar demographics. A wide variety of ethnic backgrounds make up the American and Canadian populations, with recent arrivals being relatively young. While these different ethnic groups exist in harmony in both countries, Americans have adopted a "melting pot" philosophy where citizens develop strong allegiances to the country they have immigrated to. Canada on the other hand has a "mosaic" philosophy, where individuals are encouraged to retain customs and traditions from "the old country" while adapting and blending into Canadian ways.

Canada and the United States also share many cultural and social factors. For example, as North Americans we watch the same TV programs, go to the same movies, eat the same fast food, shop at the same types of malls, and enjoy the same sports. New fads for music and fashions spread quickly throughout the continent. There are subtle nuances in day-to-day living of which each country's citizens are rightfully proud. It has often been observed that communications and collaborations are easier north/south than east/west, irrespective of country boundaries. For instance, distances may be shorter, transport and travel may be easier, and occupations may be more alike. Certainly, American and Canadian economies are interconnected, which tends to be reflected in similar business and job opportunities and unemployment rates in both countries.

In terms of politics there are many similarities. Canada and the United States both have democratic governments with nationwide decision making as well as semiautonomous regional (state/provincial) bodies; however, Canada's political system is based on a parliamentary model that has evolved from its historical roots in Britain, whereas the United States has a balance-of-powers approach (see: Chapter 1). These differences influence the ways in which health policies are created, adopted, and modified.

The health of the populations in both countries has similar characteristics, with the major causes of illness and death being heart disease and cancer. The population in each of these countries is aging and, as in most developed countries, governments are trying to figure out how to finance and manage the health problems of the elderly. New medical technologies are developing that can also add to the possibilities of people living longer. All of these factors have led to common concerns about how to contain health care costs while sustaining the quantity and quality of services that meet the public's expectations. Neither country seems to have found the perfect solution, so both countries are engaged in attempts to cap expenditures, eliminate waste, and improve efficiency.

The Systems in Brief

There are substantial differences in the two countries' approaches to health services financing and delivery systems. While health care systems in the United States and Canada began in the same way as a mechanism to ensure citizens had medical and hospital care when needed, in more recent years the systems have become quite diverse (Raffel, 1997). In Canada, in the 1960s, health care services evolved as a "right" for all citizens and health care became symbolic of equality and liberalism. A national health care program emerged with joint funding by federal and provincial governments. Voluntary hospitals, with their community-based governance structures that encouraged community participation, flourished. Dynamics hinged upon relationships between governments and the medical profession. The medical profession was successful in negotiating a fee-for-service payment structure as well as maintaining independently constituted medical staffs within the hospitals. In contrast, health services in the United States have evolved through entrepreneurial market structures with both private and public payers competing to contain costs (Tuohy, 1999).

In the United States, the federal government has responsibility for the provision of services to military personnel, veterans, Native Americans, and persons in prisons. The state governments are able to raise taxes to provide for health services. States are responsible for licensing hospitals and health professionals, public health services, and services for individuals with mental health problems. Government spending accounts for about 43 percent of health expenditures; the rest is from the private sector. Privately funded insurance, obtained through employers, is the most common source of health care funding as well as the organization and delivery of health services. Most of the care is provided through managed care organizations that contract with individual organizations, agencies, and physician groups to serve an enrolled population. The United States spends more on health services than any other country. Still, there are unsolved problems of access. It has been estimated that there are between 40 and 50 million people from vulnerable populations who are not insured.

For those citizens who do not have health insurance, or who need supplemental insurance, Medicare and Medicaid are available. Medicare covers services for the elderly such as hospitalization for inpatient services, skilled nursing facilities and rehabilitation, and some home care, including nursing, physical therapy, or rehabilitation. Coverage also provides for physician services, laboratory tests, medical equipment, flu vaccinations, drugs that cannot be administered by the patients themselves, most supplies, and diagnostic tests. Medicare does not cover long-term care, dental services, hearing aids, or eyeglasses. Medicaid, which serves about 40 million of America's poorest people, covers acute and long-term care, including inpatient and outpatient hospital services, physicians, nurses, and laboratory services.

Managed care organizations, such as Health Maintenance Organizations and Preferred Provider Organizations, provide a range of health programs to an enrolled population for a fixed fee, with the goal of reducing health expenditures while maintaining quality. Over 50 percent of persons with insurance are in some type of managed care arrangement. These organizations are competitive and try to control unnecessary use of medical services. Funding is usually by capitation and physicians are usually paid by mixed methods of capitation and fee for service. Historically, citizens have placed a high value on choice in obtaining health services; most recent observations suggest managed care now tends to operate by decreasing individual choice and by determining which doctors and hospitals their enrollees can use without paying out-of-plan rates (Starr, 2000).

In Canada, the publicly financed health system is very popular with Canadian citizens and has been widely regarded as the nation's most cherished social program (Naylor, 1999). Canada has a "single payer" health system without formal recognition of a private sector provision of services. The federal government contributes to the funding for health services on a cost-sharing basis with the provinces. Similar to the United States, the federal government retains direct responsibilities for health services for Canada's First Nations people and veterans. Through the Canada Health Act, provincial governments are delegated responsibility for the delivery of health services. The act mandates that health services shall be provided free at the point of service to cover hospital and medical services. Health services will be guided by principles that mandate comprehensive services that are equally accessible to all Canadians, portable across provinces, and publicly administered.

Although Canadians have expressed pride in the health care system they have built, in recent years questions are being raised as to whether the system can be sustained in its present form, given escalating costs. Canadians are concerned that the public system will not be available when needed and there are complaints that waiting lists for certain procedures and specialty services are too long. Public opinion has suggested that a market-driven system with parallel private services is not acceptable to many Canadians. Yet, at the present time, approximately one-third of the total cost of health services is provided by private sector sources.

In summary, in both countries, political leaders face difficult times in meeting the expectations of the public in terms of their health care needs. The problem is to find solutions to health system issues that will be acceptable to the electorate but will not cause undue economic difficulties (Raffel, 1997). Donna Shalala, the longest serving secretary of health and human services in U.S. history (1993–2000), summed up her experiences with health policy change by saying: "All my experience as a political scientist told me that you can enact sweeping health reform only when the public agree with the proposed solution. Simple dissatisfaction with the current system is not enough to drive through a major change" (Shalala & Reinhardt, 1999). Effective government relationships that bring together politicians, bureaucrats, health care providers, and the public must become an important priority.

ORGANIZATION OF THE BOOK

We have organized this book around three sections. The first section provides a broad framework for thinking about government relationships from a systemwide perspective. Chapter 1, by Raisa Deber and A. Paul Williams, gives an introduction to politics in the United States and Canada and a description of policy processes in each. Chapter 2, by Beaufort Longest, provides insights into principles of strategic planning and management as they apply to government relationships in health care. Chapter 3, by Colleen Flood, consists of an in-depth discussion of issues of accountability in health care in several different countries.

The second section of the book focuses on processes used by individuals and organizations as they attempt to exert influence over policy-making processes. In Chapter 4, Gary Filerman and D. David Persaud describe approaches to advocacy, including some examples from the United States and Canada. Mary Jane Mastorovich, in Chapter 5, elaborates on processes of negotiation and their use in interactions between health care organizations and governments.

In the third section of the book (Chapters 6–11), we draw upon the experiences of experts in government relations to illustrate a variety of strategies and techniques that have shown some success. Chapter 6, by Thomas Ricketts and Melissa Fruhbeis, provides the experiences of a federal/state coalition to meet the health needs of a particular population. Chapter 7, by Bruce MacLellan, describes the relationships between government bureaucracy and hospitals that were experienced in Ontario during a period of major reform. Owen Adams and Kevin Doucette outline in Chapter 8 the tough processes needed to maintain working relationships with the Canadian Medical Association and government. In Chapter 9, Darlene Burgess and Gail Warden describe the experiences of the Henry Ford Health System in establishing a department with specific responsibilities for developing and maintaining effective government relationships. Chapter 10 by Pamela Jeffery is able to capture the perspective of consumers and describes how to engage individuals at the grass roots in working with governments. We conclude this section of the book with Chapter 11 by Ginger Graham, who explores the important role of a CEO and other corporate leadership in creating and maintaining government relationships.

In the conclusion we provide our synthesis of what has been learned during the process of putting together the information and experiences in this book. We stress the importance of a strategic approach to effective government relationships and the advantages of including such strategies in the strategic plan of every health care organization. We give examples of some goals for developing and maintaining effective government relationships in health care, and emphasize the importance of monitoring the effectiveness of this type of program.

MAIN AUDIENCES FOR THE BOOK

This book is written for health care leaders in the United States, Canada, and elsewhere, who spend a large portion of their work life trying to figure out how to establish comfortable working relationships in health care that promote good health policy. We hope that health care executives, who must be conversant with the principles, practices, and strategies of good government relations, will find the experiences of other practitioners helpful. The number of M.B.A. programs that now incorporate this subject in their curricula is evidence of the growing importance of this topic. Our informal sampling of health care executives in both the public and private sectors suggests they spend a significant portion of their time on activities that promote their own organization by influencing health policy directions. This book may be of interest to politicians who may be struggling to understand the complexities of overt and covert relationships among individuals and organizations in health care. Professional bureaucrats, who are often put in the difficult position of interpreting various interest groups' perspectives to both the political and health care arena, may also gain insights from the candid experiences described. We hope that consumer and other interest groups find solace in the description of strategies, and that they will be encouraged to continue their struggles to have their say and to make their mark on health policies.

There may be members of the business community with an interest in government relations, such as suppliers of technologies, pharmaceutical companies, and consulting firms, who will find the text of value in their attempts to venture into the complex maze of government interactions.

One last word; in this book we sought to combine practice and theory in a way that could not be achieved alone. Thus, we are very grateful to our contributors, each of whom offers unique insights. Special thanks must also be offered to Rose York Jones who thoughtfully improved this text with useful suggestions and provided valuable assistance and coordination.

REFERENCES

Longest, B.B., Jr., (2002). *Health policymaking in the United States* (2nd ed.). Chicago: Health Administration Press.

McDonough, J.E. (2000). *Experiencing politics: A legislator's stories of government and health care*. Berkeley: University of California Press.

Naylor, C.D. (1999). Health care in Canada: Incrementalism under fiscal distress. *Health Affairs, May/June 18* (3): 9–26.

Raffel, M.W. (Ed.). (1997). *Health care and reform in industrialized countries*. University Park, PA: Pennsylvania State University Press.

Shalala, D.E., & Reinhardt, U.E. (1999). Interview. Viewing the U.S. health care system from within: Candid talk from HHS. *Health Affairs, May/June 18* (3): 47–55.

Starr, P. (2000). Health care reform and the new economy. *Health Affairs, November/December 19* (6): 23–32.

Tuohy, C.H. (1999). Dynamics of a changing health sphere: The United States, Britain and Canada. *Health Affairs, May/June 18* (3): 114–143.

Part I

Systemwide Perspectives

Chapter 1

Government, Politics, and Stakeholders in the United States and Canada

Raisa B. Deber and A. Paul Williams

INTRODUCTION

In both Canada and the United States, hospital leaders find themselves in an environment of rapid change, new expectations, challenges, and uncertainty, an environment aptly characterized by one prominent observer as "permanent white water."

On the demand side, aging and more culturally diverse populations, biomedical advances, and changing social values and expectations generate new and more complex pressures to deliver care. Patients, communities, and funders call more loudly for greater influence over decisions affecting their health and their budgets. The scope of what is considered health care continues to expand, reflecting both technological advances and an increasing emphasis on health promotion and community-based care. A declining proportion of such care needs to be delivered to inpatients in conventional acute care settings, radically changing the meaning and purpose of hospitals. Indeed, the health system itself is increasingly seen as only one, and perhaps not even the most important, determinant of health. On the supply side, seemingly unpredictable swings in requirements for and availability of health human resources pose challenges not only for long-term planning, but for day-to-day operations. Hospital leaders, under pressure from consumers and funders, must look for ways to manage within constrained budgets, and demonstrate "efficiency" by what seems like the management innovation of the month (Decter, 1994; Kleinke, 2001). Health providers are caught between two often conflicting sets of expectations—those inherent in running a cost-effective business, and those inherent in providing needed services to often vulnerable populations.

In this chapter, we focus on how governments and their policies shape the health care environment and how these policies can be understood. In all developed nations, governments have long been critical players in the business of health care, wearing the sometimes conflicting hats of *funder, regulator,* and even *deliverer* of health services, as well as the badge of *guardian* of the public interest. In Canada, for instance, the vast majority of hospital expenditures derive from public sector sources. Precise figures vary—the Canadian Institute for Health Information (CIHI), the national body that acts as a custodian for health data, places the value at about 90 percent of expenditures (2000) whereas the data set from the Organization for Economic Cooperation and Development (OECD) estimates it as 86 percent of expenditures for inpatient care (2001). Even in the United States, which purports to be a private system, the OECD reports that 60 percent of expenditures for inpatient care come from public sources (2001). Such massive investments do not come without strings attached; all funders are pressing for greater accountability in how these resources are spent. But governments are also highly involved in the role of *regulator* and generate complex sets of rules affecting hospitals. Although the precise rules vary, governments affect most aspects of a hospital's operation, from how it must behave as an employer, through its impact on the environment (e.g., how it disposes of potentially hazardous wastes), to how, if at all, it must operate "in the public interest" (e.g., mandatory treatment of emergency patients). As health costs increase, the population ages, technology beckons, health care workers agitate, and demands increase, government as, at least in theory, the *guardian* of the public interest comes under increasing pressure to square circles and reconcile often incompatible policy goals.

Of course, governments and their policies are notoriously complex. Wags have commented that no one should observe how sausage or policy is made. Yet it is possible to clarify key elements of policy making that allow hospital leaders not only to understand what shapes current policy realities, but to anticipate and influence future policy directions. To do this, we offer an analytical "tool kit" that identifies and elaborates on three main elements of policy and policy making: *ideas, institutions,* and *interests.* As discussed in the sections that follow, *ideas* refers to the beliefs and values that define "the public interest," shape the policy agenda, and point toward appropriate solutions to problems; ideas about the respective roles of public governments and private markets within health care are particularly important in this connection. *Institutions* refers to the internal "machinery of government," the legislation, offices, and agencies of government that bear not only on what government does in health care, but on how it does it; at the very least, hospital leaders need to know how key parts of this machinery impact on them and their organizations, and where they need to go if they wish to shape, and not simply react to, policy. Finally, *interests* refer to other stakeholders—including professional associations, unions, provider organizations, insurers, and consumers—who perceive themselves to have a claim in health care policy, and may pursue these claims using a range of strategies and means, including sophisticated lobbying campaigns. Hospital leaders are not alone in having an interest in what government does in the health care arena;

they must be able to identify potential allies as well as possible opponents in looking to understand how policy is made, or how it may be influenced.

In developing this "tool kit" we consider differences as well as similarities in the health policy environments of Canada and the United States. These countries share a common border and have reasonably similar cultures, economies, and social structures. Doctors and other health professionals have similar training and the health care systems in both countries are committed to the tenets of curative, technologically driven scientific medicine. Nevertheless, hospitals in the United States and Canada have moved along fundamentally different policy pathways. In the United States these pathways have contributed to the rise of massive for-profit health care corporations that pursue their interests in domestic and global markets. By contrast, hospitals in Canada continue to operate on a not-for-profit basis, largely financed by the single-payer, universal health insurance plan. To the extent that mergers have occurred in the industry, these have usually been in conjunction with the establishment of publicly funded geographically based regional health authorities in all provinces except Ontario. What accounts for such differences? While there are many possible factors and explanations, we think that attention to differences in ideas, institutions, and interests provides an important framework for hospital leaders to understand and influence their policy environment.

IDEAS

Ideas are crucial. They structure how we see the world and influence what we think is important. They describe the "good" society and the role of government in achieving it. They also clearly differentiate the health systems of Canada and the United States, each of which is based on quite different ideas about the nature of health care and how it should be funded. It is increasingly understood that health systems in the industrialized countries do not create health; they provide medical treatment for illness. But more than that, they also determine who bears the costs of illness—those who are ill or the society at large. As U.S. economist Uwe Reinhardt observes, health systems are in essence redistributive mechanisms, with different national systems building upon different assumptions about how the costs of illness should be paid (1996). In Canada, health care tends to be viewed as a public "good" with universal access to medically necessary hospital and doctor care guaranteed on the basis of need, and paid for by the publicly funded provincially organized health insurance plans. In the United States, by contrast, care is more likely to be viewed as a "commodity" subject to market forces, and access to care is more likely to be governed by the ability to pay, with provision for public or charitable payment as a "safety net" for those unable to do so.

Differences in ideas are not merely cosmetic; they have played crucial roles in defining the evolution of hospitals in both countries. As Paul Starr observed in his groundbreaking examination of American health care, few institutions have undergone as radical a metamorphosis in modern history as hospitals (1982). He shows how, through the incorporation of the ideas of scientific medicine, hospitals were transformed in the late nineteenth and early twentieth centuries from places of "dreaded impurity and exiled human wreckage" to "awesome citadels of science and bureaucratic order" with a status in the secular world analogous to that of churches in the religious world. Further, ideas have played a key role in shaping the evolution of the health care systems in which individual hospitals exist. While in the United States the presiding logic of the nineteenth and early twentieth centuries conditioned legislators to view hospitals as local or private concerns, a more collectivist logic in Canada meant that government action came to be viewed as a means of achieving a public good.

While such ideas are clearly critical, they remain almost "invisible," precisely because they are taken for granted. Important ideas are often contested—they are the subject of legitimate argument and debate—and they may conflict with each other. For example, Deborah Stone has identified four policy goals, all of which are desirable, but which sometimes are incompatible (1997). She defines these as follows:

equity—"treating likes alike";

efficiency—"getting the most output for a given input";

security—"satisfaction of minimum human needs"; and

liberty—"do as you wish as long as you do not harm others."

As noted previously, differences on such fundamental ideas have pushed the Canadian and U.S. health care systems along quite different pathways. Even within national jurisdictions, policy making often involves a careful balancing of these different goals. How, for example, can one ensure that sick people are able to get needed care (security) regardless of their ability to pay (equity) without in effect coercing others to pay their bills (liberty), while avoiding the introduction of inefficiencies into how care is organized and financed (efficiency)? Clearly, one will often be faced with the question of how best to trade off among these goals. In determining which goals will get priority, ideas about the roles of public government and private markets become critical underpinnings of health policy. Consider, for example, a person with health needs and limited resources. Whose responsibility is it to ensure that the person receives care? An enormous range of views is possible, each of which has implications for policy responses. For example, a libertarian places considerable emphasis on individual liberty; he/she would not support compulsory charity. (Indeed, most libertarians believe that taxation for such purposes is morally equivalent to theft.) Instead, they would stress that responsibility lies only with the individual and his/her family, with others free to extend charity if they wish to (and equally free to deny it). Socialists would place responsibility with society as a whole. In between is a vast array of ways in which to balance individual liberty and social responsiveness, which will in turn affect which policy responses are seen as legitimate in that society. Ideas accordingly shape the possible.

Both Canada and the United States are countries with strong regional differences, and heterogeneous political views. To dramatically oversimplify, however, there are some identifiable differences in the "ideas" about politics and government in the two countries. As a country with a smaller population living in an often hostile climate, Canadians have been far more accepting of a role for government than have their neighbors to the south, particularly those in the southern and western states. Canadians also tend to be more suspicious than Americans about the ability of markets to deliver optimal results, and hence may be more likely to mistrust for-profit delivery of certain goods and services. However, Canadians also are advocates of diversity, which is often expressed in a suspicion about "central government" control, and in giving support to provincial/local autonomy. Canada is less populist than is the United States, and more trusting of experts. It is also hyperaware of its powerful neighbor, and can be both attracted and repelled by U.S. policies.

Before September 11, 2001, it was clear that the United States had become far more suspicious about the legitimacy of government itself, and hence about the appropriateness of government involvement in most policy arenas; more recent events suggest that the pendulum may be swinging back. Nonetheless, the Reagan-Thatcher revolution was characterized by a greater emphasis on individual liberty, more faith in market forces, and less willingness to socialize policy (Yergin & Stanislaw, 1998). Although these views have certainly found resonance in parts of Canada—including in the provincial governments of Alberta (Ralph Klein), Ontario (Mike Harris), and British Columbia (Gordon Campbell)—survey results suggest that Canadians remain more favorably disposed to government actions in support of societal goals (Adams, 1997; Reid, 1996).

Ideas are not all-powerful; facts often intervene. Nonetheless, even facts are often seen through the prism of ideas. For example, one can collect empirical data about how well market forces work to allocate particular goods under particular circumstances. If, however, one believes that markets are always preferable to governments (or, conversely, that markets should have no role in how "needed" resources are distributed), those facts will be irrelevant.

INSTITUTIONS

Ideas clearly need to be taken into account when analyzing policy. But if ideas shape the goals of policy, institutions constitute the operational means for achieving these goals.

All governments must perform at least three key functions. First, they must make laws and regulations (the *legislative* function). Second, they must administer and carry out existing policies (the *executive* function). Finally, they must have a mechanism to appeal and interpret the law (the *judiciary* function). In Canada and the United States, different ideas about the role of government and the nature of health care not only have resulted in different policies that have created different institutional "structures" (e.g., reliance on employer-based insurance in the United States, and tax-based financing in Canada), but also have themselves been influenced by different structural arrangements in the two countries. As a prime example, the ability to implement universal insurance for hospital and physician services in Canada, but not in the United States, was the product not only of differing ideas, but also of different institutions of government. It was far easier for Canadian governments to implement policies that they believed to be in the public interest. Indeed, some Canadian observers have argued that Canadian Medicare was possible not just because Canadians "trust" government more than their American neighbors, but also because the Canadian constitution gives the executive branch of government more powerful tools than are available within a balance-of-powers system (Maioni, 1998). In the United States, political power is intended to be diffused through complex systems of executive, legislative, and judicial branches; in Canada, power is relatively concentrated in the power of the prime minister and cabinet. Such institutions matter.

Parliamentary Versus Balance-of-Power Systems

Canada and the United States both adhere to an ideology of democratic government, in which the ability to govern is legitimized by the "consent of the governed." Furthermore, both are federal systems, with national (federal) governments in Washington and Ottawa, and a series of states/provinces with their own autonomous powers. Both countries watch the same television programs, see the same movies, hear the same music, and at first glance appear quite similar. However, although there are nuances and variations, Canada (at the federal and provincial level) and the United States (at federal and state levels) have each chosen a different model of government, and these structural differences considerably affect how policy is made and implemented. We will term Canada's model the "parliamentary" model, and the U.S. model the "balance-of-powers" approach. It should be noted that these models are not pure. Within Canada, many municipal governments are based on a balance-of-powers model; within the United States, strong party loyalty, such as that brought about in the U.S. Congress by the Republicans under the leadership of Newt Gingrich, can begin to approximate a parliamentary model. Nonetheless, the following general principles apply.

The parliamentary model derives from the model of a constitutional monarchy, with a council of advisers. In Canada, the monarch is represented by a governor general (federally) or lieutenant governor (provincially). This model intertwines the executive and legislative functions; indeed, Parliament (the legislative authority) accordingly consists of the legislature plus the Crown, whereas the executive branch consists of the cabinet (who must all be members of the legislature) plus the civil service. In theory, the governor general is the executive and holds final authority. This formalism can be seen in rules and nomenclature. For example, no bill can become a law without being passed by each legislative house (three readings are required) and then receiving Royal Assent before being proclaimed. In practice, however, the governor general's power cannot be used to withhold assent; the powers of the governor general have long been more ceremonial than actual. These powers, deriving from those accruing to the British monarchy, have been described in the same terms—"to be consulted, to encourage, and to warn" (Dawson, Dawson, & Ward, 1971). Nonetheless, nothing compels that this counsel be sought out.

If the bills to be signed by the governor general require parliamentary approval, it is a short step to choosing a group of advisers to tell him/her what Parliament is likely to approve. This group of advisers is called the "cabinet" and is chaired by the prime minister. (Analogously, at the provincial level, it is chaired by the premier.) Although there is no mention of political parties in the constitutions of either country, they are an undoubted convenience. It is far easier to have ready-made support than to have to assemble a new coalition each time one wishes to take action. In the parliamentary model, each political party chooses a leader, elected by its own members, using its own processes. Those members elected to the legislature can then form a party caucus. By convention, the party that has elected the most members can seek to form a government; its leader (assuming he/she has won a seat) becomes prime minister or premier. If the party's elected representatives constitute more than half of the legislature, it forms a majority government. If it does not, it forms a minority government and must attract support from other parties. (If it cannot maintain that support and is defeated on a major vote in the legislature, it is deemed to have lost the confidence of the legislature, and the monarch's representative is expected to call another election.) The governing party can then select a cabinet from among its members. The cabinet members are deemed to be advisers to the governor general (or lieutenant governor), and join the Privy Council. Each cabinet member takes the Privy Council oath, and in theory is a member of it for life. Thus, in a parliamentary system, one cannot be a member of the executive branch without being a member of the legislature.

In Canada, cabinet members are given responsibility for a particular department (ministry) of government, and work with the civil servants (bureaucrats) to run their departments. The civil servants are expected to be "nameless and blameless" and to support their minister. In the Canadian system (although not in the United Kingdom), all ministers sit in the cabinet, and policy making is the collective responsibility of the cabinet rather than resting with the individual ministers. In practice, the office of the prime minister/premier can thus assert substantial policy authority (Savoie, 1999).

Note that much of this model rests on custom. There is little mention of political parties in the formal documents establishing and governing Canada. Indeed, the cabinet exists on paper as the active committee of the Privy Council of the cabinet. In practice, of course, no decisions would be made by the full Privy Council—one cannot really envision members of a defeated government seeking to attend cabinet meetings.

In contrast, the balance-of-powers model (sometimes termed the "presidential" model) separates the legislative and executive functions entirely. Whereas a Canadian cabinet member must be a member of the legislature, a U.S. cabinet member cannot. Indeed, on the occasions where presidents have selected senators or congressmen to assume cabinet positions, those so designated had first to resign their seats. In Canada, in contrast, should the prime minister/premier wish to have a particular individual in the cabinet, the potential member must first become a member of the legislature. At the national level, the prime minister can, in a pinch, take advantage of the appointed Senate, but this is considered somewhat inappropriate, and also requires that the prime minister appoint a *de facto* shadow minister to introduce the appropriations bills for that department (since these must always be introduced in the House of Commons), as well as to answer questions about that department's operations in the House's question period. This process is accordingly not common and is saved for difficult situations (e.g., the need to include a voice from regions that have not elected members to the governing party). At the provincial level, that option is not even available; regions or groups that do not elect members of the governing party cannot be represented in the cabinet at all.

The parliamentary system is set up to encourage a governing party to develop and carry through a platform. Very few checks and balances are in place if the party in power holds a majority in the legislature. (Under minority governments, where any defeat on a major piece of legislation can lead to the dissolving of the legislature and the calling of a new election, the executive must be far more cautious.) The bias is toward action, with the assumption that governing parties will be constrained by fear of electoral consequences should they go too far. The system assumes that governments will be prudent and bound by anticipated reactions rather than by structural constraints. When that does not happen, change can be dizzying, and government can resemble an elected dictatorship.

Presidential systems, in contrast, incorporate numerous checks and balances. The executive can propose legislation, but this must be passed by the legislature. In turn, the executive can veto legislative acts (while the legislature, in turn, can seek to overturn the veto). The courts also have a voice, with the ability to determine what matches their view of the Constitution. The system is set up to block action until a sufficient degree of consensus has been built up. When that does not happen, change can be impossible, and the status quo can persist even when a large proportion of the population wishes otherwise. Consider, for example, the fact that Canada was able to introduce universal insurance for hospital and physician services while the United States was not. Although we have discussed differences in values between the two countries, these explain only a very small piece of the picture; at the time Canada introduced hospital insurance, public opinion in the United States also favored similar initiatives. As noted previously, most observers suggest that the primary reasons for the different policy paths were that the Canadian government could act on its policy preferences, while policy makers in the United States were unable to move beyond the numerous blocking points built into their political structure (Maioni, 1998).

A related point involves who should be lobbied. In Canada, elected legislators have power only if they are members of the cabinet, and even then, only to the extent that they can sway their cabinet colleagues. By definition, members of the opposition parties are virtually powerless. Except in minority government situations, they can view with alarm and cause fusses, but cannot bring about policy changes unless the government agrees; it rarely does. Even "back bench" members of the governing party—the term applied to representatives who are not part of the cabinet—have little power. They may raise issues at their party "caucus," but again, they have influence only to the extent that the cabinet deems it wise to listen to their advice.

Because the loss of a vote in the legislature can lead to the defeat of a government, it is rare for governments to reverse themselves on major policy stances. The civics standby—How a Bill Becomes a Law—notes that all such bills must pass three readings in the legislature. The first reading is notice that the bill has been introduced. The second reading is approval in principle. After the second reading, bills traditionally go to a legislative committee for hearings and amendments. It is extremely rare for major alterations to happen at that stage, although minor tweaking is common. Finally, the bill may be introduced into the legislature for a third reading, which is usually a straight up-or-down vote along party lines.

Under such circumstances, it is clear that the successful lobbyist must anticipate legislation, rather than try to amend it once introduced. The parliamentary system places a high premium on access and knowledge. If a lobbyist knows that a particular issue is under study, he/she can attempt to meet with those drafting the policy alternatives to make sure his or her group's views are known and, if possible, incorporated. A successful lobbyist must, therefore, have ongoing contact with the key bureaucrats charged with that policy arena. In addition, the lobbyist should have contacts within the political staff of the minister and prime minister/premier, as well as with key cabinet members. A truism is that any group demonstrating in front of the legislature, or even mounting a letter-writing campaign to members of Parliament, has already lost the key battles. Most issues never get onto the political agenda; as such, they tend to be decided within the bureaucracy. Good ongoing relationships between the key bureaucrats and interest groups can thus be critical in helping to shape policy options. If a group is satisfied with these policies, they have a strong interest in helping the bureaucrats to keep the issue out of the press and off the radar screen.

A classic statement of this occurs in a major Canadian politics textbook—
"When I see members of parliament being lobbied, it's a sure sign to me that
the lobby lost its fight in the civil service and the cabinet" (Van Loon & Whittington, 1987, p. 412).

Another truism is that a successful lobbyist must be persistent, and present
those preparing policy options with solutions rather than just problems. Interest groups without the resources (time, human resources, and money) to keep
tabs on how government is thinking are thus severely disadvantaged in the
parliamentary system.

In contrast, a balance-of-powers system gives considerable influence to individual legislators. Legislation is frequently rewritten on the legislative floor.
Successful lobbyists may thus be able to cultivate individual politicians,
through a variety of mechanisms (including campaign contributions), to ensure
that these changes are to their liking. In striking contrast to the Canadian situation, public campaigns are common, and often effective.

Exceptions to these general rules, of course, abound. For example, under the
leadership of Newt Gingrich, a student of political science, the Republican party
used the powers of the House leadership to set up a quasi-parliamentary system
within the U.S. House of Representatives, and even within the notoriously independent Senate. Party members agreed to keep a united front and vote together.
The proportion of block votes increased considerably. Gingrich accordingly super-
imposed the ability of a parliamentary system to carry through a party platform
onto a system designed for checks and balances, and was able to implement considerable portions of his Contract with America. Nonetheless, to the extent that
the presidency was controlled by the opposite party (as it was under President
Clinton), parts of the agenda were blocked. Similarly, the Supreme Court retained its ability to rein in proposals that it felt opposed its view of the Constitution. However, the conventional depictions of U.S. politics as requiring continual
coalition building within legislatures must be modified in light of the ability of
the Republican party to maintain this party discipline, particularly at the national
level. Indeed, once the Republicans also held the presidency and could count upon
sympathetic courts (the majority of whom had been appointed under Republican
presidents), Senator Jeffords, a moderate Republican who did not share the congressional Republican agenda, felt himself compelled to take the drastic step of
leaving his party in order to shift control of the Senate from his party and introduce an additional blocking point. Similarly, Canadian interest groups have made
increasing use of the media in an effort—not always successful—to set the political agenda and constrain governmental policies.

Federalism

An additional complexity arises in determining what is meant by government; both Canada and the United States are federal systems, containing multiple levels of government. In both countries, there are considerable disparities

among the major subunits (ten provinces and three territories in Canada; fifty states in the United States), both in terms of population and in terms of fiscal capacity. Federalism is one way of attempting to reconcile two conflicting desires—that for uniformity and national standards, and that for flexibility and recognizing diverse regional identities. As such, both countries are faced with a constant balancing act about which policies and powers should rest at the national level, and which should be decentralized.

When Canada was established in 1867, the Fathers of Confederation spelled out the powers for the federal and provincial levels in the British North America Act (Government of Great Britain, 1867). Municipal governments were an afterthought, and were placed entirely under the control of the provinces; they were given no independent authority. Coming on the heels of the U.S. Civil War, the architects of Canada clearly envisioned giving control over all items of national importance, plus those likely to be expensive, to the national government in Ottawa. Section 91 read:

It shall be lawful for the Queen, by and with the Advice and Consent of the Senate and House of Commons, to make laws for the Peace, Order, and good Government of Canada, in relation to all Matters not coming within the Classes of Subjects by this Act assigned exclusively to the Legislatures of the Provinces; and for greater Certainty, but not so as to restrict the Generality of the foregoing Terms of this Section, it is hereby declared that (notwithstanding anything in this Act) the exclusive Legislative Authority of the Parliament of Canada extends to all Matters coming within the Classes of Subjects next hereinafter enumerated; that is to say ...

Twenty-eight specific categories followed, including "Quarantine and the Establishment and Maintenance of Marine Hospitals."

In the next section, Section 92, they attempted to restrict provincial authority to those things thought to be of purely local interest. Section 92 read:

In each Province the Legislature may exclusively make Laws in relation to Matters coming within the Classes of Subject next hereinafter enumerated; that is to say ...

Among the enumerated items were "The Establishment, Maintenance, and Management of Hospitals, Asylums, Charities, and Eleemosynary Institutions in and for the Province, other than Marine Hospitals," as well as municipal institutions and "property and civil rights in the province"; Section 93 also gave the provinces jurisdiction over education.

Not surprisingly, the future did not turn out as envisioned. Court decisions gave an expansive reading to "property and civil rights" and handed the residual power to provincial governments. Policy makers were able to interpret "hospitals" as encompassing almost all of health care, which accordingly was made to fall under exclusive provincial jurisdiction. Neither did the "soft services" of education, health care, and welfare prove as inexpensive as envisioned in the Victorian era. A specific constitutional amendment was needed to allow the federal government to run an unemployment insurance program after their initial effort to introduce that program had been struck down by the courts as unconstitutional. No such redistribution of power was to occur for health care. Instead, the federal government used the power of the purse, giving resources to the provincial government to allow them to run their own programs. Some of these grants were linked to particular programs (e.g., National Health Grants for building hospitals or training health workers). Others involved various forms of cost sharing (e.g., for insuring hospital care), with or without national standards. Accountability frameworks were more or less rigid, depending upon the temper of the times, the sensitivity of provincial governments to federal "incursion" into their jurisdiction, and the willingness of the federal government to pick fights with the provinces.

Some programs were introduced with all-party support; others were highly contentious. All operated against a background that, in U.S. terms, would be seen as extraordinarily deferential to states' rights. From a structural viewpoint, Canada does not have any structure by which federal-provincial issues can be debated and binding decisions taken. Although each level of government can debate such issues within its own legislative structure, relationships across levels resemble what Richard Simeon termed "federal-provincial diplomacy"; that is, representatives from the executive branches of each level meet together, in a manner reminiscent of the interactions among sovereign states (1972). These mechanisms are now well codified, if not always successful. For example, provincial/territorial ministers of health will meet and seek to achieve a common front against Ottawa; federal/provincial/territorial meetings will then attempt to achieve consensus that will be acceptable to all governments involved. Similar meetings will be held on a ministry-by-ministry basis, with the entire apparatus reaching its apex in "first ministers meetings" of provincial premiers and the prime minister. No mechanisms exist to bind the parties involved, other than their unwillingness to give the appearance of failure. The resulting agreements tend to be strong on generalities, and short on enforcement mechanisms. In that connection, the fact that Canada has only fourteen key players (ten provinces, three territories, plus the national government) makes such informal mechanisms more feasible than the fifty-one-plus player system in the United States.

The Current Health Care System in Canada

Canada has no unified health care system; it has a series of provincial insurance plans that cover, at minimum, physician and hospital services. These services are delivered by private providers, although most of them are not-for-profit organizations. However, the providers receive much of their funding from government and are highly regulated. What Canada calls "public hospitals" are accordingly private not-for-profit bodies, in that their employees are not civil servants and their managers have considerable autonomy about how they manage their resources. However, approximately 90 percent of hospital budgets come from public sector sources, and there is a widespread perception that the resources are inadequate to achieve public expectations. These organizations thus fall firmly within the category of "mediating structures"—nominally private organizations carrying out public objectives, often in a highly regulated manner. Similarly, although physicians are independent entrepreneurs, usually reimbursed fee-for-service, 99 percent of the resources to this sector come from public sector sources, according to CIHI data (2000).

Current health policy is highly conflictual; it has become a battleground for disputes between the federal government and provincial premiers. The battle was accentuated when, in 1984, as part of the federal budget-cutting exercise, Ottawa unilaterally reduced the previously negotiated rate of growth of its transfer payments to provincial governments (Deber, 2000). Nonetheless, this acrimonious battle has become the source of considerable misinformation. Although much public attention is focused on the federal role, it is less commonly recognized that, since 1977, the federal government's contributions for health care are in fact transfers into provincial general revenues, composed of a combination of tax points plus cash transfers, and are intended to cover three formerly cost-shared programs: hospital insurance, medical care (physician) insurance, and aid to postsecondary education (Auditor General of Canada, 1999). In 1996 an additional program, the Canada Assistance Plan, which had cost-shared social welfare, was folded into the block transfer, and the new program was renamed the Canada Health and Social Transfer. There are virtually no strings attached to funds nominally intended for education or welfare; provincial governments are free to divert much of this spending elsewhere. For the two health care programs (which since 1984 are defined under the Canada Health Act, which itself replaced two earlier pieces of legislation), provincial governments must only ensure that their insurance programs comply with the famous five national conditions of Medicare (Government of Canada, 1984), which are:

(a) public administration (this provision is often misunderstood; it does not require public provision or public management of service delivery, but merely requires that the insurance plan be publicly accountable for its spending of public money);

(b) comprehensiveness (all medically required services provided in hospitals or by physicians must be insured; those provided by other providers in the community do not fall within the scope of the act);

(c) universality (all insured persons must be covered);

(d) portability (there must be provision made for coverage when insured people travel within Canada; provisions for out-of-country care are far less extensive); and

(e) accessibility (the plan "must provide for insured health services on uniform terms and conditions and on a basis that does not impede or preclude, either directly or indirectly, whether by charges made to insured persons or otherwise, reasonable access to those services by insured persons," as well as ensuring "reasonable compensation" to providers).

Within these rather permissive conditions, provincial governments are free to determine how services will be organized and delivered, precisely what will be classified as insured services, how resources will be raised to pay for them, and so on. The Canada Health Act was intended to be a floor, rather than a ceiling. Provinces were free to insure care beyond the requirements of the act; they were merely not forced to do so. However, once care was defined as necessary (e.g., once midwives were defined as "health care practitioners" under the terms of the act), then all those insured persons requiring insured services would have to receive them on uniform terms and conditions.

In consequence, lobbyists must decide where to place their efforts. The federal government can be lobbied for increased funding, as well as on issues still within their jurisdiction (e.g., approval of drugs). However, most policy decisions occur at the provincial level; indeed, many are delegated to local providers. In all provinces except Ontario, regional health authorities have been set up, which receive budgets from the provincial government and are responsible for ensuring the delivery of a defined (if variable) array of services. Ontario has regionalized particular sectors (e.g., home care), and delegated other decisions to individual hospitals and their boards (Williams et al., 2001). Physicians bill under a fee schedule. As such, resource allocation decisions are highly decentralized, within the scope of global budgets or uniform fee schedules. Lobbyists are accordingly spread extremely thin.

INTERESTS

Questions about how and where to lobby underscore a key characteristic of policy; because different policies distribute costs and benefits in different ways, policy making is often contested by groups who may see themselves as potential "winners" or "losers." As we suggested in our introductory comments, because they involve not only access to health care, but also the distribution of massive amounts of funding and resources, health policies are often of considerable interest to a range of stakeholders—including professional associations, unions, provider organizations, insurers, and consumers—who perceive themselves to have a claim on health care policy, and may pursue that claim using a range of lobbying strategies as described previously. In the United States, when stakeholders mobilize to influence policy, they are often called "lobby groups" a term that refers to the "lobby" of the legislature where those attempting to influence policy may wait to gain the ear of policy makers. In Canada, where professional lobbyists have been less common, and where they have often been looked on with suspicion, they are more likely to be called "interest groups."

Paul Pross defines interest groups as "Organizations whose members act together to influence public policy in order to promote their common interests" (1975). However, not all potential groups will successfully mobilize to work together. Political scientists have laid out a "funnel of mobilization," which progresses from latent interests (defined as "individuals and corporations with interests in common, but with no sense of solidarity with one another"), through solidarity groups (which provide informal support of one another, but no formal organization), to formal interest groups (Pross, 1992). Depending upon the time and place, latent groups may enter the mobilization process. For example, gun control proposals may mobilize gun owners. Pross has categorized interest groups in terms of their objectives (broad vs. narrow; long-term vs. single interest), organization (continuity, cohesion), knowledge of government (minimal/naive vs. extensive), and membership (stable vs. fluid), to form a continuum from the highly *institutionalized* interest groups through to those that are more *issue oriented* and amorphous. A key distinction is whether the organizational imperatives outweigh any single issue; groups that wish to survive will not sacrifice ongoing relationships with decision makers unless the stakes are extremely high. Resources are also critical, including not only money, but also number of members, time, knowledge, and credibility (an advantage possessed by such health providers as physicians and nurses). As should be clear, institutionalized groups are most likely to be successful within a parliamentary system, since only they will have the resources to do the sort of long-term and consistent monitoring that is required.

Resources do not guarantee success (although their absence can make failure more likely). Success depends on many factors, including identification of the lobby points (and hence the structure within which the groups are operating), persistence, and the issue itself, including its fit with the government agenda. Smart lobbyists have an array of proposals ready, and are skilled at understanding when they might be well received. Timing is often critical, and understanding timing is one characteristic of a good lobbyist.

Even within one jurisdiction, the precise array of interests will differ across policy arenas. Political scientists speak of policy communities (Atkinson & Coleman, 1996; Coleman & Skogstad, 1990), defined as "that part of a political system that—by virtue of its functional responsibilities, its vested interests, and its specialized knowledge—acquires a dominant voice in determining government decisions in a specific field of public activity and is generally permitted by society at large and the public authorities in particular to determine public policy in that field" (Pross, 1992). In turn, policy communities are divided into the *subgovernment*, which processes most routine policy issues, and the *attentive public*. The subgovernment consists primarily of government agencies plus institutionalized interest groups with substantial resources and interests in that area. It is usually small and tightly knit. Outside, and scrutinizing with various amounts of care, is the attentive public, defined as those affected by, or interested in, the policies in that area. They follow and attempt to influence the policies, but do not participate in policy making on a regular basis.

In health care, physician and hospital groups are generally members of the subgovernment within most provinces. They will meet regularly with key bureaucrats, political staff (from all parties), and politicians. They will be involved in helping to formulate policies and will often be charged with implementing them. Even though about 30 percent of health spending comes from private sources in Canada, employers have not yet been a major part of the policy community, in sharp contrast to the United States. Even within health care, however, there are significant differences across subfields, with interest groups playing a far more important role in making policy about physician services than they do in making policy about home care.

IMPLEMENTING POLICY

As political scientists have noted, governments have available to them a series of what are termed "policy instruments" or "governing instruments," from which they can select to carry out preferred policy directions. These instruments vary considerably in how they affect stakeholders. Political scientists have classified them on a scale that varies by what can be termed "degree of coercion" (Doern & Phidd, 1988) or "intrusiveness" (Baxter-Moore, 1987). At the extreme nonintrusive end of the scale, government can choose not to act at all. Next, it can choose *symbolic* responses—what G.B. Doern and R.W. Phidd term "exhortation." Goal-setting exercises, for example, would fall into this category. Government could attempt to control health expenditures by encouraging individuals to exercise and improve their diets. It could encourage voluntary organizations to care for the poor by praising those running exemplary programs, but without paying for the services being delivered. More intrusively, it may choose to intervene indirectly, by using *incentives* for action. These can range from attempts to secure voluntary compliance with government objectives without accompanying threats or inducements, through to what Doern and Phidd term "expenditure," either through the tax system or through direct expenditure of public money. A still more intrusive set of instruments may be termed *directives* (what Doern and Phidd call "regulation"); such direct public interventions, via regulation or public ownership, shift compliance costs from government to other bodies (including to other levels of government). Although most writing on policy instruments conceptualizes them as the extent to which government directly intrudes on *private* decision making, R.B. Deber et al. have also extended this analysis to view them as the potential intrusiveness of one level of government upon another (Deber, 1996).

From the viewpoint of hospitals, then, they are confronted by two types of policy activities by government. *Allocation* issues involve public expenditures—for example, hospitals may seek to influence spending formulas. The targets of actions may include both the amount to be spent/received and the criteria to be used for distribution. For example, in most Canadian jurisdictions, hospitals receive virtually all of their budgets from government sources. Battles can accordingly be waged about how much will be incorporated into a global budget. But battles will also occur about how best to construct these budgets—how much allowance should be made for population growth, complexity of case mix, cost-of-living issues across geographical areas, technology, and so on. In the United States, the battles will directly address such issues as how much hospitals will be reimbursed for care of the indigent, what (if any) allowances will be made for teaching and research, and so on.

But hospitals are also affected by government decisions about *regulation*. It should be noted that government does not act alone—in many cases, it delegates decisions to professional organizations (e.g., colleges of physicians and surgeons, accrediting bodies, and the like). In the final analysis, however, government retains the power to set the rules by which organizations must operate. For example, hospitals are rarely free to decide on the skill mix of those delivering services. Some body—whether accrediting bodies, professional associations, or government—is likely to require a certain number of registered nurses to be present on a shift, restrict the ability of untrained workers to draw blood, insist that surgery only be performed by certified physicians, and so on. Hospitals are also affected by government regulations about occupational health and safety, ranging from issues about how long a shift can be, to how used needles should be disposed of.

Lastly, hospitals must operate within the often unwritten public norms about how they are expected to act. The clash between the ideas appropriate to business and those appropriate to "health care" may be difficult to juggle, but there are lines that are crossed only with great peril. Hospitals may be expected to manage within their budgets, but not by turning away seriously injured patients arriving on their doorstep, regardless of their ability to pay. In the final analysis, then, hospitals seeking to fulfill their mission must be able to manage their environment, and ensure that the rules (and resources) are compatible with the expectations placed upon them. In that connection, a focus on government relations is essential.

REFERENCES

Adams, M. (1997). *Sex in the snow: Canadian social values at the end of the millennium.* Toronto: Viking.

Atkinson, M.M., & Coleman, W.D. (1996). Policy networks, policy communities and the problems of governance. In L. Dobuzinskis, M. Howlett, & D. Laycock (Eds.), *Policy studies in Canada: The state of the art* (pp. 193–218). Toronto: University of Toronto Press.

Auditor General of Canada. (1999). *Federal support of health care delivery.* Report of the Auditor General of Canada, Chapter 29, November, http://www.oag-bvg.gc.ca.

Baxter-Moore, N. (1987). Policy implementation and the role of the state: A revised approach to the study of policy instruments. In R.J. Jackson, D. Jackson, & N. Baxter-Moore (Eds.), *Contemporary Canadian politics: Reading and notes* (pp. 336–355). Scarborough, Ontario: Prentice-Hall Canada Inc.

Canadian Institute for Health Information. (2000). *National health expenditure trends, 1975–2000*. National health expenditure database.

Coleman, W.D., & Skogstad, G. (Eds.). (1990). *Policy communities and public policy in Canada: A structural approach*. Mississauga, Ontario: Copp Clark Pitman.

Dawson, R.M., Dawson, W.F., & Ward, N. (1971). *Democratic government in Canada* (4th ed.). Toronto: University of Toronto Press.

Deber, R.B. (1996). National standards in health care. *Policy Options 17* (June 5): 43–45.

Deber, R.B. (2000). Getting what we pay for: Myths and realities about financing Canada's health care system. *Health Law in Canada 21* (2): 9–56.

Decter, M.B. (1994). *Healing Medicare: Managing health system change the Canadian way*. Toronto: McGilligan Books.

Doern, G.B., & Phidd, R.W. (1988). *Canadian public policy: Ideas, structure, process*. Scarborough, Ontario: Nelson Canada.

Government of Canada. (1984). *Canada Health Act, Bill C-3*. Statutes of Canada, 1984, 32–33 Elizabeth II (R.S.C.1985, c.6; R.S.C.1989, c.C-6).

Government of Great Britain. (1867). *British North America Act (Constitution Act)*. Government of Great Britain, 30–31 Victoria.

Kleinke, J.D. (2001). *Oxymorons: The myth of a U.S. health care system*. San Francisco: Jossey-Bass.

Maioni, A. (1998). *Parting at the crossroads: The emergence of health insurance in the United States and Canada*. Princeton: Princeton University Press.

Organisation for Economic Co-operation and Development. (2001). *OECD Health Data*. Compact Disc: A comparative analysis of twenty-nine countries.

Pross, A.P. (Ed.). (1975). *Pressure group behaviour in Canadian politics*. Toronto: McGraw-Hill Ryerson Limited.

Pross, A.P. (1992). *Group politics and public policy* (2nd ed.). Toronto: Oxford University Press.

Reid, A. (1996). *Shakedown: How the new economy is changing our lives*. Toronto: Doubleday Canada Limited.

Reinhardt, U.E. (1996). Spending more through "cost control": Our obsessive campaign to gut the hospital. *Health Affairs 15* (2): 145–154.

Savoie, D. (1999). *Governing from the centre: The concentration of power in Canadian politics*. Toronto: University of Toronto Press.

Simeon, R.E. (1972). *Federal-provincial diplomacy: The making of recent policy in Canada*. Toronto: University of Toronto Press.

Starr, P. (1982). *The social transformation of American medicine*. New York: Basic Books Inc.

Stone, D.A. (1997). *Policy paradox: The art of political decision making*. New York: W.W. Norton and Company, Inc.

Van Loon, R.J., & Whittington, M.S. (1987). *The Canadian political system: Environment, structure and process* (4th ed.). Toronto: McGraw-Hill Ryerson Limited.

Williams, A.P., Deber, R.B., Baranek, P., & Gildiner, A. (2001). From Medicare to home care: Globalization, state retrenchment and the profitization of Canada's health care system. In P. Armstrong, H. Armstrong, & D. Coburn (Eds.), *Unhealthy times: Polilical economy perspectives on health and care in Canada* (pp. 7–30). Don Mills, Ontario: Oxford University Press.

Yergin, D., & Stanislaw, J. (1998). *The commanding heights: The battle between government and the marketplace that is remaking the modern world.* New York: Simon & Schuster.

Chapter 2

Strategic Management and Public Policy

Beaufort B. Longest, Jr.

When decisions are made for a health care organization or system (hereinafter called an "entity") establishing or modifying such essential characteristics as ownership; mission; organizational structure; physical location and markets; product and service lines and mixes; resource acquisition and allocation; and whether to partner or ally, and with whom, *strategy* is being determined. Those who make these decisions (generally, the entity's senior-level managers and governing board members) are its *strategic managers*. The process of making and implementing strategic decisions is *strategic management*. In effect, strategy comprises decisions reflecting what an entity's strategic managers wish it to be and to achieve, as well as how they plan to accomplish this. Strategy is vital because it establishes the entity's position and direction in relation to the overall external environment within which it exists.

If an entity is to be successful, its strategic managers must orchestrate a productive fit between the entity's potential to produce benefits through its unique set of human competencies, financial resources, corporate values, information, and technologies and its external environment (Ginter, Swayne, & Duncan, 2002). An entity's external environment includes its customers, competitors, and partners, as well as relevant technology and science, general economic and business conditions, and public policies such as pertinent laws and regulations.

Making strategic decisions that ensure a productive fit between the internal situation and external environment of a health care entity—sometimes, even decisions that ensure its survival—is a great challenge. In an attempt to provide a better fit with the external environment, such decisions may involve changes in internal capacity in such areas as the entity's human competencies, financial resources, corporate values, information, and technologies utilized. Alternatively, the decisions may involve efforts to change some component of the entity's external environment such as its customers, competitors, or partners.

These efforts might also extend to relevant technology and science as well as general economic and business conditions. Finally, the search for a better fit between a health care entity and its environment can extend to decisions intended to influence the nature and effect of public policies that affect it.

This chapter focuses on the links between the public policy components of the external environments of health care entities and the strategic management of these entities. Although public policy is only one of many components of an entity's external environment, it is an important factor, and often does not receive sufficient attention in strategic management considerations.

In order to examine the links between public policy and the strategic management of health care entities, it is first useful to define public policy and describe the process through which it emerges. Then the strategic management process is described. Finally, the interactions between these two processes, and the strategic management response to them, are discussed.

PUBLIC POLICY AND THE POLICY-MAKING PROCESS

Public policies are authoritative decisions made in the legislative, executive, or judicial branches of government, which are intended to direct or influence the actions, behaviors, or decisions of others (Longest, 2002). These decisions are made at local, state/province, and federal levels of government. Numerous public policies are relevant to the strategic management of health care entities. Some are decisions codified in the statutory language of specific public laws. Others are the rules and regulations established in order to implement laws or to operate government and its various programs. Still others are the relevant decisions made in the judicial branch.

Because public policies—the authoritative decisions reflected in laws, rules, regulations, and judicial rulings—are important to strategic managers, they must also concern themselves with the process through which public policies are established, that is, with the intricate set of actors, actions, and forces that make up the policy-making process. The most useful way to conceptualize a process that is as complex and intricate as the one through which public policies are made is through a schematic model of the process. Although such models tend to be oversimplifications of real processes, as is the one presented here, they can nevertheless accurately reflect the component parts of the process, as well as their interrelationships. Figure 2.1 is a model of the public policy-making process described more fully in Longest (2002); it applies directly to policy making at the federal level, but with minor adjustments can also apply to the process at the level of states/provinces and even in some municipalities.

Several general features of the model should be noted. First, the policy-making process is distinctly cyclical. The circular flow of the relationships among the various components of the model reflects that the process is a continuous

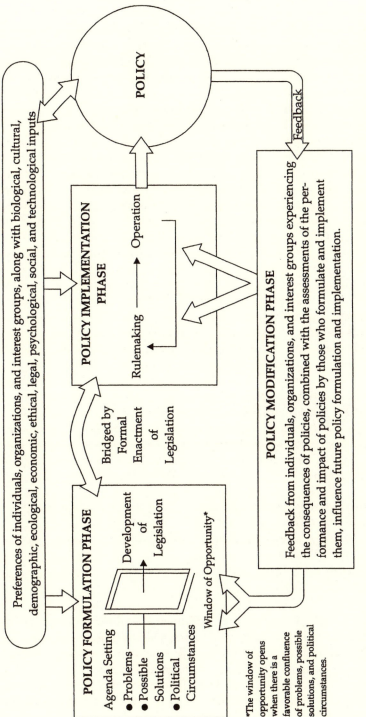

Figure 2.1. The public policy-making process (Longest, 2002). Used with permission from *Health Policymaking in the United States*, 3rd edition, by Beaufort B. Longest, Jr. (Chicago: Health Administration Press, 2002), page 115.

cycle in which almost all decisions are subject to subsequent modification. Public policy making, including that relevant to strategic managers in health care entities, is a process within which numerous decisions are reached but then revisited as circumstances change. The circumstances that trigger reconsideration of earlier decisions include changes in the way problems or opportunities are defined as well as in the menu of possible solutions to problems or avenues to realizing opportunities. The new circumstances that trigger modification in previous decisions also routinely include the relative importance attributed to issues by the various participants in the process. A problem with a low priority among powerful participants in the policy-making process may elicit a limited or partial policy solution. Later, if these participants give the problem a higher priority, a policy developed in response to the problem is much more likely. Major changes in Medicare policy in the United States or Canada Health and Social Transfer (CHST) allocations in Canada, for example, generally reflect changing concerns about the implications of these programs for national budgets.

Another important feature of the public policy-making process shown in the model is that the entire process is influenced by factors that are external to the process itself. This makes the policy-making process an *open system*— one in which the process interacts with and is affected by events and circumstances outside the process itself. This very important phenomenon is shown in Figure 2.1 by the impact of the preferences of the individuals, organizations, and interest groups who are affected by policies, along with biological, cultural, demographic, ecological, economic, ethical, legal, psychological, social, and technological inputs, on the policy-making process.

A third important feature of the model is that it emphasizes the various distinct component parts or phases of the policy-making process, but also shows that they are highly interactive and interdependent. The process includes three interconnected phases:

- *policy formulation*, which incorporates activities associated with setting the policy agenda and, subsequently, with the development of legislation;
- *policy implementation*, which incorporates rule-making activities that help guide the implementation of policies; and
- *policy modification*, which allows for all prior decisions made within the process to be revisited and perhaps changed.

The formulation phase (making the decisions that lead to laws) and the implementation phase (taking actions and making additional decisions necessary to implement laws) are bridged by the formal enactment of legislation, which shifts the cycle from its formulation to implementation phases. Policies, once enacted as laws, must be implemented. Departments and agencies in the executive branch, such as Health Canada and the U.S. Department of Health and Human Services, have primary implementation responsibilities.

It is important to remember that some of the decisions made within the implementing entities, as they implement policies, become policies themselves. For example, rules and regulations promulgated in order to implement a law, and operational protocols and procedures developed to support a law's implementation, are policies just as is the law. Similarly, judicial decisions regarding the applicability of laws to specific situations or the appropriateness of the actions of implementing organizations are decisions that are themselves public policies.

The policy modification phase exists because perfection cannot be achieved in the other phases and because policies are established and exist in a dynamic world. Suitable policies made today may become inadequate with future biological, cultural, demographic, ecological, economic, ethical, legal, psychological, social, and technological changes. Pressure to change established policies may come from new priorities or perceived needs by the individuals, organizations, and interest groups that are affected by policy.

Policy modification, which is shown as a feedback loop in Figure 2.1, might entail nothing more than minor adjustments made in the implementation phase or modest amendments to existing public laws. In some instances, however, the consequences of implementing certain policies can feed back all the way to the agenda-setting stage of the process. For example, the challenge of formulating policies to contain the costs of providing health services facing policy makers today is, to a large extent, an outgrowth of the success of previous policies that expanded access and subsidized an increased supply of human resources and advanced technologies to be used in the provision of health services.

One feature of the public policy-making process that the model presented in Figure 2.1 cannot adequately show, but a feature that is crucial to understanding the policy-making process, is the *political* nature of the process in operation. While there is a belief among many people—and a naive hope among still others—that policy making is a predominantly rational decision-making process, this is not the case.

The process would no doubt be simpler and better if it were driven exclusively by fully informed consideration of the best ways for policy to support the pursuit of health, by open and comprehensive debate about such policies, and by the rational selection from among policy choices strictly on the basis of ability to contribute to health. Those who are familiar with the policy-making process, however, know that it is not driven exclusively by these considerations. A wide range of other factors and considerations influence the process, including the preferences and influence of interest groups, political bargaining and vote trading, and ideological biases.

Strategic managers who focus only on policies (decisions) after they have been made, rather than on the larger context—with its diverse actors, actions, and forces—in which the decisions are made as well as on the process through which the decisions are made will be unprepared to make proper and timely

strategic responses to policies as they emerge. Certainly, they will have had little if any influence in the intricate process through which the policies were established.

STRATEGIC MANAGEMENT IN HEALTH CARE ENTITIES

As noted in the introductory paragraph, the process through which an entity's strategic managers make and implement strategic decisions is strategic
management. This process, which is discussed extensively in Longest (1996;
1997) and summarized from those sources here, consists of four interrelated
stages, as shown in Figure 2.2. The first two stages in this model, situational
analysis (which includes both an internal and external environmental analysis) and strategy formulation, constitute strategic planning. Adding the implementation and control stages models the entire strategic management process.
Consideration of each stage, in turn, follows, although in practice the individual stages intertwine to form a mosaic that is the whole of strategic management.

Situational Analysis

The situational analysis stage of the strategic management process has two
components: external and internal environmental analyses. In conducting these
analyses, strategic managers seek to identify and consider the opportunities and
threats presented to their entity by its external environment. They also seek to
identify and consider the internal strengths and weaknesses of their entity in
relation to these opportunities and threats.

External Environmental Analysis

The external environment for any entity includes all the factors outside its
boundaries that can influence its organizational performance. It is useful to vi-
sualize the external environment of a health care entity as a series of concen-
tric circles. At the center of this conceptualization is the focal entity and the
other similar entities with which it directly competes. These form an industry,
such as the hospital or pharmaceutical industries.

Industries exist within task environments, which form the next circle. An entity's task environment includes its industry, but extends to clients or customers, suppliers, regulators, insurers, accrediting agencies, and so on, with
which the entity has direct interactions. Finally, the external environment of an
entity includes its macroenvironment, or general environment as it is also
called. This last circle in the conceptualization is composed of everything outside the industry's task environment.

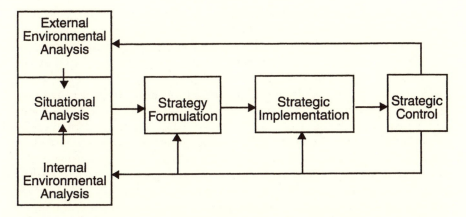

Figure 2.2. Stages in the strategic management process (Longest, 1996). From *Health Professionals in Management* by Beaufort B. Longest, Jr. (New York: McGraw-Hill, 1996), page 116. Reproduced with permission of The McGraw-Hill Companies.

In total, an entity's industry, task environment, and macroenvironment produce biological, cultural, demographic, ecological, economic, ethical, legal, public-policy, political, psychological, social, and technological information that the entity should include in its external environmental analysis.

In order to discern important information about the factors in their environments, strategic managers conduct formalized external environmental analyses for their entities. Although there are a number of approaches to conducting these analyses (Ginter, Swayne, & Duncan, 2002), they generally include five interrelated activities:

- environmental scanning to identify strategic issues (i.e., opportunities, threats, trends, developments, or possible events) that could affect the entity;
- monitoring the strategic issues;
- forecasting or projecting the future directions of the strategic issues;
- assessing the implications of the strategic issues for the entity; and
- diffusing the results of the analysis among those in the entity who can help formulate and implement its strategy.

An entity's strategic managers must apply these steps to its entire environment. For purposes of this discussion, however, we will limit the consideration to an entity's public policy environment. Effective environmental scanning of an entity's public policy environment begins with careful consideration by its strategic managers of what they believe to be strategic public policy issues. In guiding the focus of scanning, it is useful to remember the definition of public policies given earlier: they are authoritative decisions—made in the legislative, executive, or judicial branches of government—that are intended to direct or influence the actions, behaviors, or decisions of others. When these decisions influence in any way the strategic actions, behaviors, or decisions, then they can be thought of as relevant strategic public policies.

The set of strategic public policies for any entity constitutes a very large set of decisions. Remember that some of these decisions are codified in the statutory language of specific public laws. Others are the rules or regulations established in order to implement public laws or to operate government and its various programs. Still others are the judicial branch's relevant decisions.

The large set of public policies that are of strategic importance to health-related entities, however, represents only part of what must be considered strategic public policy *issues*. The problems, potential solutions, and political circumstances that might eventually align to lead to strategic policies must also be considered important strategic public policy issues. These, too, must be taken into account in complete analyses of public policy environments. Thus, effective scanning of the public policy environment involves identifying specific strategic policies *and* identifying emerging problems, possible solutions, and the political circumstances that surround them, which could eventually lead to policies of strategic importance. Together, these form the set of strategic *public policy issues* that should be scanned.

Consideration within any entity about what issues are in fact of strategic importance is largely judgmental, making the quality of the judgments quite important. For this reason, it is useful to have more than one person decide which of the scanned issues are of strategic significance. One widely used approach in making these judgments is to rely on the collective opinion of an ad hoc task force or a committee of people from within the entity. Another popular approach is to use outside consultants who can provide expert opinions and judgments as to what is strategically important.

It is also possible to utilize any of several more formal expert-based techniques. The most useful among these are the Delphi technique, the nominal group technique, brainstorming, focus groups, and dialectic inquiry (Ginter, Swayne, & Duncan, 2002; Webster, Reif, & Bracker, 1989; Jain, 1984; Terry, 1977; Delbecq, Van de Ven, & Gustafson, 1974). The starting point in any scanning activity, no matter who is doing it or which techniques might be employed, is the question of who or what to scan.

Universally, policy makers in federal, state/province, and local levels of government, and those who can influence their decisions—whether through helping shape conceptualization of problems and their potential solutions or through impact on the political circumstances that help drive the policy-making process—are the appropriate focus of scanning activities. The focus can be refined for particular situations by limiting it to strategically important policies and the problems, potential solutions, and political circumstances that might eventually lead to policies that affect the entity.

Another way of identifying who/what should be scanned in a public policy environment is to think of the suppliers of relevant public policies, and those who can influence them, as forming the appropriate focus. Members of each branch of government play roles as suppliers of policies, although the roles are very different. Each should receive attention in the scanning activity. Because policies are made in all three branches of government, the list of potential suppliers of public policies—the policy makers—is lengthy, and adding those who can influence the suppliers makes the list even longer.

Effectively scanning an entity's public policy environment identifies specific public policies that are of strategic importance. *Very* effective scanning also identifies the *emerging* problems, possible solutions to them, and the political circumstances that surround them that could eventually lead to strategically important policies. But scanning, even when very effectively done, is only the first step in the overall set of interrelated activities involved in analyzing a public policy environment.

Monitoring is more than scanning. It is the tracking, or following, of strategically important public policy issues over time. Public policy issues are monitored because strategic managers, or their support staffs who may be doing the actual monitoring, believe the issues are of strategic importance. Monitoring them, especially when the issues are not well structured or are ambiguous as to strategic importance, permits more information to be assembled so that issues can be clarified and the degree to which they are, or the rate at which they are becoming, strategically important can be determined.

The monitoring step has a much narrower focus than scanning (Ginter, Swayne, & Duncan, 2002). This is because the purpose in monitoring is to build a base of data and information around the set of strategically important public policy issues that are identified through scanning or verified through earlier monitoring. Fewer, usually far fewer, issues will be monitored than will be scanned as part of analyzing public policy environments.

Monitoring is important because it is so often difficult to determine whether public policy issues are strategically important. Under conditions of certainty, the strategic managers of entities analyzing their environments would fully understand strategic issues and all consequential implications for their decisions and actions. However, uncertainty characterizes much about the strategically important issues faced by most health care entities. Monitoring will not remove uncertainty, but it will likely reduce it significantly as more detailed and sustained information is acquired. As with scanning, techniques that feature the acquisition of multiple perspectives and expert opinions can help strategic managers determine what should be monitored; experts in the form of consultants can also be utilized for the actual monitoring if this is beyond the capacity of the entity's regular staff.

Effective scanning and monitoring cannot, by themselves, provide all the information about the strategic public policy issues in an entity's environment. Often, if the response to strategic issues is to be made effectively, reliable forecasts of future conditions or states is necessary. That is, information about issues and their effects before they occur is needed. This may provide the time needed to formulate and implement successful responses to the issues.

Scanning and monitoring the public policy environment involves searching this environment for signals, sometimes distant and faint signals, that may be the forerunners of strategically important issues. Forecasting involves extending the issues and their impacts beyond their current states. For some public policy issues (e.g., the impact on patient demand of a change in public policy redefining the eligibility requirements for programs), adequate forecasts can be made by extending past trends or by applying a formula. In other situations, forecasting must rely upon conjecture, speculation, and judgment, although these can be systematically compiled through such means as Delphi panels or focus groups. Sometimes, even sophisticated simulations can be conducted to forecast the future.

However, some degree of uncertainty characterizes the results of all of these forecasting techniques. It is especially difficult to incorporate in the utilization of any of them the fact that strategically important public policy issues never exist in a vacuum, and typically involve many issues at work simultaneously. No existing forecasting techniques or models fully account for this condition.

The most widely used technique for forecasting changes in public policy issues is trend extrapolation (Klein & Linneman, 1984). This technique, when properly used, can be remarkably effective and is relatively simple to use. Trend extrapolation is nothing more than tracking a particular issue, and then using the information to predict future changes. Public policies do not emerge *de novo*. Instead, they result from linked trains of activities that can and typically do span many years.

Even so, trend extrapolation as a technique in environmental analysis must be handled very carefully. It works best under highly stable conditions; under all other conditions it has significant limitations. When used to forecast changes in public policy, trend extrapolation usually provides predictions of general trends— such as directional trends in the number of people served by a program or in funding streams—rather than quantification of the trend with great specificity.

Significant policy changes, as well as changes in technology, demographics, or other variables, can render the extrapolation of a trend meaningless or misleading. In spite of this, however, predictions about trends through extrapolation can be quite useful to strategic managers as they seek to predict the paths of their strategically important policy issues. For those who exercise caution in its use and who factor in the effect of changes such as the introduction of a new or modified policy, trend extrapolation can be a very useful technique in forecasting certain aspects of the public policy environments of their entities.

Another technique for forecasting the public policy environment is the development, usually in writing, of scenarios of the future (Leemhuis, 1985). A scenario is simply a plausible story about the future. This technique is especially appropriate for analyzing environments that include many uncertainties and imponderables. Such features generally characterize the public policy environments of health care entities.

The essence of scenario development is to define several alternative future scenarios, or states of affairs. These can be used as the basis for developing contingent responses to the predictions; alternatively, the set of scenarios can be used to select what an entity's strategic managers consider the most likely future, the one to which they will prepare to respond (Schwartz, 1991).

Scenarios of the future can pertain to a single policy issue (e.g., policy regarding approval procedures for new medical technology) or to broader-based sets of policy issues (e.g., policies regarding funding for medical education or research, or a preventive approach to improved health). Scenarios can and, in practice, do vary considerably in scope and depth.

As a general rule, when using the scenario development technique in forecasting public policy environments, it is useful to develop several scenarios. Multiple scenarios permit the breadth of future possibilities to be explored. After the full range of possibilities has been reflected in a set of scenarios, one can be chosen as the most likely scenario. However, the most common mistake made in using scenario development is to envision too early in the process one particular scenario as "the one true picture of the future" (Fahey & Narayanan, 1986). Strategic managers who think they know which scenario will prevail and who prepare only for the one they select may find that the price of guessing incorrectly can be very high indeed.

Scanning and monitoring strategic public policy issues, and forecasting future changes in them, are important steps in a good environmental analysis. However, strategic managers must also concern themselves about the specific and relative strategic importance of the issues they are analyzing. That is, they must be concerned with an assessment or interpretation of the strategic importance and implications of public policy issues for their entities.

Frequently, this involves characterizing issues as opportunities for or threats to their entity. However, such assessments are far from an exact science. It may well be that sound human judgment is the best technique for making these determinations, although there are several bases upon which the strategic importance of public policy issues can be considered. Experience with similar issues is frequently a useful basis for assessing the strategic importance of a public policy issue. The experience may have been acquired firsthand within the particular entity where an assessment is being made, or it may come from contact with colleagues in other entities who have experienced similar public policy issues and who are willing to share their experiences. Significant variety exists among the states/provinces regarding their public policies that affect the pursuit of health; this variety can be instructive. Similarly, the experiences in other countries with various public policies affecting health and its pursuit can be drawn upon for insight. Other bases for assessments include intuition or best guesses about what particular public policy issues might mean to an entity, as well as advice from others who are well informed and experienced. When possible, quantification, modeling, and simulation of the potential impacts of public policy issues being assessed can be useful.

Making the appropriate determination is rarely a simple task, even when all the bases suggested previously are considered. Aside from the difficulties encountered in collecting and properly analyzing enough information to inform the assessment fully, there are sometimes problems that derive from the influence of the personal prejudices and biases of those conducting the environmental assessment. Such problems can force assessments that fit preconceived notions about what is strategically important rather than reflecting the realities of a particular situation (Thomas & McDaniel, 1990).

The final step in analyzing public policy environments is the sometimes very difficult one of diffusing or spreading the results of the effort to all those in the entity who require the information to carry out their own responsibilities. This step is frequently undervalued and may even be overlooked in some situations. Unless this step is effectively carried out, however, it really does not matter how well the other steps in environmental analysis are performed.

There are three basic ways that relevant information about the public policy environment can be diffused throughout an entity. Those who wish to spread the information can:

- use *power* to dictate diffusion and use of the information (this approach works best in entities whose strategic managers can, if they choose, use coercion or sanctions to see that the information is diffused, and even used, in all the appropriate places);

- use *reason* to persuade all those who are affected by the information to use it (this works as well or better than relying upon power, if the strategic managers are persuasive); or

- perhaps best of all in most situations, use *education* of participants in the entity to emphasize, and convince those who need to be convinced of, the importance and usefulness of the information as a way of improving the likelihood that the information will be properly used.

However it is done, diffusion of strategically important information about public policy issues among the relevant participants in an entity brings the steps in analyzing public policy environments to completion. Given the vital link between entities and the public policies that affect them, no contemporary health care entity can realistically expect to succeed in the absence of a reasonably effective set of activities through which its strategic managers discern and, ultimately, respond to strategically important public policy issues. However, this is only half of the task facing those responsible for situational analysis. They must also conduct an internal environmental analysis to complete the situational analysis stage shown in Figure 2.2.

Internal Environmental Analysis

An effective and thorough internal environmental analysis includes two parts: a review of current strategy, and a critical resource analysis in which both strengths and weaknesses inherent in the entity are identified and considered.

The review of current strategy (i.e., the set of decisions that determine the entity's essential characteristics and that give it position and direction in relation to the overall environment within which it exists) is conducted in order to establish a benchmark against which further strategic management takes place. In effect, strategic managers review their current strategy to determine whether the entity is moving in the desired and appropriate direction, or whether some strategic changes are indicated. At the situational analysis stage, the review of current strategy is a rather perfunctory activity. It is not until later, in the strategy formulation stage, that this benchmark information is used to help determine if changes in strategy are to be made.

The internal resource analysis conducted in this stage is a straightforward process of cataloging the entity's internal strengths and weaknesses. This information can later be used to help determine strategy by matching strengths and weaknesses against opportunities and threats.

The order in which the external and internal analyses are made in the situational analysis is important, because most internal strengths and weaknesses can be identified only in relation to the external environment. For example, an entity's "strong" financial position is defined in relation to the financial positions of other similar entities. Similarly, an entity's physical location is considered a strength only if there is ample demand for its services in the area in which it is located and if it enjoys a strong market share compared with its competitors.

The internal resource analysis, or audit as it is also called, provides strategic managers with an inventory of the entity's resource base. Although there is no universally agreed upon framework for conducting these inventories, the effort should be conducted systematically and should be repeatable over time. One useful framework is:

- A financial analysis covering the entity's financial condition, trends in its financial performance, and how it compares to industry norms.

- A human resources analysis covering the entity's capabilities in relation to its work. This analysis should provide information on the adequacy of staff, both in terms of numbers and quality, both for present activities and for possible future development.

- A marketing analysis covering all aspects of the entity's ability to distribute its services. This audit should identify the entity's markets and its competitive position (i.e., its market share) within these markets.

- An operations analysis covering the entity's various production and service delivery activities. This analysis should cover activities in the direct work of the entity, such as work done by the clinical departments and programs in a hospital, as well as work done in support and management operations.

- An organizational culture analysis covering aspects of the shared beliefs (e.g., the centrality of patient care, the importance of medical research, the primacy of quality in health care services delivery) and values (e.g., duty, integrity, trust, and fairness) that help guide the behavior of all of the participants in the entity. Although this analysis may involve a degree of subjectivity, it is nevertheless an important component of a complete internal resource analysis.

Strategy Formulation

The second stage in the strategic management process illustrated in Figure 2.2 is strategy formulation. Guided by results of both the internal and external components of the situational analysis, strategic managers can establish objectives for the entity, develop and evaluate strategic alternatives, select their strategy, and develop implementation plans for it. This set of interrelated activities comprises the strategy formulation stage of the strategic management process.

Situational analysis, in combination with strategy formulation, constitutes the strategic planning process in an entity. However, good planning, alone, does not ensure that an entity's strategic objectives will be met. It assures only their establishment. Strategic implementation and control must be added to complete the strategic management process.

Strategic Implementation

In the implementation stage of strategic management, attention is turned to what can be the significant challenges involved in carrying out strategies. There is a direct connection between an entity's capabilities to implement particular strategies and the appropriateness of such strategies for the entity. For example, strategic managers in an entity that is designed for stability and centralized decision making can have great difficulty implementing a corporate growth or diversification strategy. Similarly, people who are experienced only in implementing growth strategies will have difficulty shifting to strategies intended to stabilize or retrench.

Ideally, strategic managers will recognize the connection between strategy and implementation capability in the formulation stage and factor this into strategic decisions. Sometimes, however, they do not. When mismatches occur, whether they are imposed by external public policy or market changes or are the result simply of poor judgment on the part of strategic managers, problems invariably arise in the implementation stage of strategic management. Such mismatches can be overcome in two ways: strategies can be changed and/or the capabilities of an entity to implement a strategy can be changed. In the latter case, resources can be redirected, people can be provided with additional training and education, and new people can be brought into the situation to support strategic implementation.

Strategic Control

The strategic management process illustrated in Figure 2.2 is brought to full cycle through a final stage, strategic control. In this stage, strategic implementation is monitored and the resulting information is used to control ongoing decisions, actions, and behaviors affected by the entity's strategies. Strategic control differs from operational control, which involves such activities as job, work, or production scheduling and statistical quality control, although both strategic and operational control follow the same basic paradigm. In both, the basic control process is one in which actual results are monitored and compared to previously established objectives and standards, and deviations are corrected. In effective strategic control, strategic managers evaluate their entity's performance, and make changes when they are indicated.

Health care entities typically employ a number of strategic control systems or devices, including budgets, routine activity reports, exception reports, employee performance appraisal systems, and consumer or patient satisfaction surveys, for example. Effective strategic control systems (Goold & Quinn, 1990):

- facilitate coordination in entities;
- motivate effort toward achievement of the entity's objectives;
- provide an early detection system to warn that the assumptions and conditions underlying strategies are wrong or have changed; and
- provide a means through which strategic managers can intervene to correct an ineffective or inappropriate strategy.

The model of the strategic management process shown in Figure 2.2 illustrates that the effort to trace the source or sources of deviations and to decide where to intervene in order to correct underlying problems goes back to each stage of the process. Are the strategic assumptions that grew from the external and internal environmental analyses still valid? Are the strategies themselves still appropriate? Are the correct steps being taken to implement the strategies?

One of the important things that the model of strategic management examined previously clearly illustrates is the relationship of certain public policies—authoritative decisions made by governments in the external environments of health care entities—to the strategies undertaken by these entities. Key aspects of this intersection are explored in the next section.

THE IMPACT OF PUBLIC POLICY ON HEALTH CARE ENTITIES, AND THE STRATEGIC MANAGEMENT RESPONSE

The production and distribution of health services, whether preventive, acute, chronic, restorative, or palliative, require a vast set of resources—including money, human resources, and technology. All of these resources are affected by public policies. Furthermore, health services are provided through the health care entities that transform these resources into health services and distribute them to consumers. The entities themselves are also influenced by public policies. Public policies have a major bearing on the nature of the health services available through their impact on the resources required to produce the services, as well as on the entities through which the services are organized, delivered, and paid for.

In determining their relative interest in the impact of public policies on their entities, strategic managers might ask themselves questions such as these:

- Do public policies influence my entity's capital allocation decisions or its strategic plans for services and markets?
- Do workforce issues affect my entity and are these issues affected by public policies?
- Have previous strategic plans for my entity been scrapped or substantially altered because of changes in public policy?
- Is my entity's industry becoming more competitive? More technology dependent? Do public policies affect competition? Technology?
- Does the interplay between public policies and the other variables in my entity's external environment (i.e., general business conditions, economic performance, education) influence strategic decisions?
- Am I and other strategic managers in my entity displeased with the results of past strategic planning because of surprises resulting from changes in public policies that affected our performance?

Strategic managers who answer yes to even one of these questions most likely will be very interested in relevant public policies and the process through which they are made. If the answer to most or all of the questions is yes, as is typically the case for contemporary health care entities, they will consider interest in their entity's public policy environment to be absolutely imperative and will make strong operational commitments to understanding and effectively responding to the threats and opportunities created for their entity by public policy. To be successful, their response must fulfill two important and quite different responsibilities regarding their entity's public policy environment: analysis and influence.

Analyzing an Entity's Public Policy Environment

Effective strategic managers must *analyze* their entity's public policy environment. Such analysis forms part of the base upon which an understanding is built of the strategic consequences of events and forces in an entity's public policy environment. Effective strategic managers must accurately assess the impacts, both in terms of opportunities and threats, of public policies on their entity and position the entity to make strategic adjustments that reflect planned responses to these impacts.

The process through which an entity's public policy environment is analyzed was described earlier in the discussion of the external environmental analysis component of the situational analysis step in the strategic management process depicted in Figure 2.2. External environmental analysis, whether focused on public policy or on some other component of a health care entity's industry, task environment, or macroenvironment, incorporates the following activities: Scanning ▶ Monitoring ▶ Forecasting ▶ Assessing ▶ Diffusing.

Influencing an Entity's Public Policy Environment

Beyond analyzing their entity's public policy environment, effective strategic managers must also *influence* the formulation and implementation of public policies. Strategic managers have responsibilities to try to make their entity's external environment, including its public policy component, as favorable, and failing that, as neutral, to the entity as possible. Inherent in this responsibility is the requirement to identify public policy objectives that are consistent with their entity's values, mission, and strategic objectives and to seek through appropriate and ethical means to help shape public policies accordingly.

Typically, the strategic managers of effective health care entities not only make commitments to discern and utilize relevant information from their public policy environments, but also develop strong operational commitments to devise ways to exert influence in them. There is nothing innately wrong with a strategic manager establishing an operational objective of being influential in the entity's public policy environment. However, it goes almost without saying that activities directed to this objective can easily be tainted by overzealous attempts to influence the policy-making process for self-serving purposes. This is an area of activity where adherence to ethical principles is especially important.

As with analyzing public policy environments, the responsibility for seeking to influence events and outcomes in an entity's public policy environment rests predominantly with those at its strategic apex although they may be assisted by specialized staff in fulfilling these responsibilities, especially in large entities. When influencing its public policy environment is a major commitment and endeavor for an entity, a specialized department or unit is typically established to do much of the actual work. The directors of such departments almost invariably report to the chief executive officer (CEO), because CEOs play vital roles in influencing public policy environments, normally acting as the spokesperson for their entity with all outside stakeholders, including those in the public policy environment.

Departments or units devoted to governmental affairs serve mainly to enhance the ability of the entity's strategic managers, especially its CEO, to succeed in influencing the public policy environment to advantage. The organizational structure of the University of Pittsburgh Medical Center Health System (UPMC Health System) (http://www.upmc.edu), for example, includes a vice president for government relations, who reports to the system's president and who supports efforts to analyze and influence the system's public policy environment at the local, state, and federal levels. The director of federal government relations reports to the vice president and is responsible for keeping the senior managers "informed up to the minute" on relevant federal policies, including legislative and regulatory matters. This director performs the following specific functions:

- identifies and analyzes relevant legislative and regulatory matters;
- recommends appropriate responses to legislative and regulatory matters of interest;
- carries out the responses, including facilitating the participation of others in the responses; and
- advocates proactively in specific policy areas, including Medicare reimbursement, biomedical research funding, and transplantation issues.

No matter how an entity is designed internally to carry out the tasks associated with influencing its public policy environment, the bottom line of exerting influence in public policy environments is that influence actually must be exerted eventually. The exertion of influence in public policy environments is "simply the process by which people successfully persuade others to follow their advice, suggestion, or order" (Keys & Case, 1990, p. 38). But how?

Influence in Public Policy Environments: A Matter of Power and Focus

The effective exercise of influence in an entity's public policy environment depends on having a basis for influence and on knowing where and when to focus efforts. Power is the basis of influence in a public policy environment. Power is the potential to exert influence and derives from three sources:

- *Positional power* is based on an entity's place or role in the larger society. Health care entities have certain power, or potential to exert influence, simply because they exist and are recognized as legitimate participants in the policy-making arena. Positional power, alone, may gain a hearing for particular views or preferences. The exertion of significant influence, however, usually requires more and different power.
- *Reward* or *coercive power* is based on the entity's capacity to reward compliance or to punish noncompliance with its preferred decisions, actions, and behaviors by policy makers. The rewards that can be provided or withheld include money and other forms of political support such as votes, and the ability to organize and mobilize grassroots activities designed to persuade other people on particular issues.
- *Expert power* is based on an entity's possession of expertise or information that is valued by others. When seeking to exert influence in public policy environments, useful information and expertise may pertain to the definition or clarification of problems or to the development of solutions.

Entities that can marshal these bases of power, especially when they can be integrated, can be very influential indeed. The degree of influence, of course, varies from one entity to another. The relative amount of power each entity has is important in determining relative influence, but so too are reputations for being able to exert influence ethically and effectively and the strength of ideological convictions held by those who seek to influence. Whatever its bases, however, power is only one part of the complex equation that determines influence.

Strategic managers must also concern themselves with the second element of influence: where to *focus* their efforts to influence the public policy environment. Typically, they are guided in focusing by the identification of policies that are of strategic importance to their entity in the scanning efforts described previously, as well as by the identification of problems, potential solutions, and political circumstances that might eventually lead to such policies. By focusing in this way, strategic managers will seek to influence strategically relevant policy makers in all branches at federal, state/province, and local levels of government. Furthermore, strategic managers will extend their efforts to influence those who have influence with these policy makers. Both policy makers, and those who can influence the policy makers, form the appropriate focus for those seeking to influence an entity's public policy environment to greatest advantage.

The model of the policy-making process shown in Figure 2.1 can serve as a "map" to indicate where influencing efforts can be most usefully directed. Depending on the circumstances of a particular situation, the proper focus may be one or more of the various component phases, or stages within them, of the policy-making process as shown in Figure 2.3.

Using the map to show where to exert influence in their public policy environments, strategic managers may focus where the health policy agenda is shaped by the interaction of problems, possible solutions to the problems, and political circumstances. They can exert influence on policy making by helping to define the problems that eventually become the focus of public policy making, by participating in the design of possible solutions to these problems, and by helping to create the political circumstances necessary to convert potential solutions into actual policies. In short, influencing the factors that establish the policy agenda itself can influence policies.

Once issues achieve prominent places on the policy agenda, they can, but do not always, proceed to the next stage of the policy formulation phase, development of legislation. At this stage, specific legislative proposals go through a process involving a carefully prescribed set of steps that can, but do not always, lead to policies in the form of new legislation, or, as is more often the case, amendments to previously enacted legislation.

Although the path for legislation is long and arduous, it is replete with opportunities for strategic managers to influence legislation development. Both as individuals and through the interest groups to which they belong, leaders of health care entities participate directly in the actual drafting of legislative proposals and frequently participate in the hearings associated with the development of legislation.

Enacted legislation rarely contains the explicit language to fully guide its implementation. Rather, laws are often vague on implementation details, leaving to the implementing agencies and organizations the establishment of the rules

Influencing Policy Formulation at

  Agenda Setting, by

- *defining and documenting problems*
- *developing and evaluating solutions*
- *shaping political circumstances through lobbying and the courts*

  Legislation Development, by

- *participating in drafting legislation*
- *testifying at legislative hearings*

Influencing Policy Implementation at

  Rule Making, by

- *providing formal comments on draft rules*
- *serving on and providing input to rule-making advisory bodies*

  Policy Operation, by

- *interacting with policy implementers*

Influencing Policy Modification, by

- *documenting the case for modification through operational experience and formal evaluations*

Figure 2.3. Places to influence policy making.

needed to fully operationalize the legislation. The promulgation of rules, as a formal part of the implementation phase of policy making, because it invites those affected by the rules to comment on proposed or draft rules, is one of the most active points of involvement for strategic managers and others who have a stake in a particular policy. The exertion of influence at this point in the policy-making process can produce significant results.

In addition to exerting influence directly by commenting on the rules that will guide the implementation of policies, strategic managers can also exert influence indirectly. This opportunity to exert influence in rule making is occasioned by the fact that when the development of rules is anticipated to be unusually difficult or contentious, or when rules are anticipated to be subject to continuous revision, special provisions may be made. In particular, advisory bodies or commissions may be established to help shape the development of rules.

In the United States, the Medicare Payment Advisory Commission (MedPAC) (http://www.medpac.gov) is one such body. Operationally, MedPAC meets publicly to discuss policy issues and formulate its recommendations to Congress. In the course of these meetings, commissioners consider the results of staff research, presentations by policy experts, and comments from interested parties such as staff from congressional committees and the Centers for Medicare and Medicaid Services (formerly the Health Care Financing Administration), health services researchers, health services providers, and beneficiary advocates. Although the opportunities for direct service on such commissions are limited to a very few people, others can influence their thinking. The strategic managers of health care entities can and do influence the thinking of commission members, and thus the advice commission members ultimately provide about formulating and implementing policy.

An example of an advisory body in the Canadian context is Ontario's Joint Policy & Planning Committee (JPPC) (http://www.jppc.org). The JPPC is a partnership between the Ontario Ministry of Health and Long-Term Care (MOHLTC) and Ontario's hospitals through the Ontario Hospital Association (OHA). This joint undertaking between government and hospitals in Ontario serves to review the impact of public policy on health care entities. Its recent focus has been on developing a new funding formula for Ontario hospitals, a high-priority item for the hospital industry. Although there are limited opportunities for strategic managers to participate directly, the JPPC provides a number of venues for feedback, commentary, and consultation: through briefings, consultation sessions, and invited submissions. These serve as important opportunities to influence policy making.

Influence can also be exerted in the operation of policies. The policy-operation stage of implementing policies involves the actual running of programs and activities embedded in or stimulated by enacted legislation. Operation is the domain of the appointees and employees who staff the government. These people influence policies by their operational decisions and actions. Thus, policies can be influenced by interactions with those who have operational responsibility. This form of influence arises from the working relationships—sometimes close working relationships—that can develop between those responsible for implementing policies and those upon whom their decisions and activities impact directly, such as health care entities.

The opportunities to build these relationships are supported by a prominent feature of the careers of bureaucrats: longevity (Kingdon, 1995). Elected policy makers come and go, but the bureaucracy endures. Strategic managers can, and many of them do, build long-standing working relationships with some of the people responsible for implementing the public policies that are of strategic importance to their entities.

The most solid base for these working relationships is the exchange of useful information and expertise. A strategic manager, speaking from an authoritative position based on operational experience with the implementation of a policy, can influence the policy's further implementation with relevant information. If the information supports change, especially if it is buttressed with similar information from others who are experiencing the impact of a particular policy, reasonable implementers may well be influenced to make needed changes. This is especially likely if there is a well-established working relationship, one based on mutual respect for the roles of and the challenges facing each party.

An obvious, and very limiting, problem for those wishing to influence the policy-making process through either the rule-making or operation stages of policy implementation is the enormity of the bureaucracy with which they might need to interact. Consider how many components of the federal government are involved in the rule-making and policy operation that is directly relevant to health care entities. Add to this the relevant units of state/province and local government and the challenge of keeping track of where working relationships might be useful as a means of influencing policy making—to say nothing of developing and maintaining the relationships—begins to come into focus. Obviously, selectivity in which of these relationships might be of most strategic importance is required.

Although some health policies are developed *de novo*, the vast majority of them result from the modification of existing policies in rather modest, incremental steps. Policy modification occurs when the outcomes, perceptions, and consequences of existing policies feed back into the agenda-setting and legislation-development stages of the formulation phase, and into the rule-making and policy-operation stages of the implementation phase, and stimulate changes in legislation, rules, or operations (see the feedback loop running along the bottom of Figure 2.1). There are continuing opportunities to influence policies as their outcomes and consequences trigger policy modification. Those who would influence policies have an opportunity to do so in the initial iteration of the policy-making process in regard to any particular policy, but they also get additional opportunities to exert their influence through the subsequent modification of existing policies.

By following the feedback loop in Figure 2.1, it can be seen that because agenda setting involves the confluence of problems, possible solutions, and political circumstances, strategic managers can be influential in policy modification by making certain that problems become more sharply defined and better understood through the experiences of those who are impacted by the policies. Strategic managers of health care entities often are among the best sources of feedback on the consequences of policies, including the effects of policies on individuals and populations they serve. Similarly, possible new solutions to problems can be conceived and assessed through the operational experiences entities have with particular policies, especially when the results of demonstrations and evaluations provide concrete evidence of their performance and impact. Finally, strategic managers—guided by their experiences and interactions with ongoing policies—become important components of political circumstances surrounding the amendment of these policies.

Strategic managers' experiences with policies also equip them to help modify policies by directly influencing the development of legislation. Experience with the impact of implemented policies on their entities help strategic managers routinely identify needed modifications. The history of the Medicare program in the United States is a good example of this phenomenon. Over the program's life, services have been added and deleted; premiums and co-payment provisions have been changed; reimbursement mechanisms have been changed; features to ensure quality and medical necessity of services have been added, changed, and deleted; and so on. The inputs from entities directly affected by these changes played a role in each of these amendments to the original legislation, although other influences also helped guide these changes.

Strategic managers also have extensive opportunities to influence the modification of policies in their implementation phases, in both the rule-making and policy-operation stages. The modification of rules, as well as changes in the operations undertaken to implement policies, often reflects the actual experiences of those affected by the rules and operations. This feedback can be provided directly to those with rule-making or operational responsibilities. Strategic managers can also take their views on the rules and operational practices that affect their entities to the courts or to the legislative branch. Both can be pathways to modifications.

CONSEQUENCES

The ability to develop effective responses to the strategic consequences of public policies, and to changes in them, is greatly enhanced when strategic managers are able to anticipate such changes months—or better still, years—ahead of when they actually occur. Beyond giving themselves the advantages of longer lead times to prepare for such changes, strategic managers who understand the inevitability of particular policy changes, even before the debate over the specific nature of the changes begins, can be positioned to exert influence on emerging policies to the advantage of their entities.

But how is such prescience to be achieved? The answer lies within fulfillment of the two fundamental and interrelated responsibilities that strategic managers face regarding public policies that affect the entities they manage: analysis and influence. Strategic managers who do their jobs well foresee both the emergence and impact of relevant public policies on their entities. This foresight enables them to begin to help shape the nature and scope of policies that will impact on their entities, often to the strategic advantage of the entities.

One important aspect of fulfilling their dual responsibilities regarding the public policy environments of their entities is for strategic managers to look beyond specific decisions reflected in public policies to the environments from which policies derive. That is, they must focus not only on the policies that affect their entities, but also on why and how these policies emerge. Strategic managers who focus broadly on the public policy environments of their organizations increase their chances of anticipating policy changes far in advance of when the changes actually occur. This focus also facilitates the effective exertion of influence on the factors that lead, ultimately, to policies. It provides opportunities to influence policies in their emergent states.

There is no doubt that strategic managers who understand the public policy environments from which the policies that affect their entities emerge are better equipped to both anticipate and influence these policies than their less informed counterparts. There is always a vast difference between strategic management based on solid predictions of future public policies versus that based on reacting to announced changes, or even on soon-to-be-announced changes. With enough foreknowledge and proactive preparation, the opportunity exists to exert influence on the ultimate shape of policies. After changes occur, only reaction is possible, typically with inadequate time for thoughtful responses if managers are caught by surprise.

REFERENCES

Delbecq, A.L., Van de Ven, A.H., & Gustafson, D.H. (1974). *Group decision making techniques in program planning*. Glenview, IL: Scott Foresman.

Fahey, L., & Narayanan, V.K. (1986). *Macroenvironmental analysis for strategic management*. St. Paul, MN: West Publishing Company.

Ginter, P.M., Swayne, L.E., & Duncan, W.J. (2002). *Strategic management of health care organizations* (4th ed.). Malden, MA: Blackwell Publishers.

Goold, M., & Quinn, J.J. (1990). The paradox of strategic controls. *Strategic Management Journal 11* (1): 40–50.

Jain, S.C. (1984). Environmental scanning in U.S. corporations. *Long Range Planning 17*: 117–128.

Keys, B., & Case, T. (1990). How to become an influential manager. *The Executive 4*: 38–51.

Kingdon, J.W. (1995). *Agendas, alternatives, and public policies* (2nd ed.). New York: HarperCollins College Publishers.

Klein, H.E., & Linneman, R.E. (1984). Environmental assessment: An international study of corporate practices. *Journal of Business Strategy 5*: 66–77.

Leemhuis, J.P. (1985). Using scenarios to develop strategies. *Long Range Planning 18*: 30–37.

Longest, B.B., Jr. (1996). *Health professionals in management*. Stamford, CT: Appleton & Lange.

Longest, B.B., Jr. (1997). *Seeking strategic advantage through health policy analysis*. Chicago: Health Administration Press.

Longest, B.B., Jr. (2002). *Health policymaking in the United States* (3rd ed.). Chicago: Health Administration Press.

Schwartz, P. (1991). *The art of the long view*. New York: Doubleday/Currency.

Terry, P.T. (1977). Mechanisms for environmental scanning. *Long Range Planning 10*: 2–9.

Thomas, J.B., & McDaniel, R.R., Jr. (1990). Interpreting strategic issues: Effects of strategy and the information-processing structure of top management teams. *Academy of Management Journal 33* (2): 288–298.

Webster, J.L., Reif, W.E., & Bracker, J.S. (1989). The manager's guide to strategic planning tools and techniques. *Planning Review 17* (6): 4–13.

Chapter 3

Galvanizing Publicly Funded Health Care Systems through Accountability

Colleen M. Flood

INTRODUCTION

Surprisingly little attention is given to ensuring excellent governance and effective government relationships in publicly funded health care systems. On the one hand, publicly funded systems address key justice concerns by ensuring that access to health care is uncoupled from ability to pay. However, public and centralized management of health care systems has been associated with concerns about timeliness in the delivery of care, inflexibility, and bureaucratization. To some extent, the success of publicly funded systems in containing health care spending may be overstated since costs may be shifted to others. For example, the public sector does not incur the cost of long waiting times; these are largely private costs borne by individuals.

Despite these concerns the answer is not, as some would argue, to move away from public governance and toward more private financing. Private financing does not further the goals of ensuring an efficient, responsive system that allocates health care on the basis of need and not ability to pay. Instead, we must look to ways to improve effective government relationships *within* publicly funded systems and galvanize decision makers in the public system so that they are responsive to the larger public interest and eliminate opportunities for cost shifting. In this chapter I try to address the various mechanisms through which to enhance accountability on the part of delegated decision makers in publicly funded systems to the governments that appoint them, and to improve accountability of decision makers in general to the citizens they ultimately represent.

A common complaint about publicly funded health care systems is that they are not responsive enough to the concerns and needs of citizens and patients and that there is insufficient accountability on the part of decision makers. This may manifest itself, as it does in the United Kingdom and New Zealand, in long waiting times for care (since the cost of waiting does not come out of the public sector budget). It may also manifest itself, as some allege is the case in Canada, in shifting the cost of care on to patients and their families by, for example, significantly reducing the capacity of public hospitals and shifting to greater reliance on informal home care provided by family members or home care that is privately financed. Not surprisingly, then, improving accountability is often touted as a goal of health reform, but its advocates are surprisingly unclear by what is meant by accountability and, more specifically, "for what," "to whom," and "how."

Usually when speaking of accountability, whatever the context, the goal is to improve the quality of decision making. While this almost always involves a situation where both discretion and power of decision making have been entrusted to others, the question remains of how to ensure the quality of the decisions made as a result. What mechanisms can governments use to ensure that delegated decision makers achieve desired goals? What mechanisms can we, as citizens, use to make sure those decision makers, whether governments, health authorities, hospitals, doctors, nurses, or other health providers, do the best job possible on behalf of the public they are meant to represent? Perhaps it is already obvious that the kinds of mechanisms will depend on the kind of decision maker and the decisions he or she is responsible for.

In the health sector it is possible to identify at least three spheres of accountability: political, market, and professional (Emanuel & Emanuel, 1996). In this chapter I will examine these three types of accountability and their potential for improving government relationships. We can also make a distinction between accountability for the overall quality of the system and accountability for the quality of specific services delivered. Existing health care systems have tended to gear accountability mechanisms toward ensuring the quality of specific services rather than the *overall* quality of the health care system. Here we will focus on how to ensure accountability for the design and operation of the *entire* health care system. In doing so we will refer primarily to publicly funded health care systems found in Canada, the United Kingdom, and New Zealand, but also, where appropriate, references will be made to the U.S. context.

POLITICAL ACCOUNTABILITY AND AGENCY

If we look first at accountability of government decision makers in the political sphere, then we can also speak of "governance" and "stewardship." The importance of governance was recently emphasized by the World Health Organization (WHO), which spoke of the need for "good" and "smart" stewardship on the part of governments, and stated that "the ultimate responsibility for the overall performance of a country's health system must always lie with government" (2000). The WHO stressed that this responsibility included oversight not only of publicly financed care, but also of *privately* financed care; that is, it includes the entire health care system. Although words like "governance" and "stewardship" convey the idea of government guiding an entire system, they do not go to the heart of what we really mean or what we really want when we talk about "accountability."

J. Donahue's (1989) definition, in my mind, speaks to the heart of the concept of accountability, which he defines as being where

government action accords with the will of the people the government represents—not the will of individuals who happen to work in the government and not what those individuals think the citizens should want but what the people, by their own criteria, count desirable.

Thus, accountability can be thought of as how responsive government decision makers are to the people they are meant to represent. We can think of this in terms of a question of agency—the agent being the government, the principal being the citizens of a particular country or province. In entrusting government with decision making, citizens must allow the government discretion. Unfortunately, there is the prospect that what is in the government's best interest is not in a citizen's best interest or, cumulatively, in the public interest (Trebilcock, 1994).This means that "agency costs" may occur; that is the gap between what government does and what is actually in the public interest. Donahue argues that the question of agency (and reducing agency costs) engages the root social challenge of accountability, and devices such as the law, ethics, and the market may all be utilized with a view to ameliorating the problem. So, if that is the challenge, how then do we go about it?

The key problem with accountability in publicly funded health care systems (and the public sector in general) is that if government does not do a good job, then the costs are spread among many citizens. Consequently, citizens may often not have a strong incentive to band together to lobby government to improve its performance, and citizens may also decline to act in the hope that they can free ride upon the efforts of others (Donahue, 1989). By contrast, members of particular interest groups, such as physicians, nurses, drug companies, etc., who individually have much more to gain or lose from a particular government decision, will have a much greater incentive to lobby the government. Any resultant policy change may not, however, reflect the more diffused interest of the public at large. In these instances there is the danger that the kinds of policy changes that are made may reflect the interests of particular groups, rather than the more diffused public interest (Trebilcock, 1994).

How then can we structure a system so as to ensure that government decision makers do a good job and always work toward the larger public interest without being captured by particular interest groups? Of course, the first question to answer is what do we mean by "a good job?" We can't hold anyone accountable unless we are sure what it is we wish to achieve. This is part of the problem with the functioning of health care systems. No one is 100 percent clear about what the goals are, who should be responsible for them, and how to hold them responsible.

THE GOALS OF GOVERNANCE OF A HEALTH CARE SYSTEM

The WHO's 2000 report on health care systems argues that governments should have three fundamental goals in running a system: good health, responsiveness to people's expectations, and fairness of contribution to financing the health care system. The report also speaks of the need for a health care system to strive for horizontal and vertical equity, that is, "treating alike all those who face the same health need and treating preferentially those with the greatest need." The report also goes on to state that allocating resources on the basis of cost-effectiveness is the most relevant criterion for achieving the best overall health. It contends that while cost-effectiveness is never the *only* justification for spending public resources, it "is the test that must be met most often in deciding which interventions to buy."

I have argued in an earlier work (2000) that a government's goals in governing a publicly funded health care system should be as follows:

a. determining the most allocatively efficient level of resources to be devoted to health care services, which requires balancing expenditures on health care services against other needs, and recognizing that improved housing, education, and nutrition, and increased employment opportunities, may have as important an effect on health outcomes as the consumption of health care services (Evans, Barer, & Marmor, 1994);

b. satisfying justice in terms of fair access to health care services for everyone, but otherwise determining priorities for treatment of health needs on the basis of cost-effectiveness;

c. choosing the most cost-effective services or treatments to serve patients' needs;

d. ensuring the technically efficient production of services;

e. ensuring that the quality of services provided is adequate and meets society's expectations;

f. ensuring that providers are sensitive to patients' concerns and that a patient's circumstances, values, and attitudes toward risk are factored into the decision-making processes at the point of supply.

One can see that there is significant overlap between the goals or objectives articulated by the WHO and by myself in the earlier work. Both, however, stress that government's goals or objectives may be in conflict. The WHO states "equity and efficiency can easily be in conflict ... because the cost of treating a given health problem differs among individuals ... or because the severity of disease bears little relation to the effectiveness of interventions" (*Report*, 2000, p. 56). I have also argued that "to an extent these accountability requirements will conflict and thus a balance must be struck between what is in society's interests and patients' interests and, more broadly, between equity and efficiency" (2000, p. 130). Consequently, government and its varied agents must also be responsible for resolving conflicts or tensions between different goals.

Achieving these goals and resolving conflicts between them is undoubtedly a difficult task, but some changes could be effected in most health care systems to facilitate this. For example, in most health care systems the lines of accountability between government and those it empowers to perform tasks are often blurred, and there is confusion as to who among central government, purchasers, and providers is ultimately responsible for realization of goals for the health care sector. Where goals are clearly specified, often there are not matching incentives to ensure the realization of those goals. The WHO criticizes the "tunnel vision" of ministries of health in countries around the world where regulations or policies are promulgated, but then little is done to implement them or follow them through (*Report*, p. 120).

EFFECTIVE RELATIONSHIPS BETWEEN GOVERNMENTS AND DELEGATED DECISION MAKERS

Although governments should have ultimate responsibility for governance of publicly funded health care systems, clearly, they must and should delegate many aspects of management and delivery to public, quasi-public, and private bodies. As the Institute for Research in Public Policy (IRPP) Task Force on Health Policy in Canada wrote:

[p]resently, the provincial governments, through their departments of health, micromanage their healthcare systems. The primary accountability mechanism for health services, therefore, is through the ballot box. But while answering to the electorate at the polls is a good mechanism for ensuring accountability for "big-picture" performance, it does not enhance accountability for the multitude of decisions that have to be made to ensure an equitable and efficient system. Joan Citizen is not likely to shift her vote in a provincial election because her local hospital has not streamlined its information systems, or because more resources than is optimal are devoted to "me-too" drugs, or because a local gynecologist performs far more cesareans than are medically indicated. We need other mechanisms of accountability for these various decisions. (2000)

In this section I will explore the lines of accountability that flow from central government to ministries of health, insurers, regional health boards, primary care teams, hospital boards, and so on.

While there are multiple factors responsible for different decisions in any given health care system, I will focus on those entities that governments empower to buy or otherwise procure health care on behalf of citizens. For convenience' sake, whether these entities are ministries of health, health authorities, social insurers, or other purchasing agents such as health maintenance organizations

(HMOs), I will refer to them as health care purchasers, unless it is important to make a distinction. The responsibility of the purchaser (funder, fundholder, social insurer) is to purchase or otherwise procure primary and secondary health care services to benefit the people they represent within the public budget allocated or received by them. In contracting for health care services, purchasers are expected to fulfill a complex matrix of responsibilities. There are four key factors by which governments can ensure that purchasers perform their functions efficiently and exercise their discretion in the interests of the people they represent. Each of these is discussed below in greater detail with reference to experiences in different countries.

Governments Should Clearly Identify Goals and Objectives

Since the late 1980s, both the United Kingdom and New Zealand have had very mixed experience with "internal market reform," designed to improve the internal efficiency of their publicly funded health care system. The reform process proved to be volatile, with each new government bringing in another wave of reforms. However, one feature of the initial reforms that seems to have survived all governments and new reform initiatives is the shift toward clearly articulating broad goals and objectives at a central level and then monitoring their obtainment. For example, under the 1997 New Labour reforms, health authorities in the United Kingdom are responsible for drawing up three-year "Health Improvement Programs." The government sets out objectives to be met in the health and social services sector (the most recent document is *Modernizing Health and Social Services: National Priorities Guidance, 2000/01– 2002/03*) and health authorities must base their health improvement programs on the priorities set out in this document. Similarly, in New Zealand, the minister of health is required by legislation to determine a "New Zealand Health Strategy" that is a framework for the overall direction of the health sector. The strategy sets out seven fundamental principles that are to be reflected across the entire health sector and highlights thirteen population health objectives (chosen on the basis of the degree to which they can improve the health status of the population and reduce health inequalities between different population groups). The ministry of health and district health boards are required to focus on these objectives for action in the short to medium term.

Unfortunately, the hard-won lessons from the United Kingdom and New Zealand regarding the importance of clearly identifying goals and objectives do not seem to have been absorbed by other jurisdictions that are now experimenting with internal market reform. For example, in Ontario, Canada, there is little public articulation of the goals and objectives of the Community Care Access Centres (CCACs) to which the government has delegated the power to contract out for publicly funded home care services. There is no specific legislation or regulations setting out how CCACs are to undertake their purchasing responsibilities, and little transparency regarding their goals and objectives. The only specific regulation impacting on the CCACs sets out the maximum entitlement for any individual for home care services. The government and the CCACs enter into budget agreements each year, but the standard form contract does not mention the requirement to contract out, nor provide any detail on how CCACs should approach their purchasing responsibilities. Instead, one must look to government "guidelines" that are issued from time to time to find any content for the CCACs' purchasing roles.

An initial step toward improving accountability is to be explicit about what it is that is expected to be achieved. This would seem likely to be a more rigorous process (and not replete with conflicts of interest) when ministries of health are not setting their own objectives, but instead are setting targets for arm's-length agencies (health authorities or budget-holding groups of health care providers), while retaining the roles of oversight and governance. As discussed below, one of the benefits of devolution is that it enables a series of checks and balances, such that the central government can monitor the performance of an independent agency rather than attempting to fulfill the multiple roles of regulator, manager, and purchaser. Clearly articulating goals and objectives facilitates monitoring by the central government of purchasers' performance relative to those objectives. It also makes it difficult for both the central government and the purchasers to recant from these at a later date without at least justifying their actions to their citizenry.

Integrating Funding in the Hands of Decision Makers to Reduce Opportunities for Cost Shifting

A key factor recognized by a number of commentators is that "silos" of financing result in inefficient cost shifting. In New Zealand, overcrowding in accident and emergency rooms may be linked to the fact that hospitals are fully publicly funded and family doctor care is, at best, only partially publicly funded. In Australia, the fact that states have financial responsibility for hospital care, but not for physician services or drugs, may result in efforts to shift patients from the hospital sector and, to a greater degree (whether this is efficient or not), to rely on physician services or drugs. Similarly, in Canada, there is a significant degree of private financing for home care services and drugs. The risk is that purchasers in the publicly funded sector (ministries, health authorities, and hospitals) will overemphasize the need to reduce hospital stays (which are fully publicly funded) and put more emphasis on home care and drug therapy, since funding for these services does not have nearly as great an impact on public sector budgets.

An important aspect of accountability is to ensure that the purchaser has or is responsible for the funding for a broad range of health care services and is able to make efficient substitution decisions between different services. It has been argued that some of the benefits of New Zealand's 1993 internal market reform, namely "increased service integration" and "increased accountability for primary care," can be attributable to integration of financing for secondary and primary services, and of health and disability services. These gains, it is said, could have been achieved independently of other more controversial features of the reform process, e.g., mandatory contracting out by regional health authorities (N.Z. Minister of Health, 1996). Similarly, the benefits of integrated funding are viewed as key in the most recent U.K. reforms with primary care groups being charged with managing the budgets for primary and community care. They will also, eventually, be responsible for purchasing hospital services from the National Health Service (NHS) trusts. Noticeably, however, the primary care groups will not hold the budget for physician services. Similarly in Canada, S.J. Lewis et al. note that no province has included payment for physicians' services or drugs within regional boards' budgets (Lewis et al., 2001). Thus, these new devolved authorities are impeded from cost-effective decision making, since they do not receive funding to purchase a comprehensive range of services.

Although integration of funding seems to be well recognized in the literature as an important factor in achieving good decision making, the *extent* to which funding should be integrated is tied to the key question of who should be accountable for what. There may be a case, for example, for separating funding for public health from the rest of the health care budget or at least "ring-fencing" the public health budget, i.e., the public health budget is still kept within the general health budget but a specific amount is designated for public health and this money cannot be reallocated to other health care needs. This is because the payoffs from investment in public health are often long-term and difficult to measure, and there can be pressures to underinvest in public health so as to reduce short-term pressures in the acute care sector. This is what has occurred in New Zealand—first, through an independent public health commission charged with managing the public health budget and commissioning services, and subsequently, through ring-fenced budgets for public health within the budgets of regional health authorities. Similarly, in the Netherlands, earlier versions of the managed competition reform proposals had provided for the integration of acute and long-term care, and proposed extending the Exceptional Medical Expenses scheme so that it covered all general medical expenses. However, there was concern about how to assess accurately the risk of the need for long-term care services, since the assessment requires a projection many years into the future. It was determined that it was better for these sorts of services to be provided independently of a competition-oriented scheme (Van De Ven & Schut, 1994). As a consequence, the 1995 reforms provide for the retention of a separate Exceptional Medical Expenses scheme, albeit restricted to long-term care and mental health care.

Monitoring of Performance by Government of Delegated Decision Makers

It is not enough for a government to simply fix goals and objectives and to facilitate their achievement by devolving funding for a broad range of health care services. It is also necessary for government to monitor the obtainment of these goals and objectives. However, there is a danger in the monitoring process that the focus will be upon those indicators that are easy to measure such as increased turnover or reduced waiting lists. This was a clear lesson that emerged from the experience with internal market reform in both the United Kingdom and New Zealand. However, simply because something is not readily measurable does not mean that it does not matter. To avoid having the system skewed, it is key that more abstract or broader measures (such as maintaining people's satisfaction with the health care system or maintaining and improving the quality of services delivered) be seen as important performance indicators. In the United Kingdom, the 1997 New Labour proposals promised to broaden performance measures to "things which count for patients, including the costs and results of treatment and care." In Canada, the Ontario provincial government does seem to be alert to the fact that quality is a significant issue in tendering for the supply of home and community care services. The regulatory framework must also ensure that monitoring occurs to make sure those quality indicators are realized and that there are incentives to ensure their realization (Ministry of Health, 1997).

Incentives to Ensure Performance on the Part of Delegated Decision Makers

It is also important to ensure that there are incentives for management within the purchasing entities to achieve the goals and objectives that have been set. Margaret Thatcher's internal market reforms in the United Kingdom were criticized for not providing penalties for purchasers (the regional health authorities) that arranged "bad" contracts for supply, yet such arrangements denied patients care in the same way as the alleged inefficiencies of the old command-and-control system (Allen, 1995). Similarly, the New Labour reforms do not require any penalty or sanction for primary care groups that do not perform well, apart from firing management. In New Zealand, there were no incentives built into contracts for managers of regional health authorities (the purchasers), apart also from the prospect of dismissal. Dismissal is a crude mechanism by which to seek to ensure performance, particularly since whether or not sanctions are imposed may depend on the politics of the day and determined on an arbitrary and unprincipled basis. More recent reforms in New Zealand remove the rigid purchaser-provider split and largely return the system to its pre-1993 configuration (returning both purchasing power and management control of public hospitals back to "district health authorities"). This restores, however, the problem that the district health authorities have had. They have no incentive to purchase care from other, potentially more efficient, public or private providers, but instead may use their funds to artificially prop up the public hospitals they are responsible for managing. Very little attention has been given in any Canadian province to designating incentives to ensure that regional or district health boards are responsive and accountable to the citizens they ultimately represent. Often what limited measures are proposed to ensure accountability for performance do not come to pass. For example, although in many provinces it was intended that regional boards would eventually be elected, all remain government-appointed except for Saskatchewan's thirty district health boards.

In the absence of incentives trained on purchasers, there is no engine to drive smart decision making. In the public sector, the hope seems to have long been that the appointment of "good" people alone would be sufficient to achieve the larger public interest. The appointment of good and skilled decision makers is a necessary but not sufficient condition for decision making that works toward the larger public interest. Apart from skills and necessary resources, decision makers need incentives to make decisions that strike the right balance between patients' needs and societal interest and between equity and efficiency.

There is not room here to discuss all the possibilities in terms of designing incentives to ensure good decision making on the part of purchasers, but this exercise would seem key to galvanizing and reenergizing public health care systems. I would note here that despite well-crafted incentives, a central government's propensity to monitor a purchaser's performance may be limited by political factors. Thus, it is important to consider what incentives purchasers have, in order to be *directly* accountable to the people of the region they represent. Below I discuss two broad types of incentives, "voice" (political accountability) and "choice" or "exit" (market accountability). Professional accountability is discussed as a means to ensure the quality of particular services. I focus first on "voice" and "exit," as I am hoping to explore how to ensure accountability for the governance and management of a health care *system*, as opposed to the quality of individual services.

THE PUBLIC'S VOICE AND CHOICE

Although most publicly funded systems allow patients free choice of their family doctors, there is usually no ability to choose their insurer or the decision maker that will purchase, manage, or procure publicly funded care on their behalf. Consequently, citizens have to rely on lobbying or using whatever political clout they may have—what Albert Hirschman in his seminal work, *Exit, Voice and Loyalty* (1970), would describe as "voice"—to try to improve the performance of governments or of their health care purchasers in governing and managing the health care system.

Recent competition-oriented reforms in a number of jurisdictions have moved toward enabling citizens to choose a purchasing agent for health care. Choosing purchasers or insurers sounds like the free market at work and would seem to raise all sorts of concerns about access and justice. However, in both internal market reform (implemented in the United Kingdom and New Zealand) and managed competition reform (implemented in the Netherlands and proposed by President Clinton in the United States) the goal is that citizens should be able to shift from purchaser to purchaser or insurer to insurer with a risk-adjusted share of funding: What was paid into the pool would reflect capacity to pay (the system would be progressively funded, e.g., by individual contributions set to a fixed percentage of annual income); what would follow the individual would reflect that individual's risk of needing health care. Both these reform models attempt to harness the discipline of the market (if purchasers didn't perform then people would, in Hirschman's term, "exit," causing loss of revenues) and achieve social justice by *progressively* funding health insurance coverage.

So there seem to be two fundamental routes to select from in terms of ensuring accountability of purchasers in a system that is progressively financed—through voice or political accountability or through exit/choice as a quasi-market means of accountability (Flood, 2000, Ch. 4).

VOICE AND POLITICAL ACCOUNTABILITY

How might the use of lobbying and political voice work to improve the accountability of government-appointed purchasers such as health authorities and, now, primary care groups in the United Kingdom, district health authorities in New Zealand, and health authorities in provinces within Canada? Here I will examine five mechanisms to improve voice: (1) devolution, (2) election, (3) consultation, (4) charters of rights or bills of rights for patients, and (5) maximizing the use of voice in the public sector by discouraging those with resources from opting out to the private sector.

Devolution of Authority to Regional and Local Levels

Devolution of responsibilities for planning, setting priorities, allocating funds, and managing health care services from central health ministries to regional authorities is a phenomenon that has occurred more or less in every province in Canada. In both the United Kingdom and New Zealand, purchasing and procurement functions have been devolved away from central ministries to health authorities. Both are also experimenting with devolving budgets to groups of primary care providers.

The benefits of devolution are often said to be:

1. Decision making is shifted closer to those most affected by the decisions and thus the process becomes more reflective of local needs.

2. In terms of the use of political voice and lobbying, arguably it becomes easier for citizens to talk to decision makers about their concerns the closer and more connected decision makers are to the citizen's community.

3. Devolution shifts responsibility for certain aspects of the system away from central governments. It is not appropriate for central government to be held to task for the multitude of small health care decisions that have to be made. Governments should instead be accountable for the overall governance of the health care system.

4. Devolution helps to install a series of checks and balances into a health care system, such that central government can monitor the performance of delegated decision makers rather than attempting to fulfill the multiple roles of regulator, manager, and purchaser.

Although the advantages of devolution seem to speak strongly to the goal of improving accountability through use of political voice, there are some disadvantages to devolution that must be weighed against these benefits, such as:

1. Increased transactions or administrative costs. Concerns over rising administrative costs resulted in British Columbia's provincial government abandoning its original plan for devolution to twenty regional boards and eighty-two community health councils. Now the province will be divided among eleven regional boards (McInnes, 1996). Similarly, in December 2001, the Saskatchewan government announced it was eliminating its thirty-two district health boards and replacing them with twelve regional health boards. This being said, extra administrative costs should not be of concern provided that the benefits of devolution outweigh the costs.

2. Loss of ability to coordinate centrally and the difficulty in handling specialized services in smaller regions (but of course not all functions need to be devolved).

3. Loss of bargaining power that accrues from being a single large buyer of health care (although it is not in every market that there will be problems of monopoly on the supply side).

4. Potential difficulties of citizens moving from region to region in search of services to which the recipient region has decided to give priority.

5. The danger that government will avoid responsibility for increases in health funding, blaming the devolved authority for poor management instead.

In terms of how devolution has actually worked in practice, the first question to consider is what opportunities citizens have to influence their purchaser's decision-making processes. In New Zealand and the United Kingdom, although responsibility has been shifted away from central ministries, the large size of the new purchasers that have been created raises the question of just how much easier it will be to communicate with and influence these decision makers.

In New Zealand, the most recent trend has been to increase the number of purchasers. Prior to January 1, 2001, there was one central health funding authority, albeit with four branches, responsible for the whole population of 3.78

million (Statistics New Zealand, 1999). Since that date, there are now twenty-three district health authorities, charged with purchasing care for the individuals in their geographic areas ranging from approximately 46,000 people to 400,000 people. In the United Kingdom, the trend has been to reduce the number of purchasers. The 100 health authorities are responsible for varying populations ranging from roughly 125,000 up to just over a million. In addition, there were 3,500 general practitioner fundholders responsible for purchasing a range of health care services on behalf of the patients enrolled with them. The New Labour proposals provide for the abolition of the GP fundholders and the establishment of approximately 500 primary care groups (PCGs) as well as the gradual transfer away of purchasing responsibility from the 100 health authorities to the PCGs. On April 1, 1999, 481 PCGs began life in England, with a patient population ranging from 46,000 to 257,000, with an average of 100,000. A typical PCG includes between fifty and sixty general practitioners from twenty or so different practices. In Canada, a similar story has occurred, with devolution to multiple authorities at one level, and regionalization of management of hospital boards at another. Thus, while the number of purchasers within many provinces in Canada increased (moving from the ministry of health to several health authorities), at the same time regionalization and consolidation were happening (as the management functions of dozens of hospital boards were consolidated into the new health authorities).

Election of Members of Purchasing Authorities

Election of purchasing authorities may improve accountability because elected members know that if they are not responsive to their constituents they may well be voted out of power at the next election. Also, locally elected members may be more responsive to the voice of people within the communities they represent as well as more representative of the communities they serve. Of course, the right to elect governments is the ultimate sanction in terms of the overall governance and responsibility of the health care system. However, these elections do not ensure accountability for all the smaller, invisible webs of decision making that occur in a health care system.

Neither the United Kingdom nor New Zealand embraced the idea of electing the members of the various health authorities—they were predominantly government-appointed. As well, more recently, New Zealand reinstituted district health boards, which provides for the election of seven members, and for the appointment of up to four members by the minister of health. The legislation also states that the Minister must endeavor to ensure that Maori membership of the board is proportional to the number of Maori people in the local population and that, in any event, there are at least two Maori members on the board.

In Canada very little attention has been given to designating incentives to ensure that regional or district health boards are responsive and accountable to the citizens they ultimately represent. In Saskatchewan, where elections were introduced, a recent survey found that 76 percent of board members believed that they were more accountable to all the residents in their district than to special interest groups, ward residents, provincial ministries of health, or local health care providers, and that elected board members were more likely to state this than appointed members (Lewis et al., 2001). Nonetheless, in December 2001, the Saskatchewan government announced that it was abandoning the concept of having two-thirds of the health board members elected on a ward system and now would simply appoint board members (Saskatchewan, 2001). Meanwhile, recent regulations in Alberta allow for two-thirds of all regional health authority board members to be publicly elected, while the remaining one-third are appointed. The variety of approaches taken across Canadian provinces and across other jurisdictions suggests it is very important to conduct better research on the benefits and costs of different forms of accountability mechanisms, such as elections.

The argument against allowing elections is that government-appointed purchasers will be above the political fray—although, of course, this argument ignores the fact that the government-appointed members may seek to please, in their decision making, the government that appointed them. I have argued in an earlier work that the primary problem with reliance on election as a means of ensuring accountability is that many citizens will have to rely on members for whom they may not have voted and with whose policies they do not agree. Moreover, it is unclear whether the decisions made by an elected body can reflect the preferences of any citizen, or would result instead in a series of compromises that satisfies no one. There is also the potential problem that elected boards would be dominated by members of the medical profession or other particular interest groups, who clearly would have a much greater interest in these positions than ordinary members of the public. Despite these problems, in a democracy the means of enhancing accountability of decision makers to citizens must be seriously considered.

Consultation by Purchasing Authorities with Citizens

A feature of internal market reform in both the United Kingdom and New Zealand was the imposition of a duty to consult on government-appointed health authorities. In the United Kingdom, health authorities were required to consult with "community health councils" on any proposal that the authority had under consideration for any "substantial development" or "substantial variation" in the provision of health care services in a particular area (U.K., 1996). The 204 community health councils in England and Wales were appointed in part by local governments and could not include health care professionals. The New Labour reforms of 1997 give more emphasis to consulting with health care professionals, and require health authorities in conjunction with primary care groups to formulate "health improvement programs," which are to be "jointly agreed by all who are charged with planning or providing health." There is no mention made of consultation with the public with respect to formulation of these strategic programs. Moreover, on July 27, 2000, it was announced, as part of a new national plan for the NHS (the publicly funded health care system in the United Kingdom), that the community health councils are to be abolished and replaced with a range of new mechanisms to enhance "voice" on the part of citizens in the NHS. Unfortunately, the proposed new system of citizen consultation has been criticized as "fragmented" and the proposed new bodies have been criticized as lacking independence and statutory powers.

In New Zealand, the new district health boards (DHB) must prepare district strategic plans that set out how they will fulfill their objectives and functions. Before determining or making a significant amendment to a district strategic plan, each DHB must prepare a draft and consult its resident population. Consultation must also take place to change the policies, outputs, or funding for outputs stated in their most recent annual plan.

Consultation with citizens is one means to counteract the problem of having large, distant purchasers. Because of the various interest groups involved, the process needs to be structured to limit numbers and to ensure that the views of ordinary citizens are given serious weight. Moreover, consultation will ultimately be meaningless if the purchasers do not respond to the views they receive. Annual reporting, explaining the results of the consultation processes, and making transparent how purchasers plan to respond, may help to put in place the necessary incentives.

Charters of Rights and Health Services Commissioners

Another means of improving the accountability of health care purchasers to the citizens they represent is to empower citizens through articulation, at a central level, of a health care charter of rights and an independent method of enforcing these rights, for example, through a health service commissioner or health service ombudsperson.

New Zealand and the United Kingdom have both been experimenting with Patients' Bills of Rights. Australian states each have a "Public Patient's Hospital Charter" and a complaints body. To ensure the safety of private patients, there is a "Private Health Insurance Ombudsperson." In Canada, patients' bills of rights are under consideration in Ontario and Manitoba. In the Netherlands, there are appeal mechanisms in place for each of the compulsory insurance programs administered by Sickness Funds. In New Zealand, the United Kingdom, and Australia, the rights articulated focus primarily on the health care provider and patient relationship rather than that between the health care purchaser and citizen. To a large extent, these rights are codification of existing rights (or duties owed by health care providers) in common law. However, setting out these rights in a central document with independent enforcement (that does not involve patients having to bring expensive litigation or complain to the self-regulating colleges) should facilitate patients' concerns and complaints being aired and resolved, and help to restore confidence in publicly funded systems.

In terms of patients' rights to a fair and efficient health care system, the U.K. Patients' Charter (since 1997 the U.K. Patients' Guide) sets out national standards regarding what patients can expect in terms of access and treatment from the publicly financed system, including how long a patient should expect to have to wait for different kinds of treatment. At the regional level, health authorities and NHS trusts (which manage the public hospitals) are encouraged to negotiate even higher standards, and every year health authorities publish an annual report on each hospital's performance on charter standards.

The chief criticism made of publicly funded systems, whether in the United Kingdom, New Zealand, or Canada, is a lack of responsiveness to the public's needs and preferences, particularly as reflected in long waiting lists and times. In my opinion, this is because there is a problem with cost shifting as the costs of waiting for care (loss of productivity, loss of salary/earnings, pain, etc.) are not incurred by the central health care budget—a problem that bedevils all publicly funded health care systems. There would seem to be scope to address some of the concerns through articulation of a patient's charter of rights that does not simply speak to rights of patients vis-à-vis providers, but also rights of citizens vis-à-vis their government and health care purchasers, to have a just and efficient health care system.

On the other hand, concerns in the United States have primarily focused on explicit and implicit rationing by private managed care plans. As a consequence, there has been a flurry of federal and state legislation aimed at protecting those with insurance from limitations on access to and diminishment in quality of health care. It should be noted that these regulatory measures do not generally seek to expand the number of people covered by private insurance, but rather comprise a set of consumer rights protecting those who already have private insurance.

Explicit rationing by managed care plans, regarding scope of coverage, duration of benefits, premiums, and choice of providers, is regulated—mostly at the state level—by legislative minimum standards as well as by Patients' Bills of Rights in many states. In 1996, the U.S. federal government enacted the Health Insurance Portability and Accountability Act in an effort to reduce the worst effects of risk-avoidance techniques by private insurers and to improve the portability of health insurance for the employed. Both the U.S. House of Representatives and the U.S. Senate have passed bills providing for a Bill of Patients' Rights. While both bills provide national standards of entitlements for those who currently hold health insurance (e.g., ensuring access to specialists, government-sponsored clinical trials, and emergency services), and enable patients to appeal decisions of a managed care plan to an independent review board, the bill passed by the Republican-controlled House of Representatives varies from that passed by the Democratic-controlled U.S. Senate regarding patients' ability to sue health care plans in state courts (Flood, Stabile, & Tuohy, 2002).

Implicit rationing may occur where private managed care plans give incentives to health care professionals to contain costs. This rationing is more difficult to regulate, although measures have been proposed and adopted to attempt to ensure a proper balance between medical necessity and cost factors in the patient-provider relationship. For example, forty-eight of the fifty U.S. states ban the use of "gag clauses," which prohibit physicians from discussing matters such as treatments the plan does not cover, attempted referrals from the doctor refused by the plan, and financial incentives under which doctors deliver care (Schwartz, 1999). Similarly, the bills providing for a federal Patients' Bill of Rights provide for the prohibition of gag clauses.

Maximizing Voice in the Public Sector by Discouraging those with Resources from Buying Private Services

In Australia, the United Kingdom, and New Zealand, citizens may purchase private insurance, allowing them to buy faster or higher-quality care than is available from the public system. In the Netherlands, even though private insurance plays a significant role in financing the system, it runs counter to physicians' ethical codes of treatment. Canada has a complicated series of regulations designed to deter the existence of "two-tier" health care, where individuals can skip queues in the public system to get faster or better treatment in the private system (Flood & Archibald, 2001). Private insurance, however, is available for all other health care goods and services that fall outside the definition of "medically necessary" hospital and physician services.

In systems such as those in the United Kingdom, New Zealand, and Australia, where those with private insurance or sufficient funds jump queues and purchase care privately, the number of voices calling for the maintenance of standards in the public system may be reduced or diluted (Flood, 1996). This being the case, there is little incentive for holders of such private insurance to lobby and use their voice to maintain the quality of care in the public system, since their own particular quality and timeliness needs are being met in the private system.

Some argue that allowing a two-tier system reduces pressure on the publicly funded system (e.g., waiting lists and times). In a recent study, C. Tuohy, C.M. Flood, and M. Stabile examined this issue and concluded that there are no grounds for such an argument (2001). Each of the systems that allow for such a sector have waiting lists that are similar to or longer than those in Canada, and indeed New Zealand and the United Kingdom are significantly worse on these issues. Waiting times declined in the United Kingdom in response to infusions of public funding, such as the "Waiting List Initiative" of the late 1980s and early 1990s, and mechanisms to change incentives within the public sector (Ham, 1992). Some might wish to argue for supplementary private insurance citing this as the basis on which the U.S. system relies predominantly, and waiting lists are not a problem there. This is, however, comparing apples with oranges, since the United States does not attempt to achieve a universal insurance system ensuring access on the basis of need as opposed to ability to pay.

While it could be said that people buying private insurance and skipping queues in the public sector could be a means to enhance accountability through choice/exit, this is not so, for there are no *repercussions* for public sector decision makers/purchasers. Thus, there is more scope for productive inefficiency or slack as the purchasers in the public system have fewer demands placed upon their resources once quality-conscious individuals have exited to the private sector.

How could one change the incentives inducing quality-conscious and wealthier individuals to buy private insurance covering services available in the public sector and to enhance the use of voice? One method would be to make exit to a supplementary private insurance system more difficult. The first step is to remove all government subsidies of private insurance and private supply of services that are already provided in the public sector. All Canadian provinces have mechanisms in place to stop cross-subsidization of the public sector to the private sector by preventing physicians from billing both the public and private sectors for services that are meant to be publicly funded (Flood & Archibald, 2001). Taking matters a step further, government could seek to reduce the incentive to obtain private insurance for services that are provided in the public sector, by imposing a surcharge on premiums that purport to provide coverage for those classes of services. A more radical step would be to prohibit private insurance from covering those services that are available in the public sector. Exit is made more difficult because only those individuals who can afford to pay directly for the cost of private care are able to exit the public sector. Anecdotal evidence suggests that as a consequence, voice is strongly used as a mechanism to enhance the quality of Canada's health care system and to protect what are perceived to be core values (National Forum on Health, 1997).

ACCOUNTABILITY THROUGH CHOICE OR EXIT

Another means to enhance accountability is to allow citizens a choice of decision maker in a publicly funded system. If individuals were (to use Hirschman's terminology) entitled to "exit" or shift from purchaser to purchaser, taking with them a risk-adjusted share of government funding, then this would send a clear financial signal to purchasers to improve their performance or risk further loss of public revenues. Efficiency would be enhanced, and justice concerns would be satisfied, since the system would be largely progressively financed. This is the premise of managed competition reform proposals that were unsuccessfully proposed by President Bill Clinton in the United States, and implemented in a piecemeal fashion in the Netherlands. Some choice of purchasers was provided for in the internal market reforms that occurred in both the United Kingdom and New Zealand. In the United Kingdom, GP fundholders (in theory) competed with each other and with health authorities with regard to the purchase of a limited range of services—drugs, diagnostic tests, outpatient care, community services, nonemergency surgical services, and listed appliances. GP fundholding improved accountability not only through devolution (a political accountability mechanism) but also, *theoretically*, through choice/exit, as citizens/patients who did not like their fundholder could shift to another or instead choose to enroll with a family physician who was not a fundholder, in which case the patients would rely upon their relevant health authority to purchase other kinds of care. I emphasize that the choice/exit option was available in theory but, in fact, very few individuals in the United Kingdom exercised this option. In New Zealand, "independent practice associations" (subsequently known as "budget-holders") were groups of general practitioners who received budgets for a limited range of health care services (drugs, diagnostic tests, etc.). In theory, New Zealand citizens can choose their own budget-holder and if they don't like the budget-holder's performance, they can shift to another, taking with them a risk-adjusted share of public funding.

Managed competition reform is essentially a sophisticated form of voucher scheme. It is appealing in theory since it offers the spontaneous order of competitive markets but with distribution inequities corrected. Individuals dissatisfied with their current purchaser may "exit" to another, taking with them a risk-weighted share of public funding. It also means that individual preferences are given expression through individual choice, whereas ensuring accountability only through voice satisfies the preferences of the majority or those with political clout. Moreover, as Hirschman notes, ultimately voice does not have much impact unless an individual can threaten to exit or choose another purchaser. As explained further below, "exit" is not as appealing as it first appears because of the continued need for government intervention to facilitate competition on price and quality dimensions.

The Achilles' heel of managed competition reform is whether or not government regulators have the ability to deal adequately with the cream-skimming problem so as to encourage price and quality competition among purchasers. A smart regulator is required to risk-adjust the premiums paid so that competing purchasers are compensated for the risk they bear as a result of the characteristics of the people who have chosen to enroll in their particular plan. In the absence of purchasers' receiving a premium on behalf of each person enrolled with them that reflects that enrollee's risk of subsequent utilization of health care services (as is able to be assessed by purchasers), the incentive is for purchasers to engage in cream-skimming tactics, that is, trying to attract the young and healthy and not serve high-cost patients. The technical difficulties, importance, and need for effective resolution of this problem are generally underestimated in managed competition proposals. Solving this problem is crucial in order to protect vulnerable populations in all health care systems, as is the need to determine how to ration health care services and how to assess what services are cost effective (Matsaganis & Glennerster, 1994).

A managed competition system offers the prospect of a mix of regulatory, political (voice), and market (exit) mechanisms that can be tailored to ensure the accountability of purchasers. D. Dranove argues in favor of competition or exit for "[a] regulated approach will lock in existing institutional arrangements, with all future changes dictated by the whims of the political process, rather than by the demands of consumers" (1993). But a politics-free health allocation system is an impossible goal unless one is willing to sacrifice the goal of justice (redistribution—so that care is allocated on the basis of need and not ability to pay). In managed competition models, government must manage or regulate competition between purchasers to ensure universal coverage; to eliminate cream skimming; to stimulate competition on price and quality dimensions; to facilitate choice by consumers among competing purchasers; and to ensure that the quality of services provided is adequate (Brown & Marmor, 1994). It is a serious mistake to assume that the government's role is not as critical where there are competing purchasers as it is where governmental agencies act as the sole purchasers of services. Political accountability and voice continue to have a large and important role to play.

PROFESSIONAL ACCOUNTABILITY

So far we have been talking about accountability geared toward ensuring the good governance and management of the whole health care system—something that has long been overlooked in most publicly funded health care systems. This is not the case in professional accountability, which speaks more to ensuring the quality of *individual* services and the treatment of *individual* patients.

It is generally agreed among health policy scholars that patients may often not have the information with which to judge the quality of a diagnosis made or of the care recommended or provided. Health care providers generally have more information than patients, resulting in an information asymmetry problem and concerns that providers may take advantage of vulnerable patients. Although a response would be for a government to *directly* regulate the interaction between physicians and providers, this has long been perceived as too costly and too difficult. As a result, regulatory responsibility has been devolved to health care professionals themselves. In every jurisdiction there is legislation that gives members of the health care professions powers to set conditions on the training required to enter and remain in the profession, to establish ethical codes and professional standards, and to discipline those members of the profession who do not comply with the relevant codes and standards. Most systems also rely upon the deterrent effect of medical malpractice actions to ensure quality in the delivery of care by health care providers, hospitals, and other institutions. Moreover, historically it was thought that the quality of care provided by health professionals and hospitals was assured by the fact that public and private insurers indemnified health care providers on a fee-for-service basis. Thus, hospitals and health professionals had no incentive to reduce or restrict the range, effectiveness, or volume of services supplied.

Increasingly there has been growing concern over the conflicts of interest involved in allowing health care professions to regulate themselves (Jost, 1995) and in the real deterrent effect of medical malpractice actions. The shift in most systems to paying hospitals by way of a fixed annual budget has increasingly meant that hospitals have had to choose between different health care needs. In systems where publicly funded hospitals do not face competitors, concern grew that management was finding it easier to allow waiting lists to grow rather than to strive for improvements in efficiency (Saltman & Von Otter, 1992). There has also been a concern that connections and social status were influencing physicians' decisions regarding preferential treatment. Concomitantly with these trends there has been a growing awareness that quality cannot be measured by the supply of all possible health care services irrespective of costs and marginal health benefits. Increasingly there is a sense that when speaking of "quality" in terms of health care we should not just be thinking of quality of individual service delivery (both in terms of the technical skill with which a service is delivered and matching the appropriate treatment to the medical need) but quality in terms of *prioritizing needs* within a system.

In response to the concern that physicians have little incentive to be sensitive to the costs and benefits of the treatments they recommend, countries have been shifting toward paying physicians on a capitation basis. Training financial incentives upon a physician brings into focus the conflict between a physician's personal financial interest and his or her fiduciary duty to his or her patients. The intensity of this conflict will depend upon the strength of the financial incentive and the physician's ethical norms. Thus professional accountability may become of increasing importance as physicians are put under pressure to factor cost into their decision-making considerations. In any system there is a need to inculcate within physicians strong ethical norms to protect their patients' interests. These norms should include the duty of the physician to advise the patient not only of the range of treatment options, but also of the reasons why he/she is recommending or prescribing a particular treatment. Of course, there will always be tension and a physician, in reality, will strike a balance between her or his patients' needs and the resources available. However, the development and enrichment of strong ethical norms for physicians will provide a general assurance to patients that, within the confines of the resources received, physicians will do their utmost to satisfy all the needs of their patients in the fairest manner. Moreover, physicians should act as advocates on the part of their patients, ensuring that they receive a fair share of available resources in proportion to their relative health needs. The balance between this advocacy and the incentives to contain costs on the part of competing insurers/purchasers in a sense reflects the need of a system to balance individual patient needs against the larger needs of the population being served by the insurer/purchaser. Ethical norms and the bonds of collegiality developed between health providers can undoubtedly help to protect the quality of health care services, particularly in times of change and transition within a health system. For example, in the context of New Zealand's internal market reforms, P. Gorringe (1996, p. 5) notes:

Luckily, however, cooperation evolved before formal contracting. We can call on such things as commitment of people to professional goals, to caring and to cooperation and loyalty within organizations to bridge the motivational gap left by the incompleteness of contracts and their associated incentive structure.

In sum, it would be unwise to underestimate the importance of physicians' and other health providers' altruistic concerns for patients and the importance of their relationships with each other in any system of accountability.

CONCLUSIONS

Keys to improving accountability and effective relationships between government and delegated decision makers (e.g., health authorities, groups of providers, social insurers, etc.) include clear identification of goals and objectives; integration of funding to reduce opportunities for cost shifting; monitoring of performance; and instituting a system of incentives for decision makers to achieve the goals and objectives. Many of these key principles of accountability seem obvious but are so often ignored in practice.

There are a range of possibilities whereby the accountability of decision makers directly to the citizens they represent can be improved. The possibilities can be roughly categorized as those that enhance political "voice" and so result in pressure on decision makers in the public sector to improve their performance, and those that enable "exit" or choice and provide incentives for decision makers in the public system to perform with a threat of a loss of public funding.

With regard to accountability mechanisms that can be categorized as enhancing political voice, I first discussed the benefits of devolution of purchasing responsibility from central government to health authorities, groups of providers, social insurers, or other entities. Devolution has the advantage of enabling a system where roles are clarified and there are checks and balances on performance, with central government assuming the role of regulator and the devolved entity (be it a health authority, hospital, or group of providers) having responsibility for the day-to-day management of the system. Consultation is another means of improving political voice, but there are difficulties with ensuring that vested interest groups do not "capture" purchasers. There is also a need for incentives to make sure that purchasers give more than lip service to a requirement to consult. Election of members of purchasing boards is, in a democracy, the most obvious way of ensuring accountability through political voice. There are problems, however, since more complex measures of performance, such as the quality of services supplied, may be lost in the political process. Moreover, although the majority of the population may be satisfied with their elected members, there will still be a significant portion of the population who will not. Ombudspersons and charters of rights are important mechanisms through which to improve voice of patients and citizens but presently they speak to patients' rights vis-à-vis physicians and other health care providers, rather than patients' and citizens' rights vis-à-vis those who govern and manage the system. A key means by which to improve voice in a publicly financed system is to capture those quality-conscious and politically influential individuals. This may at first glance seem to be reducing choice and competition, but one must recall that if citizens participate in a supplementary private insurance sector this does not have any financial ramifications for decision makers in the public system. Thus, unlike in the private sector, where shifting to another firm sends a strong signal to the first firm to improve its performance or at the limit face insolvency, this is not the case where citizens purchase supplementary private insurance to get higher quality or faster care than is available in the public system.

Unfortunately, there is very little evidence about the effectiveness or otherwise of the various voice mechanisms discussed. It is possible that the many different mechanisms for voice could be combined to ensure the accountability of government-appointed purchasers to the citizens they ultimately represent. The fact that across jurisdictions and within countries the kinds of mechanisms adopted change back and forth, with little evidence supporting the new change, is suggestive of the need for not only a much greater emphasis on designing effective mechanisms, but much greater research into the effectiveness of these mechanisms.

With regard to accountability mechanisms that can be categorized as enhancing choice or exit, I discussed the managed competition model, which seeks to ensure social justice by ensuring that the health care system is progressively funded by facilitating choice of insurer/purchaser. This *prima facie* is a very attractive model as it ensures redistribution and harnesses the efficiency of the market. At the same time, sophisticated governance and regulation is required in order to achieve the goals of ensuring social justice while enhancing efficiency in a managed competition model. This is a task to which academics and policy makers must address themselves in the future.

REFERENCES

Alberta Regional Health Authorities Act. (1994). Section 2, RSA 2000, c. R-10.

Allen, P. (1995). Contracts in the National Health Service internal market. *Modern Law Review 58* (3): 321–339.

Australia. Private Health Insurance Ombudsman, *Who are we*. Web site: http://www.phio.org.au/onlineaction.htm. Accessed January 29, 2001.

Bipartisan Patient Protection Act (placed on the calendar in the Senate). HR 2563PCS, HR 2563PCS: in general, Subtitle B. In particular, S. 114: Timely access to specialists; s. 119: Coverage for individuals participating in approved clinical trials; s. 113: Access to emergency care. In general, Title 1: Improving managed care, ss. 101–105. In particular, s. 104, which amends ERISA to include s. 503 C.

Brown, L.D., & Marmor, T.R. (1994). The Clinton reform plan's administrative structure: The reach and the grasp. *J. Health Polit Policy Law, Spring 19* (1): 193–199.

Community Health Councils. (n.d.). Web site: http://www.achcew.org.uk/perspectiverel.htm. Accessed February 22, 2002.

Community Health Councils. (n.d.). Web site: http://www.ukpc.org/pub/chclist.htm. Accessed March 9, 1999.

Community Health Councils. (n.d.). Web site: http://www.achcew.org.uk/Discussion.htm. Accessed February 22, 2002.

Donahue, J. (1989). *The privatization decision: Public ends, private means*. New York: Basic Books.

Dranove, D. (1993). The case for competitive reform in health care. In R.J. Arnould, R.F. Rich, & W.D. White (Eds.), *Competitive approaches to health care reform* (p. 79). Washington, DC: The Urban Institute Press.

Emanuel, E., & Emanuel, L. (1996). What is accountability in health care? *Ann. Intern. Med* 124: 229.

Evans, R., Barer, M., & Marmor, T. (Eds.). (1994). *Why are some people healthy and others not?: The determinants of health of populations*. New York: Aldine De Gruyter.

Flood, C.M. (1996). Will Supplementary private insurance reduce waiting lists? *Canadian Health Facilities Law Guide* 11: 1.

Flood, C.M. (2000). *International health care reform: A legal, economic and political analysis*. London: Routledge.

Flood, C.M., & Archibald, T. (2001). Legal constraints on privately financed health care in Canada: A review of the ten provinces. *Canadian Medical Association Journal*, March.

Flood, C.M., & Archibald, T. (2001). The illegality of private health care in Canada. *Canadian Medical Association Journal 164* (6): 825–830.

Flood, C.M., Stabile, M., & Tuohy, C.H. (2002). The borders of solidarity: How countries determine the public/private mix in spending and the impact on health care. Forthcoming in *Health Matrix*, vol. 12, no. 2. University of Toronto.

Gorringe, P. (1996). Secondary health care: contracting, people and politics. Draft of November 5, 1996, prepared for the Central Regional Health Authority, New Zealand.

Ham, C. (1992). *Health policy in Britain: The politics and organization of the National Health Service* (3rd ed.). London: Macmillan.

Hirschman, A. (1970). *Exit, voice and loyalty: Responses to decline in firms, organizations, and states*. Cambridge, MA: Harvard University Press.

Institute for Research in Public Policy. (2000). *IRPP Task Force on Health Policy, Recommendations to First Ministers*. Montreal.

Jost, T. (1995). Oversight of the quality of medical care: Regulation, management, or the market. *Arizona Law Review 37*: 825–000.

Lewis, S.J. et al. (2001). Devolution to democratic health authorities in Saskatchewan: An interim report. *Canadian Medical Association Journal 164* (3): 343–347.

Matsaganis, M., & Glennerster, H. (1994). The threat of "cream skimming" in the post-reform NHS. *Journal of Health Economics 13* (1): 31.

McInnes, C. (November 20, 1996). New plan, new slogan, same objectives. *The Globe & Mail*.

Ministry of Health. (1997). *Provincial requirements for the long-term care: Request for proposals process* (September 1997) (revised), p. 6.

National Forum on Health. (1997). *Canada Health Action: Building on the Legacy*. Ottawa.

New Zealand Minister of Health. (1996). *Healthy New Zealanders: Briefing papers for the Minister of Health, 1996*. Vol. 1, *Key Policy Issues*. Wellington.

Saltman, R., & Von Otter, C. (1992). *Planned markets and public competition: Strategic reform in northern European health systems*. Buckingham: Open University Press.

Saskatchewan. (2001). *Healthy people. A healthy province. The action plan for Saskatchewan health care*. Regina, SK. Web site: http://www.health.gov.sk.ca /hplan_health_care_plan_skhealth.html.

Schwartz, S. (1999). How law and regulation shape managed care. In D. Bennahum (Ed.), *Managed care: Financial, legal and ethical issues*. Cleveland, OH: Pilgrim Press.

Statistics New Zealand. Web site: http://www.stats.govt.nz. Accessed March 11, 1999.

Trebilcock, M. (1994). *The prospects for reinventing government*. Toronto: C.D. Howe Institute.

Tuohy, C., Flood, C.M., & Stabile, M. (2001). The impact of private finance on public health care systems: Evidence from OECD nations. University of Toronto. [unpublished].

United Kingdom. (1995). Health Authorities Act (U.K.) 1995, c.17, ss. 4–5, and Sch. 6.

United Kingdom. (1996). Community Health Councils Regulations, S. I. 1996/640, s. 18. Section 18(3).

United Kingdom Department of Health. (1997). The new NHS: Modern, dependable. *White Paper 3807* (December 8, 1997). Web site: http://www.official-documents.co.uk/document/doh/newnhs/contents.htm. Accessed March 15, 1999.

Van De Ven, W.P.M.M., & Schut, F.T. (1994). Should catastrophic risks be included in a regulated competitive health insurance market. *Soc. Sci. Med. 39* (10): 1468.

World Health Organization. (2001). How is the public's interest protected. *World health report 2000*. Geneva. Web site: http://www.who.int/whr/2000/en/report.htm.

Part II

Dynamic Processes for Influencing Policy Making

Chapter 4

Advocacy

Gary L. Filerman and D. David Persaud

ADVOCACY IS A FUNDAMENTAL DYNAMIC OF
HEALTH SERVICES POLICY AND ORGANIZATION

The focus of this chapter is a discussion about advocacy, the direct impact of interest group advocacy on the health care systems in Canada and the United States, and some key issues that are the subject of current advocacy initiatives. There is a tendency within health services organizations and among health policy makers to identify advocacy as an element of the external environment, a category of forces and influences to be managed, at best, or at worst to be contended with. In fact, advocacy is a core dynamic of the organization, the fuel it runs on, and it is the raw material of policy making in a democratic system. It is important that the student of health services recognize that every practitioner, administrator, policy maker, and policy implementer is an advocate Every one of them is a "special interest," as is every health services organization. The constant process of articulating positions (wants, preferences, hopes) and aggregating the resources (energies, money, access) to communicate them, and trading off preferences in exchange for accomplishments, explains why the American and Canadian health care systems are what they are. It would be so much simpler to have an omniscient czar dictate what the system will be, but that presumes that the czar can either ignore or selectively accommodate all the advocates.

An analysis of the process and agents of advocacy begins at the micro level, focusing on the level of the individual. It most frequently takes the form of one individual who takes on a cause as a result of a personal experience or that of another person with whom he or she has a relationship, such as a parent, child, or friend. The important stimulus is the one-to-one relationship. The objective is to allow those who are disadvantaged to be treated as individuals rather than being categorized into a group. Examples include advocating for better treatment on behalf of someone in a long-term care facility or pushing for faster service for someone waiting for cataract surgery. Often the advocate's role as friend, counselor, and legal adviser makes it difficult to focus on the real issues (Bateman, 2001).

At the professional micro level, every health professional claims to be the advocate for the patient. The interests of the patient are usually described in terms of access to the services that the provider deems appropriate and necessary, sometimes identified as the "paternalistic dimension" of advocacy. The interest of the patient and interest of the professional often become blurred by the interjection of such professional values as autonomy of practice and adequate payment to sustain optimal practice conditions. Or, the interest of the professional may reflect the desire for more income, "the self-serving dimension" of advocacy. Take, for example, the case that nurses have made in recent labor actions, arguing for improved pay, better hours, and improved working conditions, all couched in terms of advocating for improving or protecting the quality of patient care.

Advocacy is an important lens through which to view how disciplines and professional boundaries have been established. How is the case presented by anesthesiologists relative to the role of nurse anesthetists, or ophthalmologists relative to optometrists, or in the myriad other domain issues that have defined the contemporary pattern of the professions? Again we see the blurring of values and goals through advocacy. At the institutional level, be it the hospital, health center, nursing home, hospice, or any other place where providers work together to serve the public, each component pursues its interests through advocacy for space, money, staff, or authority. Management is, in part, the process of managing among the competing advocates by understanding their motivation, negotiating among them, rationing resources, and allocating managerial attention to their agendas. For example, radiologists often advocate for a major investment in new technology that will improve patient care. This investment may preempt spending on new technologies advocated by other services, all arguing on behalf of quality patient care. The institution as a whole should also promote and protect itself. Every institution invests energy in convincing the public and the policy makers that it is important to the community and merits support, politically and economically. Advocacy is a responsibility of the executive leadership of the organization and is often an explicit requirement for membership on a board of directors, who are well networked to decision makers in government, industry, and the community.

These interests, and others, converge at the national, state/provincial, or macro level of advocacy in the form of organized associations, some of which have advocacy as their only mission and others of which have broader agendas such as promoting professional standards or providing services. They compete for the attention of the public, policy makers, regulators, investors, and opinion leaders of every description. They are joined by organizations articulating the aspirations of segments of "consumers" (e.g., women, the elderly, children, minorities), those committed to conquering specific diseases (e.g., breast cancer, prostate cancer, Alzheimer's disease) and improving conditions (e.g., for the blind), educators (e.g., medical and nursing schools), and those who want improved services (e.g., blood supply, family planning).

The businesses that depend on the health sector (e.g., pharmaceuticals, devices, equipment, accounting, information systems, insurance) are particularly important players. Business in general is clearly the "heavyweight" in interest group politics. It aligns its interests with the general economic welfare and has the most money and capacity to allocate to the effort (Lindbloom, 1980). In the health sector there appears to be a degree of balance among the influences of health-related business, consumer interests, and professional groups. The growing strength of the consumer movement is a relatively recent development, resulting from an increased use of consumer interest groups to advocate for a particular health cause. Often employing a variation on the name "Citizens for ... ," they may be directly or indirectly supported by a business, business group, union, or professional organizations. Public relations companies or consultants are often retained to establish such initiatives. Thus, "Citizens for Better Hospitals" may be sponsored by hospital associations seeking higher government subsidies, or by hospital equipment manufacturers advocating more investment in their products. As "Citizens for ... " groups have proliferated, policy makers have developed a healthy skepticism toward them, although sometimes using their support to justify policy actions.

C. Lindbloom (1980) identifies two additional interest groups: influential individuals and bureaucrats. There are many cases where prestigious individuals from business, religion, science, or academe have put their influence and resources behind a cause. A recent example is the role being played by George D. Lundberg, the highly regarded and fiercely independent former editor of *The Journal of the American Medical Association*. In speeches, television appearances, and through his book, *Severed Trust: Why American Medicine Hasn't Been Fixed*, he is putting his considerable prestige behind a call for reform of the medical profession and substantial changes in public policy (Lundberg, 2000). Civil servants, stretching their formal authority, frequently advocate for or against the policies of their governments or agencies. They also hold great power as writers of regulations that translate policy or law into action. Contacts with civil servants at all levels are an important aspect of advocacy. They are lobbied with as much vigor as are the legislators. Many interest groups allocate a substantial portion of their resources to developing relationships with bureaucrats (McNiven, 1997).

Advocacy is therefore a part of almost every job and entity in the health services of a democratic state. It is also big business: involving hundreds of organizations, absorbing substantial resources, and employing thousands of individuals. The goal is to persuade and advocacy is the vehicle. Advocacy is a continuous iterative process which includes identifying issues and problems, specifying and modifying desired outcomes, research and analysis, securing and retaining the support of the constituents, monitoring and responding to changes in the situation and, above all, communication. Advocates for cancer research, for example, constantly monitor research developments, respond to the interests of their subgroups, and collate their interests with other interest groups, such as those who support genetic research.

Coalitions enhance influence. Coalitions are either general in purpose, such as support for research, or specific and short-term, advocating for the solution to a particular problem or to address a policy initiative. Sometimes, coalitions bring together diverse interests producing "strange bedfellows." For example, the not-for-profit hospitals might join in coalition with the for-profit hospitals to gain increased reimbursement, while opposing each other on issues of tax relief—in both cases each arguing that they are advocating for the public interest. While much advocacy takes place within the professional and legislative arenas, most of the effort addresses the "court of public opinion" (McNiven, 1997). The health care system, in its form and priorities, is largely driven by public policy. Public policy is ultimately shaped by what policy makers perceive the public will support, or tolerate. Public support is the ultimate arbitrator of competing values and objectives.

Health advocacy attempts to influence the policy agenda by shaping opinion through the media using the tools of public relations and advertising. A high priority is placed upon engaging the participation of the media, by encouraging TV, newspaper, or magazine coverage. Editors are "informed" about the issue with the goal of securing a favorable editorial. Letters to the editor are generated and articles submitted, all with the objective of garnering attention. Polls are commissioned and are quoted as authoritative reflections of the public's opinion, or letters to legislators are generated to demonstrate grassroots support. Other marketing tactics include public forums, community meetings, and educational workshops. Fundamentally, public policy advocacy depends upon trust and the power to influence opinion. The policy maker, often not an expert in health affairs, must depend on experts for advice about the best course of action. Depending on the cause, the advocate must convince the policy maker that the direction being advocated represents the experts, and the informed judgment of constituents. For the politician, the question is, will the advice, information, or evidence point to the "right" decision with a minimum of unforeseen and undesirable technical or political consequences?

Finally, it has been argued that for interest group advocacy to drive change in public policy, political, social, and economic forces must be aligned. In other words, a window of opportunity arises, often opened by advocacy, when these forces converge (Nestman, 1996). This has occurred at several stages during the evolution of the Canadian and American health care systems. In fact, the character and structure of the systems can be correlated to direct influence of advocacy groups. The evolution of the two systems is instructive and informs us of the vitality of advocacy.

THE ROLE OF ADVOCACY IN CANADIAN HEALTH CARE

The issues in Canadian health care revolve around the principles of the Canadian Medicare program established in the early 1970s (Taylor, 1987). These principles were enshrined as part of the Canada Health Act in 1984 and form the basis of the act. They include universal coverage of all provincial residents on uniform terms and conditions; public nonprofit administration; portability of benefits among provinces; comprehensive coverage of all "necessary" services provided by medical practitioners and hospitals; and maintenance of reasonable access to insured services, "unprecluded or unimpeded, either directly or indirectly, by charges or other means" (Canada Health Act, 1984). In order to understand the impact of advocacy on the key principles of the Canadian health care system, an analysis of the historical context is informative.

A seminal milestone in Canadian health care occurred in 1946 when the Saskatchewan Co-operative Commonwealth Federation (CCF) provincial government developed North America's first compulsory state-sponsored universal hospital insurance program (Taylor, 1987). This program resulted from a grassroots advocacy movement initiated by vast numbers of citizens unable to pay for the health services they needed in a province having woefully inadequate hospitals as a result of the lingering effects of the Great Depression (Klatt, 2000). The grassroots movement resulted from an agglomeration of several interest groups. These included returning World War II veterans who strongly expressed the view that they and their families had medical coverage during the war and felt it should be available when they returned. Immigrants to Canada during this era came from countries where the health concepts of Bismark to Beveridge were in place; hence they had expectations that reasonable access to health services would be available (Nestman, 1998). Finally, most citizens of Saskatchewan found it difficult to pay for catastrophic medical services and looked to government to provide insurance for medical care (Klatt, 2000). Advocacy groups composed of these citizens, through strong, publicly organized action, effectively influenced public opinion. Their techniques included communicating with politicians and interacting with government bureaucracy (McNiven, 1997). As a result of the advocacy of this grassroots movement, the party in opposition made the provision of hospital insurance a major focus of its political platform. They were elected in 1944, and initiated the process that would lead to the legislation of a universal hospital insurance program in 1946.

By 1955, five provinces had enacted universal hospital insurance plans. Although politically popular, the plans were expensive and the federal government was pressed to honor a 1945 hospital insurance cost-sharing offer (Vayda & Deber, 1992). In 1957, federal legislation known as the Hospital Insurance and Diagnostic Services Act was enacted. It called for fifty-fifty cost-sharing coverage between the federal and provincial governments for hospital care and related diagnostic services in all provinces. This occurred despite opposition by the Canadian Medical Association, the Canadian Chamber of Commerce, and the Canadian Hospital Association to a publicly funded program. The popularity of Medicare was heightened by increased public awareness, and the Canadian Labour Congress advocated continued adoption with submissions of briefs to the federal and provincial governments. News and other media coverage served to galvanize public opinion in favor of government action (Taylor, 1987).

In 1962, the Saskatchewan government legislated a provincial medical care insurance program known as the Saskatchewan Medical Care Insurance Act, which represented the first universal, tax-supported medical care insurance plan administered by public authority in any province or state in North America. This legislation was the direct result of government advocacy by focused interest groups representing labor, farming, and concerned citizens (Taylor, 1987). This legislation occurred in spite of immense opposition from the College of Physicians and Surgeons of the province, which culminated in a twenty-one-day withdrawal of services by physicians. In 1964, after considerable consultation with interest groups throughout Canada, a royal commission advocated that the federal government enter into an agreement with the provinces to operate a compulsory, tax-supported, state-operated, comprehensive, universal program of personal health services (Taylor, 1987).

The commission made this recommendation after hearing briefs by hundreds of interest groups, including the Canadian Medical Association and the Canadian Health Insurance Association. Both groups were not in favor of a publicly funded system and advocated for a private insurance system with the government providing a subsidy to individuals or families who were below a predetermined threshold in earnings. On the other hand, the Canadian Labour Congress and the Canadian Federation of Agriculture advocated for a publicly funded system with no means testing for individuals or families. Both of these groups made recommendations that were the result of decisions that had been accepted by local, provincial, and national conventions (Taylor, 1987). All four organizations advocated their interests at public hearings and royal commissions while also working to obtain the support of political parties, thereby influencing the legislative process. They essentially favored a system that was universal in application and comprehensive in coverage, that presented no economic barrier between the provision of health services and those who are in need of it. Finally, as with all programs that require legislation, political advocacy was necessary. This came from ministers within the ruling Liberal government and members of the opposition who supported the implementation of a publicly funded system. National medical insurance, known as the "Medical Care Act," became a reality in 1971, with all provinces becoming full participants in the combined medical and hospital services program referred to as "Medicare" (Naylor, 1999). It is important to reiterate that before the 1970s a substantial amount of advocacy for public medical care insurance came from the grassroots level. Citizens achieved their goals by petitioning their politically elected officials directly, as well as through their memberships in organizations such as the Canadian Labour Congress and the Canadian Federation of Agriculture.

During the 1970s, provincial governments began to take a hard line on collective bargaining with physicians over fee structures for medical services because of the overall rising cost of medical care. This resulted in a sizable minority of physicians levying charges (known as "extra-billing") to patients over and above provincially negotiated fee schedules for fee-for-service charges. This caused concern about the accessibility to the Medicare system (Naylor, 1999). The federal government responded in 1984 by legislating the Canada Health Act with its accompanying principles. The act consolidated previous health insurance legislation and reduced federal financial transfers to provinces that allowed hospitals to levy user fees or doctors to charge more than negotiated tariffs. There were forces advocating on both sides of the extra-billing issue before the Canada Health Act was legislated. Vigorous advocacy for the continuance of extra-billing was led by the Canadian Medical Association on behalf of physicians. However, the 100,000-strong Canadian Nurses Association (CNA) advocated against extra-billing and was a factor in determining the federal government's policy on this issue. This also marked a turning point in terms of the advocacy of the nursing profession in Canada (Nestman, 1998).

ADVOCACY AND THE CURRENT ISSUES IN CANADIAN HEALTH CARE

In Canada, discussions concerning the financial sustainability of Medicare have become a national pastime. This concern generally embodies aspects of the Canada Health Act related to access and comprehensiveness of care. The boundaries of "comprehensiveness" are expanding because of scientific advances and because of expectations of what is medically necessary. Demands for coverage of home care, prescription drugs, and preventive care are increasing (Klatt, 2000; Naylor, 1999). These services are not provided under Medicare, which covers hospital and medical costs. Currently, the private component of total health care expenditures has increased from 23 percent in 1983 to nearly 31 percent in 1997 (Klatt, 2000). Providers and governments at the federal and provincial levels perceive a crisis in the health care system. When the system is carefully scrutinized in terms of patient satisfaction and services provided, however, the charges of crisis seem to be generally unfounded (Roos, 2000; Vayda & Deber, 1992). In addition, what is seldom mentioned is that this is a concern of every developed country.

In general, advocacy in Canadian health care has now become the general preserve of large well-funded interest groups. For the past two decades there has been a growing number of interest groups on the political right that have been advocating on the future of Medicare in Canada. Examples of these groups include the Fraser Institute, The C.D. Howe Institute, and the Atlantic Institute for Market Research. These groups have capitalized on the weaknesses of the public system and the perceived benefits of a market-driven approach. On the other hand, there are interest groups such as the Canadian Health Coalition that seek to protect Medicare. In addition, professional groups such as the Canadian Medical Association and the Canadian Nurses Association have continued to advocate on behalf of their members.

In response to the concern over the sustainability of Canada's publicly funded health care system, the prime minister announced the appointment of former Saskatchewan premier Roy Romanow in April 2001 to chair a commission to study the future of health care in Canada. The commission was charged to focus on four major themes: Canadian values, sustainability of the health care system, managing change, and cooperative relations in health care. Essentially, the commission's recommendations are intended to reflect the kind of health care system Canadians want and need and the implications of these wants and needs for Canadian health care. The commission held meetings with various groups throughout the country. These meetings provided a forum for presentations from such groups as the Canadian Healthcare Association, the Canadian Medical Association, the Canadian Nurses Association, and the Canadian Health Coalition. Hearings held by the commission presented an excellent opportunity for groups to have their concerns heard and to influence the future provision of health care. The profiles that follow are intended to provide insights into the characteristics and approaches of some of the predominant advocacy groups in Canada.

The Canadian Healthcare Association (CHA) is the federation of provincial and territorial hospital and health organizations across Canada. The CHA represents a broad spectrum of organizations that include acute care, home care, community care, long-term care, public health, mental health, palliative care, addiction services, children, youth and family services, housing services, and professional and licensing bodies. The CHA's mission is to improve the delivery of health services in Canada through policy development, advocacy, and leadership. In advocating for its members, the CHA utilizes the Fisher (1977) framework (which emphasizes multiple points of influence on the legislative process). Specifically, discussion papers such as "The CHA's Framework for a Sustainable Healthcare System in Canada" are produced. These publications are then disseminated to the public, media, government bureaucrats, cabinet ministers, and political parties. The CHA also advances its agenda by writing letters outlining its health care priorities to the minister of finance prior to budget announcements as well as by sending letters to the prime minister regarding such issues as funding for Canada's health system.

The Fraser Institute was founded in 1974 to focus public attention on the role markets can play in the economic and social well-being of Canadians. The institute's main sources of income are from private donations and its publications. The institute's publications are in the areas of welfare reform, privatization, education, taxation, the role of government, deregulation, and health care. One of its most notable publications related to health care is *Waiting Your Turn: Hospital Waiting Lists in Canada*. This yearly publication uses telephone interviews to physicians and hospitals to determine waiting times for specialists and various types of services such as cataract surgery, cardiovascular surgery, radiation oncology, and general surgery. Although this method of determining waiting times is controversial, the results of the annual study have helped the institute to advocate for some form of private medical services within the general Canadian Medicare framework.

The Canadian Health Coalition (CHC) is dedicated to preserving and enhancing Canada's public health system for the benefit of all Canadians. Its members include health care professionals, consumers, unions, seniors, churches, women, and students. The CHC has developed ten goals in order to improve the health of Canadians, and to ensure the future of a publicly funded health care system in Canada by utilizing various methods to affect the legislative process. Among the CHC's goals are to provide for an environment that creates good health; protect Medicare from the for-profit health industry; strengthen and expand public health care; introduce a universal public drug plan; undertake primary health care reform; restore the federal role in health care; exclude health and social services from trade agreements; and make the health care system more accountable. In order to achieve its goals, the CHC uses several methods to affect the legislative process. These methods include providing reports and briefs to the media on topics that they feel directly affect the health of Canadians in order to influence public opinion and hence the government. Other methods involve making presentations to task forces and commissions. The CHC also makes regular submissions to government departments. For example, they made a submission to the federal Department of Finance regarding the future of Canadian Medicare, and produced a document on home care in Canada, which they circulated widely to all levels of government and the media. This combination of methods serves to advocate the interests of the CHC with the eventual goal of affecting the legislative process.

The Canadian Medical Association (CMA) is the voice of Canadian medicine and advocates for the rights of the medical profession. The CMA develops policies on major health issues and produces reports, policy statements, and discussion papers on the future of Medicare, physician supply in Canada, alternative medicine, and waiting lists in Canada. Like the CHC, the CMA utilizes the media to publicize its reports, as well as making presentations to task forces and commissions. It also lobbies the government, its ministers, and representatives of the other national political parties.

The Canadian Nurses Association (CNA) advocates for registered nurses on nursing and health issues to the public, governments, and other organizations. It does this through political action and utilizes policy statements and press releases. The CNA commissions studies on important health care issues and makes them available to the public, various media, and the government. Position and policy statements of the CNA are in areas such as financing Canada's health system, determinants of health, the role of nurses in various settings, and primary health care. It also lobbies on behalf of its members by sending open letters to the federal minister of health, provincial ministers of health, other influential members of the national cabinet, and conferences where elected provincial and federal representatives meet to determine the direction of health care in Canada. It has created ACTION 301, which is a network of nurses working at the grassroots level in all 301 Canadian federal constituencies to ensure that the voice of nursing is heard. The CNA strongly supports the Canada Health Act and put its considerable clout of 110,000 members behind the federal government in that government's legislation against physician user fees in the 1980s. It advocated strongly for the implementation of the Canada Health Act. The CNA also works with the CMA and the CHA to advocate collectively on certain issues of mutual importance. An example of this was an open letter to the chairman of the Conference of Premiers in August 2000 from all three groups. It urged the provincial premiers to consult the public, the CNA, the CHA, and the CMA to address the challenge facing the health care system.

Unquestionably, the future of Canadian health care will be affected by the positions and influence of these advocacy groups, particularly if their messages are aligned with prevailing public thinking and the government's political agenda. For more than a decade there have been significant tensions between the federal and provincial governments regarding health care funding and the significantly diminished leverage enjoyed by the federal government in its enforcement of the Canada Health Act. This situation has arisen because the average proportion of provincial health expenditures provided by Ottawa fell to 21.5 percent in 1996, from 30.6 percent in 1980 (Naylor, 1999). Furthermore, the closing of hospitals and other cost-cutting measures by provincial governments in an attempt to contain health care costs has fueled the public perception that there is a "crisis" in health care. This sentiment could pave the way for market-based advocacy and reform by bolstering the case of those groups advocating that market mechanisms should have a role in the Canada Health Act. If, on the other hand, advocates for the preservation of Medicare and its core values are successful, any innovation will need to take place within the existing framework.

THE ROLE OF ADVOCACY IN AMERICAN HEALTH CARE

In the early 1960s Medicare became an international term describing some form of governmentally assured or insured medical care for all or a component of the population. At that time the U.S. Congress conjured up an ingenious and complicated package of legislation that was designed to respond to what was, even by American standards, an extraordinary intensity of advocacy. Almost every interest that had any real clout was able to claim victory in some form. The package, of which Medicare was only one part, took the wind out of the sails of the universal health insurance movement, pleased organized labor, turned the American Medical Association (AMA) into a partner of the government, protected states' rights, enhanced civil rights, protected private practice, and made the insurance industry happy.

Interest in national health insurance has a long history in the United States, but until the administration of John F. Kennedy (1961–1963), it was a slowly rising and marginal tide. Shortly after World War II it emerged as the pet theme of some public health officials and organizations such as the American Public Health Association and several welfare organizations and of some labor economists concerned about income maintenance. The notion of government involvement in medicine did not gain much popular support in an era of preoccupation not only with big government but with the "threat" of socialism and communism. As support and visibility increased, opposition, led by the American Medical Association, took two tacks. One was ideological, suggesting that health insurance through government was "creeping socialism." The other was that almost everyone was getting the medical care they needed, and that national health insurance would inevitably mean intervention in the doctor-patient relationship.

By the early 1960s, the alignment of interests had changed significantly. Study after study demonstrated that health services were confusing, inadequate, and expensive. The American governmental system had spawned a plethora of piecemeal health programs at the federal, state, and even local levels. When viewed from the individual or community level, health services were uncoordinated and there were significant gaps in access as well as very uneven quality. A strong case for comprehensiveness and continuity had emerged in professional circles. Private health insurance was working well for some of the people and not very well for many of the people. Costs to the employer and to the individual were going up. A powerful civil rights movement had developed, calling attention to inequities of widespread poverty in an era of unprecedented scientific progress and prosperity.

Demography had emerged as a driving force for change. The proportion of the aged among the population was growing rapidly and medical expenses were impoverishing many. The elderly had also become a more active political force, with a high percentage voting, particularly in certain jurisdictions. The labor movement, led by the American Federation of Labor-Congress of Industrial Organizations (AFL-CIO), had made health insurance a priority issue, creating and subsidizing the National Council of Senior Citizens to be in the forefront of advocacy for the elderly. Health care of the poor was, and is, the business of the states. The federal government paid part of the bill, but welfare programs were becoming increasingly expensive to the states. Benefits of all kinds were uneven, with frequent stories in the press about poor people moving from state to state in search of better deals. Some advocates for the poor were arguing that the federal government should take over the programs in order to assure equity and to curb abuses by both the recipients and the administrators. The governors were asking Washington for relief.

Organized medicine was becoming disorganized. The AMA had lost much of its influence with the public by repeatedly appearing to be more concerned about doctors' incomes than about access to care. Very importantly, medicine had become increasingly specialized over the previous decade. Many doctors were more closely identified with their specialty organizations than with the AMA, and the specialty groups had become politically active in their own right, reducing the AMA's claim to speak for the profession. Proponents of health insurance had become adept at calling attention to physicians' high incomes in contrast to the many that could not afford to pay for care.

Legislative initiatives calling for national health insurance, long a congressional perennial, had gradually moved from the periphery to the center, getting serious presidential attention from Eisenhower. By the time Kennedy was elected, it had become a liberal vs. conservative issue (there were members of both parties on both sides), and he made insurance for the aged a centerpiece of his agenda. Before he died, it had become a major public and legislative issue and rallying point for all of the advocates, for and against. Lyndon Johnson (1963–1969) declared a "War on Poverty" to establish the "Great Society" that eluded many Americans. Freedom from the fear of medical impoverishment was a key component of his plan. Democrats were in control of the Congress. A powerful coalition of advocacy groups had become articulate in favor of health insurance through Social Security, including the labor movement, organized elderly, religious groups, public health workers including some physicians, welfare reform advocates, and the civil rights movement. It was the great debate on campuses and in the press. Most of the supporters of universal coverage had adopted an incremental approach, accepting care for the aged as the most achievable first step, agreeing that "half a loaf is better than none."

Faced with rising public sentiment and political support, the AMA backed away from the position that there was no real problem and began to advance solutions that protected their interests. They sided with the U.S. Chamber of Commerce, the National Association of Manufacturers, and the insurance industry in supporting subsidies for expanding private health insurance. Basically, they argued for more money flowing into the existing system and no interference with the doctor-patient relationship. They proposed various schemes for doctors to be involved in whatever oversight the federal funds would require, thereby becoming partners with government in making the proposed new system work. The social, economic, and political forces were in alignment, and Kennedy and Johnson had opened the window.

The Congress produced a three-part package that responded to the concerns of the most powerful advocates. Medicare consisted of two components: Part A, the hospital insurance program; and Part B, the medical insurance program. The third part of the package was Medicaid, which addressed the need to strengthen the state welfare programs, essentially through an infusion of money, accompanied by improved standards. The critical role of advocacy is clear in this configuration of programs. The separation allowed for distinctive responses to the interests of hospitals, doctors, and the states. Part A is mandatory for all Social Security beneficiaries. Part B is voluntary and requires a monthly premium that is deducted from the Social Security payment. It operates much like a private insurance plan. Neither covers all costs. The hospitals and doctors remain private, subject to extensive regulation relative to their eligibility to participate in the programs. Virtually all hospitals participate, but a small minority of doctors do not.

Over the years since the programs were initiated, Medicare has been expanded to cover some people with disabilities under the age of 65 and specific diseases at all ages. It is a tribute to advocacy that coverage for end-stage renal disease and amyotrophic lateral sclerosis has been added. Similarly, several categories of providers have become eligible for reimbursement. These successes have energized a small industry of interest groups to seek further expansion.

From the perspective of advocacy, it is interesting to note that the plans do not provide much long-term care coverage. Part A provides partial coverage for up to 100 days in a skilled nursing facility, and some home health and hospice care. When the law was passed, the nursing home field was relatively small and politically weak. The major financial threat to the elderly was acute hospital care. Now that the major threat has been reduced (there are still substantial hospital co-payments and coverage ends after 150 days) long-term care is one of the issues of the day. Medicaid is a major payer for nursing homes, with the result that the now relatively prosperous nursing home industry makes a large investment in lobbying the states for increased reimbursement. The insurance industry has responded to opportunity by offering long-term care insurance designed to keep people out of facilities that cater to the poor. Consumer advocates have succeeded in having federal standards established for the plans. From the same perspective, the role of dentistry is interesting. The American Dental Association (ADA) stayed clear of the debates about Medicare, keeping a low profile. The ADA took the position that paying for dental care of the aged is not a problem requiring a national health insurance program. So, to this day, dental care is not covered in spite of evidence that poor dental health is a major factor in the health status of the aged. Looking back on the impact that Medicare had on physicians' income, one must conclude that many dentists regret taking that conservative position. However, there was no visible advocacy for such coverage at the time the program was passed.

Hospitals, by choosing nongovernmental intermediaries to manage their payments, reduced the concern of the hospitals that the government would interfere with their operations. Most chose the not-for-profit Blue Cross plans that were closely allied with the American Hospital Association (AHA). As the program matured, government's direct involvement grew steadily, placing the AHA in the role of continual negotiator of detailed regulations that now affect almost every aspect of hospital operations. As had been the case in medicine, specialty groups have emerged to pursue the concerns of particular hospitals, thereby weakening the role of the AHA's spokesperson, but perhaps strengthening the overall influence of hospitals, at least when they agree. Separate associations now represent investor-owned, children's, public (e.g., city-owned), and teaching (through the Association of American Medical Colleges) hospitals.

The medical plan was originally a fee-for-service arrangement with complete freedom in choosing a doctor, which is what most participants have today. Doctors are allowed to charge more than the Medicare benefit, and there is an annual $100 deductible. In an effort to cut costs, the government recently expanded the program to include HMO coverage (Medicare+), which is attractive because it often includes extra benefits such as prescription drugs and routine physical examinations. The program is not available everywhere. In fact, it is considered by some observers to be a failure because it has not attracted many subscribers and has been withdrawn from some areas because of inadequate reimbursement.

The Medicaid program has had a rocky history. Some states were very slow to adopt it, resenting the use of the federal contribution to extract more state matching money than they were willing to spend. Intense lobbying by welfare groups was necessary to bring them into the program. The Clinton administration enlarged the scope of the program by adding the State Children's Health Insurance Program (SCHIP) that offered coverage to poor children and some of their parents. Again, the states have differed widely in their enthusiasm for the program. That initiative responded to strong advocacy for kids and demonstrates the viability of the incremental approach to universal coverage.

The three programs, Medicare Parts A and B and Medicaid, are usually viewed as constituting the core of the American health care "system," but there is much more to it. The programs have succeeded in reducing the threat of impoverishment, but have not abolished it. They have fed a huge amount of money into health services without solving the problems of continuity of care and comprehensiveness. Little has been done to contain costs and almost nothing to address the fact that much of health care is of marginal quality and value. The programs have not replaced or rationalized the many governmental programs for special populations such as veterans, Native Americans, or the poor and migrant workers served by community health centers. They have not dealt with inadequacies in mental health, public health, support for health professions' education, rural access, or academic health centers. Research continues to be funded without relationship to epidemiological priorities. The answer to the question of why this situation is allowed to continue lies in the dynamics of advocacy. There are many powerful stakeholders all pulling in their own direction and all identifying that direction with the public interest.

ADVOCACY AND THE CURRENT ISSUES IN AMERICAN HEALTH CARE

The American health care system is adrift. While science continues to expand the armamentaria of prevention and cure, economics, and politics are carrying the system far from the promise for many people. There is no national health plan and no consensus on how to improve the situation. The underlying faith in the free market system undermines any effort to rationalize the vast resources available to the system so as to meet the needs of the people. There are just two ways to turn the system in the right direction. The first, and least likely, is an infusion of leadership that will rise above the entrenched interests that control most elements of the system, and rally the professions, the purchasers, and the public behind total reform. The second is action by the government, which is growing more likely every day, ironically as the result of the behavior of the players who most oppose it. But as bad as the situation is, it will have to get worse before reform becomes a viable public policy; and it is getting worse.

The employer-based insurance system that serves many middle-class Americans is being challenged by economic conditions that will not sustain it. Only half of American workers have employer-provided insurance, and many of those are underinsured. With the economy in a downturn and significant unemployment, employers lose the incentive to offer coverage and have every incentive to reduce the coverage that they do offer. More costs are shifted to the employee by reducing benefits, reducing choice of plans, and increasing deductibles and coinsurance. Low-paid employees cannot afford what is offered and bypass the opportunity. Employers devote immense resources to an unrelated business that only produces high costs, high prices, and unhappy employees and retirees.

At the same time, managed care organizations squeeze the employee further in an effort to keep premiums low and market share high, and to protect dividends. They have instituted regulations designed to control utilization, many of which have become political "hot potatoes," such as "drive-by" mastectomies and deliveries. It is widely acknowledged that the much-heralded innovation is managing cost, not care. Hospitals and other providers are constantly negotiating among demands for reduced fees and special relationships with insurers that will protect their market share. There are few predictable relationships, because the market responds to financial, not health, demands. Some are doing well but many are not.

As these and other forces have buffeted health care, there have been continuing attempts at solutions to the problems through highly touted, short-lived, and often conflicting organizational, financial, and reimbursement innovations, most of them partial and self-serving. The litany is long: managed care, Diagnostic Related Groups (DRGs), health maintenance organizations (HMOs), management service organizations (MSOs), independent practice associations (IPAs), professional associations (PAs), hospital and insurance company mergers, vertical integration, capitation, and defined-contribution "insurance," to name the most conspicuous. Now the theme of national meetings is "After Managed Care," acknowledging the failure to deliver on the promise.

Reform is not on the horizon. There will be more piecemeal programs in response to the most serious issues of the day. The most pressing is relief from the high cost of prescription drugs, particularly for the elderly. The major components of the system are now hospitals, doctors, and drugs. The pharmaceutical industry is highly profitable and the recent trend to direct consumer advertising has driven up demand, as well as promotion costs. Advocacy, for and against controls and discount programs, will determine the form and impact of the partial solution, which will be through federal legislation.

Support for coverage of the uninsured has brought together coalitions of organizations that are usually opposed to each other, such as hospitals, welfare organizations, and the insurance industry. They know the political environment will not support the expansion of Medicare to younger people or the expansion of Medicaid to people with higher incomes. The short-term "solution" is likely to be a combination of tax credits, subsidies for health insurance, and expanded support for community health centers.

We will not see America's physicians set up to assume the leadership to assure the people the access and quality of care that the system is capable of delivering. The physician has the perspective, the place in the community, and the responsibility to realize the promise of American health care. That is the advocacy that is missing from this picture.

REFERENCES

Bateman, N. (2001). *Advocacy for health and social care professionals*. London: Jessica Kingsley Publishers.

Canada Health Act. (1984). Revised Statutes of Canada, 1985. C. C-6.

Fisher, J. (1977). *Money isn't everything*. Toronto: Management and Fund-Raising Centre.

Klatt, I. (2000). Understanding the Canadian health care system. *Journal of Financial Service Professionals, September*: 42–51.

Lindbloom, C. (1980). *The policy-making process*. Englewood Cliffs: Prentice-Hall, Inc.

Lundberg, G. (2000). *Severed trust: Why American medicine hasn't been fixed*. New York: Basic Books.

McNiven, J. (1997). *Action through advocacy: A guidebook on advocacy for seniors organizations*. Halifax: Canadian Pensioners Concerned Inc.

Naylor, C.D. (1999). Health care in Canada: Incrementalism under fiscal duress. *Health Affairs 18* (3): 9–26.

Nestman, L. (1996). Principles, values and health care reforms. In *Midnet, Together we can*. Fifth meeting of the Expert Network on Health and Health Care Financing Strategies. World Health Organization, Regional Office for Europe.

Nestman, L. (1998). Canadian physicians: The struggle with health reform. *Medicina Nei Secoli Arte E Scienza: Journal of History of Medicine 10* (1): 73–109.

Roos, N.P. (2000). The disconnect between the data and the headlines. *Canadian Medical Association Journal 163* (4): 411–412.

Taylor, M.G. (1987). *Health insurance and Canadian public policy* (2nd ed.). Montreal: McGill-Queens University Press.

Vayda, E., & Deber, R. (1992). The Canadian health-care system: A developmental overview. In C.D. Naylor (Ed.), *Canadian Health Care and the State*. Montreal: McGill-Queens University Press.

Chapter 5

Negotiation

Mary Jane Mastorovich

The purpose of this chapter is to explore the concept of negotiation and the attendant skills necessary for a health care leader to engage in successful negotiation preparation and practice—a vital aspect in the effective conduct of government relations. Negotiation is a process of interactions where one party desires something that the other party possesses. This chapter will explore the concept of negotiation in three dimensions. The first approach is exploration of the concept of dialogue and its application to the development of relationship building, learning, and discovery. These nontraditional elements of successful negotiation are woven throughout the chapter. The second area of concentration introduces the concept of boundary management as a strategic preparatory activity for negotiation. In the third portion of the chapter we will review principled negotiation and evaluation of the negotiation process.

Contemporary health care leaders are faced with an array of challenges. Increasingly these leaders must balance operational efficiency and financial solvency with the goals of the broader community, embracing changes in public attitudes and consumer expectations. These tensions arise on multiple boundaries in constituencies with well-defined economic, political, or professional relationships with the health care organization. The familiar organizational autonomy of leadership authority is fleeting in circumstances that demand trade-offs with external entities such as local and national governments. Additionally, managers across cultures frequently harbor narrow, stereotypical conceptions of government that impede effective negotiation on both sides. A meaningful search for common ground and shared understanding is often missing (Bolman & Deal, 1997; Vladeck, 1992). This additional level of management complexity places extraordinary demands on health care leaders and moves negotiation strategies to a central place in their roles.

One could challenge the idea that much of what passes for negotiation is more akin to what J. Conger (1998) describes as the very linear, straightforward, ineffective process of persuasion. Initially a strongly stated position is offered, followed by an outline of the supporting arguments, and then an aggressive data-based presentation is delivered. Lastly, one enters the "deal making" stage and works toward closure. These tactics are employed with the best of intentions and the utmost confidence in the position taken. But they are sterile and highly ineffective in actually persuading or moving an issue forward.

This scenario is bereft of discovery, preparation, and dialogue, all of which serve to provide the basis for effective negotiation. According to R. Fisher and S. Brown (1988), "No amount of rational thinking, clear understanding, accurate communication, trustworthy behavior, or persuasive influence will build a working relationship if each side rejects the other as unworthy of dialogue." David Bohm (1999), the distinguished scientist and philosopher, speaks of dialogue as a process of exploration where everyone who participates wins. How different from the hard-edged, competitive negotiation and persuasive tactics that dominate our workplaces. In Bohm's view, true dialogue takes place when those who participate are open to challenging and questioning their fundamental assumptions about an issue. In other words, they are open to learning and discovery. Without this openness, participants who negotiate will seldom succeed.

Frequently we enter negotiation with necessities on both sides: things that cannot be ignored or turned aside. Those absolutes fuel the conflict that precedes and, in many instances, is inherent in negotiation, leading to frustration and personal animus among the participants. What we fail to acknowledge is the interdependency among participants who are engaged in negotiation activities. This is particularly important for those who manage public organizations with heavy reliance on some form of external support such as government entities. Inevitably this interdependence leads to conflict. The root of the conflict is often the opportunistic interactions of both parties. These interactions are wrought with self-interested maneuvers, guarded information, a lack of full disclosure, and other unproductive behaviors (Lax & Sebenius, 1986). However, once acknowledged, conflict can be beneficial. The acknowledgment can unearth often ignored assumptions that may underlie an issue, but are central to its resolution.

One way that the conflict can be unearthed is through dialogue. An operational extension of Bohm's commentary on the need for dialogue and the challenge of assumptions as mediators of conflict is the conscious use of the ladder of inference. P. Senge, et al. (1994) describe the ladder of inference as a common mental pathway of increasing abstraction, often leading to misguided beliefs. The beliefs are formed by observing the behaviors of other individuals or entities and attaching meaning to those actions, meanings based upon our own long-held assumptions. These meanings and beliefs are then perceived to be obvious truths, based upon real data and incorporated into assumptions. Incorporated into action, the ladder of inference proceeds in this way: First an individual observes data or experiences. The individual then selects data from the observations, adds meaning to the data, makes assumptions based upon the added meanings, draws conclusions, adopts beliefs, and takes action based upon those beliefs. All of this takes place unconsciously, without validation, interaction, or dialogue. This contributes to, and frequently sets up, a conflictual pattern of interaction that negatively affects negotiation because untested assumptions frame the process. It is possible to overcome these inherent biases through a process of self-reflection and dialogue that leads to disclosure of the links in reasoning, in other words, making your thinking about the process or the individual with whom you will negotiate a social process, open to scrutiny and validation. Adequate preparation for negotiating sessions involves bringing many points of view forward, unpacking both support and opposition from within the organization, and from the external negotiator who will participate in the process. The quality of an organization's internal communication and negotiation can affect the outcomes of external negotiations.

BOUNDARY MANAGEMENT

Most organizations do not think systematically about their negotiating activities. Each negotiating situation is highly complicated and unique. Changes in practice and perspective are necessary so that negotiation becomes an institutional capability rather than a discreet activity (Ertel, 1999). New boundaries have been created in the postmodern organization that force managers to be attentive to a broader understanding of negotiation. Preparation for negotiation involves managing the complexities of both traditional and nontraditional boundaries. The activities that took place during the 1990s, globalization, reengineering, downsizing, and flattening of organizations, have blurred the traditional lines of authority and responsibility both inside and outside of the organization. Traditional boundaries were hardwired into hierarchical organizational structures. The roles of managers and employees in these structures were clear, simple, and relatively stable. As organizations were forced to become more flexible, nimble, and competitive, roles within them became correspondingly blurred and ambiguous and tensions arose on boundaries that were once quite clear (Gilmore, & Hirschhorn 1992). The new boundaries are at the same time less visible and, perhaps, more important. One process for increasing an organization's internal capabilities to negotiate is boundary management.

L. Hirschhorn and T. Gilmore describe four new boundaries for the contemporary organization; authority, task, political, and identity. Although their classic description is applied to internal organizational dynamics, it is also germane to external negotiations. The practice of boundary management as a precursor to formal negotiation can assist managers to think more systematically and robustly about this critical management activity. Managing boundaries is an antidote to the unstructured, undisciplined, and frequently unprincipled approaches to negotiation traditionally employed by managers in organizations.

The authority boundary is where the different status of individuals is enacted, most commonly between subordinates and superiors. In negotiation sessions, difficulty on this boundary arises in two dimensions. The first is the determination of who in the organization will engage in the negotiation process. This individual should most likely hold the same rank as the external counterpart in the process, giving legitimacy to the encounter. Organizational standing or positional power can influence the outcome of the negotiation process (Doctoroff, 1998). Consider the faith-based community hospital that must compete with a large, secular health care system in the same community for government funding for a clinic to serve the vulnerable population in their immediate vicinity. The larger system desires the same space for a free clinic so that it too can offer services to disadvantaged members of the community. Both seek government support for acquisition of the space, but the larger system is more sophisticated and powerful in the community, has paid lobbyists on staff, and can afford to purchase other space. When individual participants or organizations hold unequal power, shadow negotiations are more likely to occur. Shadow negotiations are the subtle and complex games people play before and after they move to the negotiation table. In this situation it is conceivable that the more powerful, affluent organization may attempt to employ lobbyists to win support for the space outside of formal negotiation sessions. Similarly, the smaller organization, feeling less powerful, may attempt to influence on the basis of faith-based values of caring for the poor. When these shadow negotiations are enacted by individuals without equal status, the process can become blocked and undermined by hidden assumptions and unrealistic expectations (Kolb & Williams, 2001).

Conversely, the second tension on the authority boundary can emerge because the person holding the highest position in the organization is chosen. In contemporary, highly complex organizations those individuals with formal authority may not have the most up-to-date information about the issue, project, or business problem. In these situations, subordinates must manage the task of adequately informing their superiors and helping them to think clearly and rationally about the issue. This "staff" work must be in the interest of helping the superior to acquire literacy and deep understanding of the content of the proposal or issue to be put on the table in the negotiation session.

The task boundary is where the preparation of the information for the negotiator takes place. Due to the complexity of health care organizations, work is necessarily highly specialized and at the same time team based. It is in these teams where the preparatory work of information gathering can occur. High degrees of specialization often leads to worker alienation and loss of touch with the organization's larger focus. Creation of teams of information gatherers with a clear sense of direction and common purpose of preparing the negotiator can modify the alienation of the necessary specialization. Individuals working in these teams divide the work and then coordinate their separate efforts so that the end product has integrity, is informative, and increases the knowledge of the negotiator. Some of this work will be technical in nature, such as preparation of financial impact statements. The work may also be in the interest of preparing the negotiator with a tool kit of strategies for managing the dynamics that arise in the negotiation session. In addition to helping the negotiator to deeply understand the business problem and the negotiation process, these teams can also provide valuable "scouting" of the culture and political terrain of the other party in the negotiation.

Managing tensions on the political boundary in preparation for a negotiation will enhance the negotiator's position. The political boundary is where competing interests and perspectives meet, where individuals face the challenge of presenting and defending their interests without undermining the effectiveness or coherence of the other (Gilmore & Hirschhorn, 1992). According to Peter Block (1987) we become political when we attempt to translate a vision into action and the translation requires negotiation. Prior to the actual negotiation the political terrain is mapped by determining the "players," their interests, and their power. The previously mentioned teamwork can produce answers to questions such as these: What support is needed? How is that support obtained? How can opposition be reduced? Who are true adversaries? Are there shadow players with extraordinary influence (such as the lobbyist in the prior example)? Who should participate in dialogue around these questions? The process for obtaining answers to these questions involves active engagement in the process of dialogue where assumptions are suspended and learning and listening are the primary activities. For example, in the scenario in which the large and small organizations competed for the same space controlled or owned by a government entity, the assumption by the faith-based organization that the larger facility desires the space to operate a free clinic only to maintain their nonprofit status may not be valid. Some engagement in dialogue could begin to set the stage for the building of relationships between the facilities. In the process, one organization is able to avoid treating the other as an abstraction or stereotype. Through dialogue participants begin to gain a high familiarity with the culture of the other, experience positive social interactions, and enhance the potential for establishing common ground among the participants (Weiss, 1994). Managing this boundary successfully will generate valuable information for the negotiator and will preclude the organization's tendency to view the other party as the enemy rather than a partner. It may be possible then for these two organizations to arrive at some common ground, care of the disadvantaged, and jointly sponsor the free clinic.

The tension on the identity boundary of participants in a negotiation process is manifested by an "us" versus "them" quality. All groups embody unique characteristics of sameness that shape their cultures. These identities may be produced by professional cultures, ethnicity, race, organizational affiliation, or other distinguishing associations. The identity boundary is activated when participants trust insiders in their organizations, but are wary of outsiders. Although identity relationships within an organization may be energizing and motivating, when the identity is oversubscribed it can yield arrogance, alienation, isolation, and contempt for others who do not share the same values, experience, or vision. For example, stereotyping of government workers as indolent bureaucrats by private sector employees is a classic example of oversubscribing to identities. This posture can obviously be extremely detrimental to negotiation with government agencies and significantly undermine their willingness to engage in dialogue. Positive interface at this boundary involves maintaining identity without devaluing the potential contribution of the other. Stephen Weiss (1994) identifies this as "symphony," where both parties in a negotiation are able to transcend exclusive use of either home culture by exploiting their familiarity and seeking common ground. Although his context is international negotiation, organizational cultures can be equally compelling, misunderstood, and difficult to traverse. Seeking symphony, the harmonious combination of elements, requires the cooperation of the counterparts and the development of a joint culture or "score"—the common ground of the encounter, which helps to make behavior predictable, comprehensive, and coherent. The "score" for the two hospitals previously mentioned could be care of the disadvantaged.

Management of the authority, task, political, and identity boundaries as preparation for negotiation may seem somewhat onerous. It becomes even more complex because the management of these four boundaries occurs simultaneously, not as discreet, hierarchical activities. However, adequate preparation is a precursor of success and much of the anxiety surrounding negotiation can be contained within the boundary management process where organizational skill building is also accomplished. Separate task forces or teams of individuals can be formed to assist the negotiator with this effort. For example, each of the boundaries may warrant a separate team where the expertise of the team members is suited to relieving the tensions which emerge on that boundary. Potential team membership and work are examined in the table that follows.

This boundary management schema can help individuals and organizations to approach their negotiating activities more systematically, creating institutional capabilities rather than engaging in discreet preparatory activities in the absence of a working framework. The work also helps staff to align their activity toward organization goals.

PRINCIPLED NEGOTIATION

Despite ample empirical evidence to the contrary, people enter into negotiations through positional bargaining. Each side presents its stance on an issue, argues for that position, and makes concessions or compromises to reach agreement. When concessions are not forthcoming or agreements cannot be reached, the parties sever the discussion and walk away, each harboring dissatisfaction with the encounter. This approach may suffice when the parties have

Table 5.1.
Potential Boundary Management Teams: Membership and Work

	Authority	Task	Political	Identity
Participants	Individuals with interpersonal skills. Middle managers with cross-organizational or cross-professional relationships. Individuals from the department of external or community affairs.	Technical experts within the field of inquiry, and representation from finance, planning, marketing, etc.	The chosen negotiator and senior and middle managers.	Staff who are able to suspend judgment, evaluate cultural determinants that will inform the process, and unpack interests of both parties.
Work	Prepare the negotiator to become literate re the issue. Determine who will negotiate from the other side. Deepen the understanding of the culture of both sides.	Provide the negotiator with technical information. Gather data to support the establishment of the BATNA.	Make contacts within the other organization. Determine the amount of support needed, by whom, and how that support is to be obtained. Identify adversaries and shadow partners. Develop relationships within the other organizations.	Ascertain the interests of the opposing side. Hypothesize common ground. Serve as coaches for the dynamics that may emerge in the sessions.

alternatives, such as the new-car buyer who has the option of going to another dealer in search of a better price. Positional bargaining is useful in that it informs each side of the others intentions. But this approach is much more risk laden when the two parties are interdependent and have the potential for mutual gain within the relationship.

The inability to move from a position reinforced by repeated clarification and defense of the position results in the position becoming more deeply imbedded. Eventually, the position becomes entangled with the ego of the individual. This overidentification makes it less likely that any agreement will be reached. The danger inherent in positional bargaining is that less attention is directed toward preparation and managing the dynamics of the interaction, and more attention is directed toward improving the chance of a settlement favorable to one party. Positional negotiation begins with the taking of extreme positions and progresses to stubborn attachment and deception on the part of both parties. Positional bargaining can become a contest of wills that endangers the potential for an ongoing relationship (Fisher & Ury, 1991). Anger and resentment can build, compromising work completed in the preparatory phases of the negotiation where discovery and learning take place. According to R. Fisher and W. Ury (1991), an alternative to positional bargaining is principled negotiation, which has four basic elements: separation of people from the problem; a focus on interests, not positions; generation of multiple possibilities prior to decision making; and a result based upon objective criteria.

Separation of individual negotiators from the problem involves untangling the perception of the individual from the substance of the problem. Emotions play a predominant role in confusing the person with the issue. Emotional responses get generated by attentiveness to unsubstantiated assumptions and by unintended forces of will, blame, and nearsightedness, relative to the problem. Building both a personal and an organizational relationship with the other side can ameliorate this difficulty. It becomes more difficult to attribute demonic characteristics to someone with whom you have a personal relationship. As individuals seek a common ground for the negotiation outcome, and focus on the problem, personal animus is less predominant.

Assuming a positional stance in a negotiation is rarely successful, as has been previously suggested. However, an organization or an individual must pay attention to the interests that formulate a positional stance. Interests drive positions in ways that mission and vision support strategy. It is in the exploration of interests that common ground is possible. Positions tend to be polar opposites, but interests frequently are compatible. For instance, a private health care organization may be at the bargaining table with a government agency negotiating for increased funding for a capital project. The position of the organization is that it cannot provide state-of-the-art care to the community without the additional capital. The position of the government agency may be that the capital project is unnecessary in the current environment of fiscal constraint, but both parties are committed to the delivery of quality care to the community. They share a common interest in the welfare of the community. Making their interests public, both sides move forward toward resolution of the issue of mutual interest. Sharing interests does not necessarily mean full disclosure of organizational "secrets." Negotiators who explore mutual interest are more likely to achieve higher quality results, avoiding extreme opening positions that eventually move toward mutual concessions not satisfactory to either party. Trading concessions may cause the already fixed pie to erode away without either side achieving value (Doctoroff, 1998).

Constructing options for mutual gain involves suspending judgments, being open to multiple resolutions, avoiding viewing the situation as an either/or trade-off, and using brainstorming to develop solutions that meet the interests of both sides. The development of objective criteria helps to frame a negotiation strategy because the criteria are independent of each side's will. The criteria should be both legitimate and practical and apply to both sides. The criteria can take the form of fair standards and procedures that will guide the process. Utilization of these four methodologies for negotiation assumes that the two parties are equal and that each has something to gain from the interaction. However, if one side has more leverage than the other during the process, no one method can guarantee success. The organization that was negotiating with a government agency for increased capital funding faces this dilemma. One side, the government, has domain over allocation of resources. In situations such as this, where power is unevenly distributed, Fisher and Ury suggest that the development of a BATNA (Best Alternative to a Negotiated Agreement) will prevent an individual from either accepting or rejecting an agreement inappropriately. The BATNA becomes the standard by which any proposed agreement is measured. The standard protects against acceptance of terms that are too unfavorable, and rejection of terms that are in the best interest of the individual or organization to accept. Development of a BATNA becomes protection against failure to reach agreement. The process of developing a BATNA is threefold: generating a list of actions that can be taken if the negotiation fails; enhancing some of those ideas and converting them to practical options; and selecting the one option or alternative that seems best. This cognitive evaluation activity will reduce the anxiety that can emerge during the negotiation process.

Negotiating power is not limited to the party with the most resources, influence, connections, etc. The real power in a negotiation between two parties lies with the attractiveness to each party of not reaching agreement. The individual or organization with a coherent practical BATNA can enter the negotiation less emotionally fearful of failure, and confident that alternatives exist. Therefore, the previously mentioned errors in premature closure or premature rejection are less likely to occur (Fisher & Ury, 1991). In the example of the health care institution seeking capital resources from a government agency for enhanced technological capability, a potential BATNA could be a defined fund-raising activity and/or internal cost-reduction measures to fund the project. Whatever the choice, an alternative exists.

Despite boundary management, BATNA development, and utilization of the previously mentioned four-step method, issues emerge during negotiation that have the potential to sabotage the process of reaching mutually beneficial agreement. The negotiation process is lengthy, complex, and vulnerable to collapse at many junctures. Both partners in a negotiation can succumb to what is described in game theory as the prisoner's dilemma. In this scenario, both sides fear that the other will achieve greater gains by acting opportunistically while one side acts in good faith. The result is that both sides fail to cooperate, and each is worse off than if some joint resolution had been reached (Gulati, Khanna, & Nohria, 1994; Lax & Sebenius, 1986).

The negotiator's dilemma as described by D.A. Lax and J.K. Sebenius (1986) involves negotiators who can choose between two negotiating styles. The first is one of creating value. In this style the negotiator is open and shares information about beliefs, preferences, interests, and minimum requirements. This approach is typical of the integrative dimension of negotiation. In this style both parties gain some mutual benefit. The second style is identified as claiming value. The distributive dimension of negotiation typifies this style. Usually, a fixed amount of resources is available and one side stands to gain at the expense of the other. A negotiator choosing this style is often deceptive, misleading, threatening, and self-interested. The negotiator's dilemma, then, is which of the two postures to assume at which point in the negotiation. One can hypothesize that it would be in the best interest of both parties to create value in the process by assuming a posture of openness. However, individuals face tension on this boundary throughout the negotiation process. The tension that emerges is between the cooperative impulse to create value and the competitive impulse to claim value. Effective management of this tension, then, is to create value while claiming value, with mutual gains as the outcome. For example, in the scenario with the two health care facilities competing for the same space for a clinic for the indigent, each could potentially create value by engaging in an open process of exploration of interests that would clarify a mutual desire to serve the community by entering into a partnership to sponsor the endeavor, each then benefiting. If both organizations sought to claim value, one side would win at the expense of the other, the fixed pie being the sought-after space.

Fisher and Ury (1991) describe a difficult situation where one party is open to dialogue around interests, options, and standard setting and the other party remains stubbornly attached to a positional style. When a negotiator encounters this resistance, he or she may become reactive and assume an opposing positional stance that locks both parties into a no-win posture. Instead of reacting to the positional stance, a negotiator can treat it as an option and seek to determine the interest that lies behind it. Secondly, the negotiator is advised to invite criticism and advice, turning criticism into a means for learning and improving the process of working toward agreement. And, lastly, the negotiator should resist the temptation to counter a personal attack by refocusing the attack onto the problem and away from the negotiator. This approach toward recalcitrant bargainers is difficult in the heat of battle, but with adequate preparation and anticipation of the emergence of positional bargaining in the negotiation session, the negotiator will have distinct advantages.

Evaluations of negotiation strategies should include evidence of the claiming-value or creating-value postures as they relate to success. However, currently organizations limit their evaluation methodology to financial metrics that reflect some measure of price or cost. Focusing on financial measures as an exclusive means of evaluation can impede relationship development and reduce opportunities to add value between interdependent partners such as those in both public and private organizations. Establishing broader performance measures for negotiators will support an evaluation of the process, as well as the financial outcome. A proposed set of new measures offered by D. Ertel (1999) serves as a reflection of a more robust approach to increasing organizational capacity to effectively negotiate.

The first measure addresses the issue of whether the negotiation process helps to build relationships that will endure after the negotiation is complete. Organizations and managers within them should clarify the distinction between winning individual deals and the need for ongoing relationships with the other party, such as those between organizations and government entities where both independence and interdependence are manifest. The second answers the question of how effective the communication process was in creating an environment in which both parties can engage in constructive dialogue aimed at solving future problems. The third relates to clarification of mutual interests that were honored during the negotiation. The process of dialogue around these interests keeps the process away from positional stances and individual egos. The fourth measure analyzes the search for innovative, elegant, and efficient solutions that offer joint gains. In other words, how effective was the negotiator in establishing a climate of mutual creative inquiry? The fifth measure seeks to evaluate the search for objective criteria to be used as a measure of an option that can be justified by both parties. The sixth measure relates to evaluation of the end result against the chosen BATNA—did the organization compromise or agree too quickly? Lastly, commitments are evaluated in terms of mutual understanding and feasibility of implementation. These broad categories of evaluation measures can be applied liberally with detail from within individual negotiation strategies.

This chapter has focused upon the need for adequate preparation of the organization prior to entering a negotiation session. This preparation may be more important than the dynamics of the actual session because of the dialogue that ensues during preparation of the organization for the negotiating session. Negotiation with a government entity is unique in that the process can form the basis for a necessary long-term relationship. The inherent differences in power and stature, but commonality in the health of the community, force health care leaders to acquire skills in this demanding process. This rather broad approach to negotiation does not attempt to cover all of the theories that support negotiation, or all of the strategies a negotiator may employ during the sessions. Readers interested in additional detail are encouraged to refer to the references for more information about negotiation strategies, techniques, and research.

REFERENCES

Block, P. (1987). *The empowered manager* (pp. 137–160). San Francisco: Jossey-Bass.
Bohm, D. (1999). *On dialogue* (pp. 1–31). New York: Routledge.
Bolman, L.G., & Deal, T.E. (1997). *Reframing organizations* (pp. xi–xiv). San Francisco: Jossey-Bass.

Conger, J. (1998). The necessary art of persuasion. *Harvard Business Review 76* (3): 84–95.

Doctoroff, S. (1998). Reengineering negotiations. *Sloan Management Review 39* (3): 63–71.

Ertel, D. (1999). Turning negotiation into a corporate capability. *Harvard Business Review 77* (3): 55–70.

Fisher, R., & Brown, S. (1988). How can we accept those whose conduct is unacceptable? *Negotiation Journal, April*: 125–136.

Fisher, R., & Ury, W. (1991). *Getting to yes, negotiating agreement without giving in.* New York: Penguin Books.

Gilmore, T., & Hirschhorn, L. (1992). The new boundaries of the "boundaryless" corporation. *Harvard Business Review 70*: 104–115.

Gulati, R., Khanna, T., & Nohria, N. (1994). Unilateral commitments and the importance of process in alliances. *Sloan Management Review 35* (3): 6–19.

Kolb, D.M., & Williams, J. (2001). Breakthrough bargaining. *Harvard Business Review 79* (2): 89–97.

Lax, D.A., & Sebenius, J.K. (1986). *The manager as negotiator, bargaining for cooperation and competitive gain* (pp. 1–182). New York: The Free Press.

Polzer, J.T., & Neale, M.A. (2000). Conflict management and negotiation. In S.M. Shortell & A.D. Kaluzny (Eds.), *Health care management, organization design and behavior* (pp. 130–149). New York: Delmar.

Senge, P., Kleiner, A., Roberts, C., Ross, R., & Smith, B. (1994). *The fifth discipline fieldbook* (pp. 242–246). New York: Doubleday.

Vladeck, B.C. (1992). Health care leadership in the public interest. *Frontiers of Health Service Management 8* (3): 3–26.

Weiss, S.E. (1994). Negotiating with "Romans"—Part 1. *Sloan Management Review 35* (2): 51–61.

Weiss, S.E. (1994). Negotiating with "Romans"—Part 2. *Sloan Management Review 35* (3): 85–99.

Part III

Strategies and Techniques: Lessons Learned

Chapter 6

Federal/State Coalition Initiative
for Rural Health Care

Thomas C. Ricketts and Melissa Fruhbeis

INTRODUCTION

This chapter describes the complex, formal and informal structure of intergovernmental and interinstitutional relationships that were called into play following the passage by the U.S. Congress of the Medicare Rural Hospital Flexibility Program (FLEX Program). That legislation, part of the Balanced Budget Act of 1997, was the result of the efforts of an advocacy coalition to modify Medicare payment policies for rural hospitals. The origins of the FLEX Program were in an earlier demonstration program, the Essential Access Community Hospital-Rural Primary Care Hospital program (EACH/RPCH, pronounced "each-peach"), and a companion demonstration program in Montana of the Medical Assistance Facility (MAF). Under the EACH/RPCH program, seven states received grants to develop networks that consisted of the limited-service hospital (RPCH) and the acute care referral hospital (EACH). The RPCHs provided outpatient and short-term inpatient care that was limited to an average length of stay of 72 hours. Under a demonstration waiver, Medicare was authorized to pay for basic emergency care, outpatient services, and inpatient care (limited to 96 hours) provided at these limited-service hospitals. As of August 1997, a total of thirteen Montana hospitals had become MAFs and in six EACH/RPCH states, thirty-eight hospitals converted to RPCHs (General Accounting Office, 1998).

The Rural Hospital Flexibility Act requires states interested in participating in the FLEX Program to submit a state plan that outlines their process for program implementation. This plan requires approval by the regional Health Care Financing Administration (HCFA) office—now the Centers for Medicare and Medicaid Services (CMS). Once approved, states' program foci include several activities: establishing state rural health plans, assisting small rural hospitals in converting to Critical Access Hospitals (CAHs), developing and improving rural health networks, strengthening rural emergency medical services (EMS), and improving the quality of care in rural communities.

Under the second activity of the FLEX Program, assisting small rural hospitals in converting to CAHs, the states follow particular criteria for deeming hospitals "eligible." In order to be eligible as a CAH, a facility was originally required to be a rural public or nonprofit hospital located in a state that has obtained approval for its state rural health plan; a later amendment allowed for-profit hospitals to qualify. The hospitals are required to be more than a 35-mile drive from any other hospital or CAH (15 miles in mountainous terrain or in areas with only secondary roads) or must be certified by the state as being a "Necessary Provider" of health care services to residents in the area. In addition, the facility must have 24-hour emergency services available, have a length-of-stay limit of 96 hours on average, be part of a network with at least one acute care hospital, and have no more than fifteen acute beds. An exception to the fifteen-bed limit is made for swing-bed facilities. These facilities are allowed to have up to twenty-five inpatient beds that can be used for either acute or skilled nursing-facility levels of care; however, no more than fifteen beds can be used for acute care at any one time. Existing RPCHs and MAFs were grandfathered as CAHs if they were eligible to be designated as CAHs by the state.

The FLEX Program has been remarkably successful in at least one of its components. As of December 2001, over 500 rural hospitals had taken the largely unprecedented step of restricting their size and the length of stay of their patients in exchange for cost-based reimbursement for Medicare patients. This program is an example of how the U.S. federal government supports local health care organizations using a state-level intermediary. Such a program may appear to represent a linear hierarchical relationship between the national government and the state government and thence to local authorities and institutions but, like many American policy initiatives, in reality it involves a complex web of interests and influences that reflect the reality of intergovernmental relations in health care.

The U.S. federal system of government is a delicate balance of constitutional responsibilities with the federal Constitution structured on a principle of specific powers ceded to the central government with all other powers reserved to the states or the people. In health care, this means that the states hold the primary responsibility for policy making for the licensing of practitioners, the creation and funding of institutions for the poor and dependent, and the protection of the public's health (Lipson, 1997). In the twentieth century, the federal government found more and more justification to create national policy with the implementation of food and drug regulations, grants-in-aid to states for maternal and child health programs, the creation of a central disease monitoring system, and a structure of national research institutions. By the 1960s, there was a quantum leap in the involvement of the federal government in health care when the Medicare and Medicaid programs were passed into law, the former being a centralized national health financing system that pays directly to beneficiaries or to individual practitioners and institutions for health care services. Medicaid, on the other hand, is described as a "partnership" where the federal government sets general guidelines for a health care financing program for poor people and mothers and children and transfers tax dollars to that program but allows states to set specific rules and regulations as well as share in the financing. The Medicaid program is one of the largest intergovernmental transfer programs in the United States involving a shift of approximately $100 billion from federal tax revenues to states and the states spend $70 billion on the program themselves. The proportion of state budgets dedicated to Medicaid has risen faster than any other single component. States, when considering intergovernmental relations in health policy, think immediately of Medicaid. However, there are many other programs that involve complex relationships between states and the federal government and which involve the direct delivery of care or the support of caregivers. The FLEX Program is one of these programs. It represents an innovative approach that allows the advocacy coalition that pressed for policy change a chance to take part in the implementation of the policy itself.

RURAL HEALTH POLICY AND ADVOCACY COALITIONS

Medicare and Medicaid are broad entitlement programs of the U.S. government intended to provide care for the elderly, disabled, and selected needy populations. However, much of the Congress's attention is spent working on specific legislation that benefits specific populations. This is commonly called "categorical" program support. Those programs often involve the identification of a special population or disease or a profession that can solve a specific problem. They emerge as the result of focused advocacy by an interest group or groups. The goals of many of these policies are to enhance access to health services where there is a perception that the market has created a measurable disparity in the ability of a particular group to make use of health care services, including those paid for by Medicare and Medicaid. This lack of access is combined with a situation where the states have been unable to respond to the need or close the gap in access.

The FLEX Program reflects that general category of policy; rural populations are perceived to have lower access to care and rural hospitals are seen to be at risk due to low payments. This situation is exacerbated by the chronic problem of recruiting practitioners to rural communities. The FLEX Program became a part of federal health policy as a result of efforts by what Paul Sabatier calls an "Advocacy Coalition" (Sabatier, 1988; Sabatier & Jenkins-Smith, 1999) that knits together a broad array of stakeholders including representatives from multiple levels of government, both agency bureaucrats and constituents and beneficiaries who relate closely to government programs. The FLEX coalition involved a core membership association that provides services to its constituents but also lobbies (the National Rural Health Association—NRHA), a federal agency that channels policy benefits to rural health systems (the Office of Rural Health Policy in the Health Resources and Services Administration—HRSA), and a grouping of members of Congress who are sympathetic to the needs of the members and respond with legislation and appropriations (the Senate Rural Health Caucus and House Rural Health Coalition).

Rural health may be seen as a policy domain that follows the pattern of the interest networks that bring together lobby groups, congressional committees, federal agencies, and community-based advocates in a symbiotic and relatively autonomous policy community (Peterson, 1994). Those elements fit rural health into the classic "iron triangle" model of policy making, but the triangle does not completely enclose the interests and constituents of rural health policy because there is a larger interest at stake that revolves around the overall condition of being rural. The rural health advocacy community represents a grouping of policy-linked yet professionally diverse occupations and organizations: hospitals, practitioners, clinics, public agencies, and private firms whose primary interests are often more directly represented by another association or lobbying group that falls under the umbrella of the NRHA.

The creation of the rural hospital policy initiative emerged because the FLEX Program generally followed the "standard" American policy development process. That process, described in a classic study by John Kingdon (Kingdon, 1995), joined interest groups, government agencies, stakeholders, and stake-keepers in their efforts to secure the allocation of federal funds with minimal regulatory constraints. The policy development process moved through several predictable steps: from the definition of the problem (the threat to survival of small rural hospitals caused by market forces and demographic trends), to the selection of options to solve the problem (payment reforms, institutional reforms), to the effort to bring the two steps together on the political agenda using media, lobbying, and legislative "logrolling," to eventual passage. The process of the actual implementation of the policy is not so well described. One reason for this is the great complexity of intergovernmental relations in the United States and their critical but often changing role in making legislative decisions actually work.

The emergence of population-specific programs, including those that fall under the "rural" umbrella and that developed as a result of the activity of coalitions, is a normal process in health policy making in the United States. However, the health policies most identified with advocacy networks have tended to be weighted toward stronger federal involvement. The rural constituency had traditionally seen national programs such as Rural Health Clinics legislation, the National Health Service Corps (NHSC), and Title VII funding for health professions schools as the primary pathways to solving their problems. Keith Mueller, political scientist and rural health advocate, described the balance of rural interests at the national and state government levels (Mueller, 1997). His characterizations revealed far greater activity and focus at the federal level. The FLEX Program, in contrast, emphasizes more state- and local-level activity and control, and, as such, represents a departure from the "federal-centric" viewpoints of many rural health advocates.

The characterization of the "target population," in this case rural Americans, is an awkward process (Schneider & Ingram, 1993). Making the case that rural America is deserving of special treatment in health policy is often difficult when there may be a prevailing image of rural places as healthy, stable communities with lots of fresh air and community solidarity (Ricketts, 2000). The social construction of rural America as a population at risk has been one of the biggest challenges of the advocacy coalitions that press for favorable policies. There are, to be sure, areas and parts of rural America that are very poor. Furthermore, rural communities often have the worst indicators of health status and quality of life. This makes it even more difficult to craft policy for a group that is very diverse in the nature of its need.

DEVOLUTION AND HEALTH POLICY

The acceptance of the mixed responsibility in the FLEX Program by an advocacy coalition fits into a larger pattern of "devolution" of responsibility if not power and authority from the federal government. Devolution in health policy had been a deliberate policy goal of earlier administrations. During the Reagan administration the idea of "block grants," in use in health care since 1966, became the preferred mechanism for shifting cost controls to the states but they were not broadly implemented. Block grants were lump-sum appropriations given to states on a formula basis that allowed the states latitude in achieving broadly stated goals such as "to ensure the delivery of high quality care to all pregnant women and infants" (Maternal and Child Health Branch, 2000). There was strong resistance to the idea of block grants for health programs that benefited specific populations or groups who felt that their interests could best be served in Congress rather than in the states (Sardell, 1988). By the time Bill Clinton became president, there was much broader acceptance of the idea of "devolution" of power in health policy to the states and communities, although most federal health programs remained "categorical," that is, they functioned under separate legislative authority, administration, and budgeting. The devolution came in the form of greater flexibility for states in operating their Medicaid programs through the use of projects that allowed them to work outside the normal rules—called "Section 1915 program waivers" and "Section 1115 research and demonstration waivers." There was parallel reform in the federal income support program, the Personal Responsibility and Work Opportunity Reconciliation Act of 1996.

This pattern of devolution has prompted some to observe that this amounts to a "race to the bottom" with states pressing the federal government to allow them the latitude to "fix" problems without disturbing their own systems of influence and power (Estes & Linkins, 2001; Peterson & Rom, 1990; Thompson, 1997). The devolutionary reforms have spurred private foundations and the government itself to fund projects to monitor and assess the effects of this wave of "new federalism" on health and health care (see, for example, http://www.newfederalism.urban.org/) to determine if the target populations are receiving less under the new arrangements. The reasons for devolving power from the federal government are many and, although the tendency for devolution to more local control is associated with conservative national politics, there are contradictions and paradoxes typical of the American system. Lawrence Brown et al. classify supporters of devolution into five types: substitutors—fiscal conservatives who want to block grants and cut funding; supplementers—liberals who want to use block grants to supplement funding and consolidate and expand programs; decentralizers—who want a reduced federal role in the states; consolidators—who want to reorganize funding in the interest of administrative rationality; and lastly, equalizers—who want to redress regional inequalities (Brown, Fossett, & Palmer, 1984).

In the earlier Reagan-era attempts to devolve power and control costs, the substitutors, decentralizers, and consolidators were clearly the drivers and those motivations remained at the forefront in the "Contract with America" initiatives of the Congress led by Newt Gingrich and Trent Lott and in the executive decision making of the George W. Bush administration. The FLEX Program is an example of a program motivated more by the supplementers and equalizers. The FLEX Program also sought to avoid a problem that devolution created for the states' unfounded mandates. These mandates were the transfer of responsibility for regulatory control or the guarantee of benefits and entitlements from the federal government to the states but with no or little additional funding to support the expenses the states would have to incur. The experience of the EACH/RPCH program told the states that widespread conversion of hospitals would not happen quickly, if at all, without some form of incentive for the states to participate and without funds to move the process along. The FLEX Program was initially authorized by Congress with a $25 million grant program to support the states and their role in designating and assisting the facilities; however, the money was not appropriated until a year after the initial authorization (each participating state received $200,000 in start-up funding prior to the appropriation). The fight for that appropriation was heated within the rural advocacy domain and argued on the grounds that the federal government had created the inequities in hospital payments through the Prospective Payment System (PPS) but was not willing to compensate with the cash necessary to redress the problem.

FEDERAL HEALTH CARE FINANCING: THE FLEX PROGRAM

The FLEX Program was intended to improve the viability of rural health systems as well as rural hospitals by allowing for the designation of Critical Access Hospitals (CAHs) by the Centers for Medicare and Medicaid Services (CMS), formerly known as the Health Care Financing Administration (HCFA). Most hospitals are paid through the Medicare Prospective Payment System (PPS), using fixed payments for patient diagnoses—so-called Diagnostic Related Groups (DRGs). The CAH designation allows alternative reimbursement formulas, based on real costs, for the participating rural hospitals. The switch from PPS to cost-based reimbursement offers significant financial benefit to many small rural hospitals that have higher proportions of their patients covered by Medicare. The fact that the program requires the CMS to participate in the approval of applications for conversion to the new payment plan and gives them the role for administering the payment system, yields that agency a key stake in the overall FLEX initiative. The CMS is, however, an unwilling participant. Speaking through its advocates who are part of its policy-making advisory group, the Medicare Payment Advisory Commission (MedPAC), the CMS bureaucracy and policy keepers would rather see the elimination of any special types of reimbursement or payment, especially for rural hospitals that had been included in previous exceptions (Hoyer, 2001; Kerns, 2001).

W.T. Gormley and C. Boccuti reviewed the relationship between the states and the HCFA (CMS) (Gormley & Boccuti, 2001). Their analysis scaled state-HCFA interactions according to the degree of salience and conflict inherent in the specific polices over which there was some disagreement. That study painted a picture of a relatively balanced flow of power and a pattern of compromise between the central bureaucracy and the states. That balance is not reflected in other reviews of the performance of the agency. J.K. Inglehart described the CMS as a bureaucracy that was stressed by its heavy workload and complex structure, which included many outside contractors that it could not adequately oversee; as viewed as an adversary by the physicians and hospitals it pays; and as a point of conflict between the two parties as they try to reform Medicare and the agency (Inglehart, 2001). When the administration of George W. Bush assumed power, they felt that relations between the states and the agency were strained to the point where the agency needed reorganization and renaming. As part of that reorganization, the Center for Medicaid and State Operations was created within CMS to improve state-federal relations (Thompson, 2001).

Rural hospital payment policies have struggled for a place of salience on the political agenda and have achieved that through the tie between the dominance of key committees in the Senate and leaders who represent rural states. Max Baucus of Montana succeeded Charles Grassley of Iowa as chair of the Senate Finance Committee, which writes much of the law that controls Medicare, and the Majority Leader of the Senate is from South Dakota, a mostly rural state. That salience combined with the advocacy coalition politics that have developed around rural health system issues does not fit exactly into the matrix Gormley and Boccuti developed. The intergovernmental processes that they describe as operative range from "symbolic" with bureaucrats operating in quiet isolation to "collaborative" with the federal and state bureaucracies openly but cooperatively seeking solutions. As conflict rises, the states and the federal bureaucracies and their supporting politicians may "go public" and attempt to modify policies and implementation with public and private pressure. Lastly, where the issue is of high salience and conflict, there may be an attempt to coerce the CMS through explicit and specific directives by the legislators who have been pushed hard by constituents.

The emergence of the FLEX Program has caused contention but it was not a leading or decisive policy issue, even in rural states. It was, however, a key issue at a level just below wide public attention. Key local elites are involved deeply in the affairs of local hospitals, which, in small towns and rural areas, are often the largest employer and a symbol of community pride and identity. That network of elites from businesses as well as from key institutions, including schools and social organizations, was motivated to press for "relief" from the discriminatory policies of Medicare (Size, 2001). The result was strong pressure on the CMS bureaucracy and policy allies to accommodate rural interests. The FLEX Program was a large part of that accommodation. It might easily be assumed that this political climate created some degree of strain between state and federal bureaucracies, but that has never been examined formally.

The relationship between the CMS and its policies and the states and state health policy making was not the only point of potential intergovernmental contention. Given that health financing and health care delivery are usually separated in the American system, there was a parallel arena that involved other parts of the federal and state bureaucracies. In this case, that arena was driven by a planning and coordination program. The second largest component of the FLEX legislation is a four-year, $25 million grant program, which is implemented by the Federal Office of Rural Health Policy (FORHP). The FORHP, located in another part of the federal health bureaucracy—the Health Resources and Services Administration (HRSA)—is able to provide annual awards of up to $775,000 to participating states to make improvements in rural health systems.

HRSA programs are usually characterized by a more collaborative interaction between states and the federal bureaucracy. Because of this collaboration, there are many more opportunities for agency "capture" by constituencies since the goals of the federal programs are to actually deliver services and affect change. Generally, the government agencies implementing the programs share these same objectives. The FORHP sees its role as one of working in close partnership with the State Offices of Rural Health and other state-based entities that deliver services to communities. To help with this, the FORHP formed the Technical Assistance Service Center (TASC) to advise states on FLEX Program development and CAH conversion. The FLEX Program, in its implementation, explicitly requires the creation of coalitions of stakeholders within the states to, at the very least, plan for the coordination of funds and the activities required of them under the FLEX Program. These coalitions potentially encroach on another potential field of conflict, intergovernmental relations within the states.

INTERGOVERNMENTAL INTERACTIONS WITHIN STATES

The CMS-state relationship has been drawn as contentious but the conflicts between these two relatively large governmental components may be considered mild when compared with the often internecine struggles that occur within states (Brown, 1993; Oliver & Dowell, 1994). Some states, however, have been able to craft significant broadscale reforms in health policy (Nelson, 1994a). Those reforms, which have been viewed variously as failures or successes, have all witnessed intense cross-department and cross-agency conflicts, and the intransigence of bureaucrats has often been a key factor in the failures (Nelson, 1994b). The FLEX Program required state agencies and nongovernmental organizations to cooperatively develop, first, the State Rural Health Plan and then, later, to distribute the state grant funds. Although the FLEX Program itself, when compared to Medicaid or the block grant for preventive or maternal and child health services, is quite small, it requires governmental entities, who were not used to cooperating, to agree on a plan for coordinating activities and sharing responsibilities as well as funds. This recipe could either succeed based on creative problem solving and the use of existing lines of cooperation or fail because of deep-seated hostilities and mistrust among the governmental entities.

METHOD

Since 1998, as part of an assessment of the implementation of the FLEX Program, state FLEX Program coordinators in the forty-seven participating states have been interviewed. Each state is contacted at least once a year by investigators and asked to describe the progress of the FLEX program by identifying successful as well as problematic examples of how the program has operated. The interviews make use of a structured interview protocol whose focus changes from year to year as different elements of the program are emphasized. This "tracking" is supplemented by a review of the states' rural health plans, which are required for participation, as well as their applications to the FORHP for the grant funding. These documents are then summarized within several major "themes" in a qualitative analysis of the implementation process. One of those central themes has been interorganizational and intergovernmental coordination and conflict.

DESCRIPTIONS OF SPECIFICS OF THE INTERACTIONS BETWEEN AGENCIES IN THE STATES

The programs, as they have emerged in the states, have created coalitions of stakeholders that combine both public and private entities. Most often, the hospital associations and the state rural health offices are part of the formal coordinating or governing structure for the program. Medical societies and primary care associations are the next most often included private sector stakeholders. In the formal structures for managing the FLEX funds and activities, the coordinating bodies sometimes reach a stage of inclusion that might make them less than fully effective; one state includes thirty-four entities and organizations on its oversight board. While the states generally report progress and cooperation among the groups, there are signal examples of delays and misunderstandings whose causes are more likely part of preexisting interagency and interorganization rivalries or, more simply, insularity.

The ability of the agencies and organizations to work together may have been facilitated by the size of the program itself. The funding that was involved was so small, in the range of $200,000 to $775,000 per year, that there was little to fight over. The benefits were to be felt by the individual hospitals in the form of increased payments by Medicare, and the agencies and associations were seen to be working for their constituencies. State agency officials charged with implementing the Rural Hospital Flexibility Program described the implementation process as cooperative and collegial (our sources were guaranteed anonymity when they responded to our questions):

Developing the plan was very positive from the standpoint that it was great to bring stakeholders together who had not had any opportunity to be brought together before. They understood what the goal was. We essentially, from the start, emphasized the need to leave their group's agendas at the door. It was a very collaborative process.

We brought together a state advisory board including medical examiners, the *State* Medical Association, Medicaid, the *State* Hospital Association, and the rural hospital association. A significant number of them were from the Health Department. They hammered out a plan and went back and worked out the application and certification process. It was a really good process because everyone became aware of what was going on. Although it is not quite as large, the group still meets. We have re-focused the group for the maintenance side of the program; therefore, we have hospital administrators included on the advisory board.

We have been fortunate in *State A* to have established a working relationship with the hospital association. The Hospital Association had put together a transitional hospital model; they had a committee of people working on what would become the CAH program since the mid-1990's; therefore, a lot of players had already been in place and relationships had already been built.

The problems that did arise appeared due to lack of some form of template for coordination or leadership:

[Our state] does not have a local responsibility—nobody is mandated to provide or monitor rural EMS in their communities.

The biggest problems are the multiple folks and the inability of the local administrators to make some basic change decisions.

The range of interacting agencies and organizations is illustrated by the following listing (Table 6.1).

Table 6.1.

Examples of Organizational Representation on Coordinating/Administrative Bodies for FLEX Program Implementation in States

State Health Department Agencies	Other State Agencies	Professional/Trade Associations	Community Groups
Office of Primary Care and Rural Health	License and Certification Department	Hospital Association	Congressional Office Liaison
Licensing	Emergency Medical Services (Public Safety)	Medical Society	City/County Fire and Rescue Departments
Facility Services	Statewide Health Planning	Peer Review Organization	Selected Network Representatives
Emergency Medical Services	Integrated Health Policy Coordinating Agency	Rural Health Association	
Health Planning	Area Health Education Centers Program	Community Health Centers Organization	
Mental Health Services	State Health Care Financing Agency	Primary Care Association	
Quality Assurance Agency	Medicaid Program	Academy of Physician Assistants	
District Health Offices	Office of the Governor	Emergency Technicians Association	
	Department of Consumer and Industry Services	Department of Public Transportation	
		Association of Counties	

MEDICAID AND THE FLEX PROGRAM

That type of collaboration was necessary to coordinate the program implementation with Medicaid. It was at the option of the states whether or not to have the Medicaid program match its payments with the Medicare structure—CAHs would be reimbursed for real costs by the Medicaid program. This presented the challenge of direct interaction with the political systems in the states since, in most cases, the legislatures were required to take action in order to align the payment systems.

Our DHHS folks moved pretty quickly on it and got the rules through fairly quickly (as quickly as possible). The only concern was from the hospital association. The hospitals will do a year-end cost report and assessment; however, the hospital association thought they should do it more frequently than only at the end of the year.

I think that my predecessor really formed a strong partnership with the Office of Rural Health, the Bureau of Medical Services (Medicare and Medicaid, Licensing), and the Hospital Association.

These interactions have not all worked well; less than half of the states (N = 18) have created parallel payment systems for Medicaid for their Critical Access Hospitals:

Non-participation of the Medicaid program continues to be a problem.

Low reimbursement from [statewide Medicaid managed care waiver] has placed a serious strain on many of the state's hospitals.

DISCUSSION

The experience of intergovernmental relations in health policy in the United States has been painted as "designed for failure" (Vladeck, 1979). The Medicare FLEX Program appears to support an opposite view; at some levels, coordination and cooperation can occur. It may be that the states and federal bureaucracies, including CMS (formerly HCFA) and the Health Resources and Services Administration have learned from prior health policy failures like Medicaid regulatory devolution and state health planning. It may be that the interagency and intergovernmental experiences of those failures created some residue of networking and coordination that allows a program at this scale to work well. The scale of the program is important in that the stakes are not so high as to draw the attention of competing interests. In the Medicare FLEX Program, there simply may not be enough to fight over. On the other hand, with almost one in every ten hospitals in the nation having converted to CAH status, this program has the potential to become very large and to shift substantial flows of dollars into rural institutions and rural health systems where states have a growing role as agent and coordinator.

REFERENCES

Brown, L.D. (1993). Commissions, clubs, and consensus: Florida reorganizes for health reform. *Health Affairs* (Millwood) 12 (2): 7–26.

Brown, L.D., Fossett, J.W., & Palmer, K.T. (1984). *The changing politics of federal grants.* Washington, DC: Brookings Institution.

Estes, C.L., & Linkins, K.W. (2001). Decentralization, devolution and the deficit: The changing role of the state and the community. In P.R. Lee & C.L. Estes (Eds.), *The nation's health* (pp. 129–141). Sudbury, MA: Jones and Bartlett Publishers.

General Accounting Office. (1998). Rural primary care hospitals: Experience offers suggestions for Medicare's expanded program (GAO HEHS-98-60). Washington, DC: U.S. Congress, General Accounting Office.

Gormley, W.T., & Boccuti, C. (2001). HCFA and the states: Politics and intergovernmental leverage. *Journal of Health Politics, Policy & Law 26* (3): 557–580.

Hoyer, T. (December 6, 2001). "Comments on rural networks." Paper presented as part of Collaborative Strategies to Address Critical Rural Health Issues—A National Policy Conference, Washington, DC.

Inglehart, J.K. (2001). The centers for Medicare and Medicaid services. *New England Journal of Medicine, 345* (26): 1920–1924.

Kerns, J. (2001). Existing Special Payment Programs. *Medicare Payment Advisory Commission* (pp. 154–159). Washington, DC.

Kingdon, J.W. (1995). *Agendas, alternatives and public policies* (2nd ed.). New York: HarperCollins.

Lipson, D.J. (1997). State roles in health care policy: Past as prologue. In T.J. Litman & L.S. Robins (Eds.), *Health politics and policy* (pp. 176–197). Albany, NY: Delmar.

Maternal and Child Health Branch. (2000). *Title V: A snapshot of maternal and child health 2000.* Rockville, MD: Health Resources and Services Administration, U.S. Department of Health and Human Services.

Mueller, K.J. (1997). Rural health delivery and finance: Policy and politics. In T.J. Litman & L.S. Robins (Eds.), *Health politics and policy* (3rd ed., pp. 402–418). Albany, NY: Delmar.

Nelson, H. (1994a). *Federalism in health reform: Views from the states that could not wait.* New York: Milbank Memorial Fund.

Nelson, H. (1994b). The states that could not wait: Lessons for health reform from Florida, Hawaii, Minnesota, Oregon, and Vermont. In D.M. Fox & J.K. Inglehart (Eds.), *Five states that could not wait.* Cambridge, MA: Milbank Memorial Fund.

Oliver, T.R., & Dowell, E.B. (1994). Interest groups and health reform: Lessons from California [see comments]. *Health Affairs* (Millwood). *13* (2): 123–141.

Peterson, M.A. (1994). Congress in the 1990s: From iron triangles to policy networks. In J.A. Morone & G.S. Belkin (Eds.), *The politics of health care reform: Lessons from the past, prospects for the future* (pp. 103–147). Durham, NC: Duke University Press.

Peterson, P.E., & Rom, M.L. (1990). *Welfare magnets: A case for a national standard.* Washington, DC: Brookings Institution.

Ricketts, T.C. (2000). The changing nature of rural health care. *Annual Review of Public Health 21*: 639–658.

Sabatier, P.A. (1988). An advocacy coalition framework of policy change and the role of policy-oriented learning therein. *Policy Sciences 21*: 129–168.

Sabatier, P.A., & Jenkins-Smith, H.C. (1999). The advocacy coalition framework: An assessment. In P.A. Sabatier (Ed.), *Theories of the policy process.* Boulder, CO: Westview Press.

Sardell, A. (1988). *The U.S. experiment in social medicine: The community health center program, 1965–1986.* Pittsburgh, PA: University of Pittsburgh Press.

Schneider, A., & Ingram, H. (1993). Social construction of target populations: Implications for politics and policy. *American Political Science Review 87* (2): 334–347.

Size, T. (2001). Fair Medicare payments are not subsidies. *Rural Wisconsin Health Cooperative Eye on Health* (February 1).

Thompson, F.J. (1997). The evolving challenge of health policy implementation. In T.J. Litman & L.S. Robins (Eds.), *Health Politics and Policy* (3rd ed.). Albany, NY: Delmar.

Thompson, T. (2001). *Remarks by HHS Secretary Tommy G. Thompson at press conference announcing reforming Medicare and Medicaid agency*. U.S. Department of Health and Human Services. Web site: *http://www.hhs.gov/news/press/2001pres/20010614b.html*. Accessed January 2, 2002.

Vladeck, B.C. (1979). The design of failure: Health policy and the structure of federalism. *Journal of Health Politics, Policy and Law* 4 (3): 522–535.

Chapter 7

Experiencing Politics: A Primer

Bruce MacLellan

Effective government relations may be one of the most unappreciated elements of the success of every publicly funded hospital. In both Canada and the United States, governments play a large and influential role in the affairs of hospitals—as payer, customer, regulator, arbitrator, and influencer. For health care executives, governments demand considerable attention and thought.

The most obvious reason for this assertion is the simple fact that government is a main funding source for hospital operations in Canada and the United States. Government sets overall policy directions for the provision of health services, and hospitals are key implementers of such policies. Moreover, government influences the hospital's operating environment through legislation and regulations.

FINDING COMMON GROUND

Broadly speaking, government relations (GR) works best when organizations and government can find common ground to achieve mutual goals. This win-win philosophy should always be a starting point and endgame for any GR program. The principle of mutual benefit applies to private sector businesses seeking to sell products (to government or the public) and to non-profit organizations sharing in the delivery of public services. It also applies to hospitals.

The win-win approach requires a clear understanding of current government objectives. This knowledge is critical to getting started, but it is often overlooked or inadequately handled. It can make or break your success with government depending on how well you demonstrate consideration of its priorities.

This is a frequent source of frustration for government officials. Organizations are often so parochial that they disregard government policies or constraints. They may also disregard the perspective of other related stakeholders, such as other health providers in the community. Many self-centered organizations have handicapped themselves with this attitude.

In Canada, for example, the hospital sector hurts itself by being too fractured and self-interested. Hospitals are often divided between teaching facilities, community hospitals, large hospitals, regional groups, and other segments, in addition to hospital associations. The cacophony of interests, especially when they are not organized, is counterproductive.

Hospitals need to approach government as a team, with a constructive tone and by acknowledging issues that the government faces. A simplistic demand to "give us the money and leave us alone" is not an acceptable message. This view, however, is a sentiment common within government. The challenge of balancing diverse needs and limited resources is an enormous task.

Governing is a difficult job, especially in large or diverse jurisdictions, or when budgets are under pressure. In health care, the government sees its client as the public, and specifically the patients in the system. This client group includes young and old, urban, rural or remote, male and female. In health care, government must also balance other "clients" such as doctors, nurses, home care providers, and nursing homes. I have never met a minister of health who thought his/her job was easy. As an institution, government is often stereotyped with a tarnished reputation. This should not take away from the excellent intentions of the people who serve in government, nor should you underestimate the talents and skills of politicians and public servants.

Politicians make easy targets. But let's remember one of the positive influences of the electoral system: it keeps politicians in touch with the public. In this way, politicians are more aware of public opinion regarding health policies than anyone else. They should not be dismissed by anyone. For example, public demands for better home care services could put pressure on government to increase funding in that area instead of for hospital operations. Does this make politicians misguided or wrong? Politicians must balance good governance with listening, and the two go hand in hand.

Public servants also deserve credit for the role they perform. Charged with making recommendations to the political level, these players must balance the competing interests of the health system, political pressure, and policy directions. It is often an exceedingly difficult task. To make these decisions, they need honest, understandable, and intelligent input from providers, including the hospital sector.

If public servants were to be asked about their needs, these could be summarized as solutions to complex issues and competing interests. Access to funding would also be useful. The stakeholders in the health policy area include doctors, specialists, nurses, hospitals, researchers, community caregivers, long-term care facilities, pharmaceutical companies, insurers, disease groups, and patient groups to name some. Managing this field of opinions and interests is not easy.

Hospitals no doubt argue that they also serve the same client, the public. This is true, but they must acknowledge when talking to government that the system is complex, with many care providers. Hospitals also need to deal with the scrutiny and responsibility that comes with the public sector. On the one hand, hospitals tell government that they are experts and want to be left alone in how they deliver care. But when a news story breaks about a patient left waiting in an emergency room for four hours with an untreated heart attack, it is often the politician or public servant who draws fire. Hospitals should be circumspect about their criticism when these stories happen. Inadequate funding and poor policy decisions are one dimension, but process improvements and structural self-examination should also be considered.

The dichotomy of autonomy versus responsibility is a concern to many in government. When issues flare up, the government must contact the affected hospitals to seek information. It is not helpful for a hospital to consistently assign blame to government.

Since government relations is a two-way street, the attitude of the political and bureaucratic players also needs to be examined. During my time in government, I often saw a good policy undermined by last-minute political meddling. Obviously, government will alter decisions, but it is exceedingly unfair when rules change in the middle of the process. Government works best when policies and procedures are transparent and followed with predictability. Government works poorly when the system is constantly influenced by personal connections or those who have the loudest voice.

Governing the health system should be driven by constructive analysis, discussion, and allocation of resources based on delivering results. In Canada, the Ontario government took a major step toward such a system when it created the Health Services Restructuring Commission (HSRC) in 1996. The HSRC was given absolute authority to direct the restructuring of Ontario hospitals. The result was the amalgamation and closing of dozens of hospitals. Tired, old buildings were closed, and systems of governance were established to reflect the broader community. In the final analysis, the system was depoliticized, and volunteer HSRC commissioners drawn from the health sector made decisions based on facts, not newspaper headlines or emotional or parochial interests.

This approach was alien to large segments of the hospital sector. For example, executives at Women's College Hospital in downtown Toronto were among the best at managing the news media to turn up political heat on government. Whenever a report appeared to suggest closing the old facility, the hospital used the media to engage public support with a backdrop of anxious mothers and babies.

Ontario Ministry of Health officials were frustrated during the entire restructuring process because hospital leaders refused to accept that political pressure wouldn't work. This occurred in part because it was such an unprecedented approach, and old habits die hard. The government also retained full funding responsibility, which may have been a strategic miscalculation. Professor Charles Doran, director of Canadian studies at Johns Hopkins University, analyzed the process and wrote in 1998 that a "curious separation occurred between recommendations for change and allocation of monies to make the changes feasible." Doran concluded: "As it turns out in policy terms, the extent of this gap had an impact on the perception of effectiveness of reform" (Doran, 1998, p. 17).

THE MEDIA ROLE

Few issues attract such media interest and public emotion as health care. During its operation, the HSRC was determined to communicate directly with Ontarians through news media and other communication vehicles. HSRC volunteer commissioners gave numerous interviews with the media, and reporters were actively sought as were meetings with editorial boards.

In addition, the public process for hospital restructuring included many points of access. The HSRC began its visit to each of the communities with a formal press conference. Following the release of proposed changes to the local hospitals, the lead and associate commissioners for each community were proactive in seeking to meet with members of the local media and political leaders to discuss the HSRC's decisions and address questions.

After a firestorm of criticism following release of proposals in the first few months, the HSRC decided it required a more direct approach in communicating. As a result, the HSRC purchased full-page advertising space in local newspapers the day following release of draft reports and again upon release of final directions in individual communities. These ads focused on the facts related to the HSRC's decisions and the overall reasons for them. The ads also invited questions and comment from the community and offered more information upon request. It was the view of commissioners that public interest in the health system warranted the ads to ensure that the HSRC's work was transparent and the public was informed. The advertisements helped to educate media and key stakeholders about the proposals. Not surprisingly, there was very little response from the public in terms of submissions or requests for input from the ads.

This experience demonstrates how change in health care can easily frighten people. In addition, it can bring forward the worst tendencies of the news media to oversimplify or package news in a good versus bad format. Given the complicated nature of health care delivery and the often shrill voices, it is very difficult for the public to grasp the "big picture." It is easier for people to support the system they know rather than the vision of a new and different system.

It took the Ontario government enormous self-discipline to resist the lobbying, protests, and press conferences of hospitals facing restructuring. The same is true for hospital restructuring carried out in other provinces such as Quebec and Alberta. But in the long term, the hospital sector should be driven by facts, not emotion or symbolism. A clear set of expectations and a transparent process will assist in this goal.

Indeed, the hospital sector should *insist* on a relationship with government based upon mutual respect for facts and data. This should be particularly appealing to smaller facilities, which often believe that the larger, better-connected hospitals receive more attention and resources.

Fairness is the type of treatment that any hospital executive expects to receive in dealings with government health officials. "Equity, fairness and quality service, not politics, are the criteria we want to work with," according to one Canadian hospital CEO. Smart hospitals want to see government funding regimes based on performance. Hospitals and government need to improve how quality is measured. At the same time, government needs to be clear about what it wants for its money.

For hospitals in North America, government is a key client. Government is a purchaser of services on behalf of the public, and it is both a payer and a client. Hospitals and government need to work together to serve the public, and all parties need to understand their respective roles in this partnership.

What does success look like for a hospital's government relations program? The answer to this question will vary depending on conditions and needs, but it should be assessed over time. "Success prior to the '90s used to be measured by going to government with an empty suitcase and leaving with one full of money," observes Mark Rochon, the CEO of a Toronto hospital (personal communication, July 29, 1999). The probability for health service providers to achieve success with their long-term plans increases when positive partnerships with government are based on agreed-upon expectations.

Hospitals also need to measure their success according to the complexity of their services and mandate. A small rural hospital will have different goals than a large urban teaching hospital. Small hospitals need to make every possible contact with their provincial government, because they will get fewer opportunities. They also need to leverage the influence of their local provincial legislative member, particularly if he or she is in the party in power. Small-town and rural members can be very influential, and are known for being effective advocates.

CHALLENGES FOR U.S. HOSPITALS

A number of issues create a different set of government relations dynamics for hospitals in the United States. Many of the issues in Canada do not apply in the United States because of that country's market economy for health care.

The differences begin with mandate and ownership of hospitals. About 15 to 20 percent of U.S. hospitals are privately owned, for-profit businesses. Another 5 percent are publicly owned and the remainder, about three-quarters, are private, nonprofit entities.

There are enormous differences in the payer as well. Private insurance companies, manifested through health management organizations, represent part of the revenue. Medicare payments for senior citizens from the federal government are also very important. It is estimated that between 35 and 50 percent of all U.S. hospital business is with patients over the age of 65.

The result is that U.S. hospitals share systemwide funding issues, rather than receiving direct operational grants as hospitals do in Canada. This gives greater incentive for American hospitals to participate in strong, effective associations. For example, the Federation of American Hospitals represents 1,700 owned and managed "for profit" hospitals. The American Hospital Association represents the thousands of nonprofit hospitals. These Washington-based organizations handle the main government relations activities for their members and present a strong and united front as a result. Consistent with American politics, they also engage outside lobbyists for ongoing or project work.

One such issue of common concern was the U.S. Balanced Budget Act of 1997, which led to $226 billion in Medicare spending reductions. These cuts had a massive effect on hospitals, given the large portion of their operating revenue that comes through the federal program.

There is also no significant capital funding role by government in the U.S. hospital system. The exception is a small amount from the state level, but most hospitals must rely on private financing, borrowing, and fundraising for capital requirements.

In addition, American hospitals face major regulatory concerns. For example, the Federation of American Hospitals has identified 130,000 pages of "red tape" from state and federal governments affecting hospital operations. The fifty U.S. states provide a portion of Medicaid funding with the federal government, and as a result they have accompanying federal regulations. For example, some states have contemplated laws specifying the number of nurses that must be employed in hospitals.

Labor and workplace issues make up the third major area of government activity that affects hospitals in the United States. In addition to labor legislation of various kinds, shortages of skilled workers concern many hospitals.

Government relations in the United States is dominated by associations and lobbyists. In this model, the average U.S. hospital CEO spends less time on these matters. It is estimated that government relations takes up as little as 1 to 5 percent of his/her time, and then it is mainly for local and state issues. It would be wise for all parties to ensure that legislators receive adequate exposure to frontline hospital CEOs and other personnel.

The importance of good volunteer governance of hospital associations applies in both Canada and the United States. It is common for these associations to hire presidents and other senior personnel. However, they can never be a substitute for the hospital CEO, and in fact, they rarely combine the skill and acumen of a frontline operational CEO. It is these seasoned, performance-minded executives who can best present a case for hospitals to government.

This ensures that both the Washington lobbyist (internal and external) and the legislator don't lose touch with reality.

The overriding issues for the hospital-government relationship in the future will be funding challenges and changes to health care delivery. Technology will radically alter treatment options and costs, while patient demographics will also present new challenges. Discipline will be needed on both sides to work together in a constructive atmosphere, where politics is kept to an absolute minimum.

Another interesting influence on this relationship will be the growing health knowledge of the shared client, the general public. Patients and their families have increasing access to the Internet and other new forms of consumer medical media. North American doctors already report an increasing frequency of patients citing Web sites and other Internet research as the basis for questions and concerns. This expanding consumer knowledge is not frivolous. Much of it is derived from qualified sites and experienced patients who share stories about illnesses and treatments.

An elitist attitude has existed among health care professionals and administrators that is not sustainable in the face of a smarter public. The rise of hospital report cards in the popular press and more official versions from government will further this consumer empowerment. Health care administrators cannot dismiss public evaluation. A new sense of customer service and results measurement is bound to influence the relationship with government. Demonstrating customer satisfaction will become an integral part of government relations.

SUMMARY

An effective government relations plan must take these factors into account. Every hospital's GR plan ought to be customized to its own patient needs and the community it serves, and it must operate within the government's policy agenda. In developing a plan, the following points should be considered:

- Assess and establish priority ranking of your needs from government in order to achieve excellence in the health services you provide.
- Understand the political goals of government and the political environment that prevails, and find opportunities where you can support the government.
- Understand government's own process and criteria, and hold it accountable.
- Establish dialogue with your community health provider partners to ensure you reflect the broader needs of the public.
- Build your government contacts and relations at every level from the bottom up, starting with regional staff and eventually progressing up to the senior bureaucratic and political level.
- Establish a team that will represent your hospital at these various levels, ranging from operational administrators to chief of staff, CEO, and select board members.

- Ensure government relations is overseen by your senior executive and the board, ideally including board members with relevant experience.
- Build relationships in government before problems happen. Call with good news when it happens.
- Be open and accessible when government calls in crisis situations.
- Get to know your local state, provincial, and federal representatives, and get them on your side.
- Set goals for the short term and long term, and identify issues that you can tackle alone and those that must be addressed as an association.
- Build your allies in the community, with your staff and with your own patients and their families.

Government relations outcomes will never be evaluated by the type of scientific measurement associated with modern medicine. A genomics or proteomics analysis cannot explain how it works. There is no doubt, however, that a hospital struggling in its relationship with the government is a hospital missing the full impact of the care it could provide.

REFERENCE

Doran, C.F. (1998). *A study of hospital consolidation in Toronto and Montreal.* Baltimore, MD: The Centre for Canadian Studies, Johns Hopkins University.

Chapter 8

Alliance Strategies

Owen Adams and Kevin Doucette

THE RISE AND FALL OF CONSTITUENCY POLITICS
IN CANADIAN HEALTH CARE: A RETROSPECTIVE
IN THE 1990s

The old aphorism about strength in numbers is certainly true in the lobbying business, especially where it involves health care. Its veracity was confirmed time and again through much of the past decade in the face of a strong federal government determined to stare down any contender bold enough to challenge its initiatives. This chapter takes a retrospective look at health care through the "naked nineties" and exposes the system for what it was—fragile and fraught with internal inconsistencies.

Using classic public policy analytical frameworks, we expose the vulnerabilities of the health system's integrity and how issue-specific strategic alliances can be used to overcome the most powerful opponent of change—inertia! In doing so, we examine the advisability of the "go it alone" approach to lobbying versus the effectiveness of "team" lobbying in influencing the direction of health care. Issue identification, issue definition, and options developments are key factors in swaying the decision-making and implementation process. The timing of such initiatives is shown to be as much good luck as good management.

DON'T WORRY ... BE HAPPY!

On September 21, 2000, after the ongoing posturing that accompanies most federal/provincial/territorial interactions in this country, first ministers signed the Canada Health Action Plan. This was billed by some as long-term securement of our cherished Medicare program. For example, at that time, the federal minister of health believed the plan "reflects the commitment of all governments to work collaboratively to improve access to quality health care and services for the sake of all Canadians" (Rock, 2001).

Some observers believed it was fiscal federalism at its finest, yet another example of federalism working to the benefit of all Canadians. As Prime Minister Jean Chrétien noted: "Everyone had to make compromises. It's a great day for all of us. Now that we are in a better financial position we have restored the money to the provinces" (Kennedy, 2000).

For those working in, or relying on the system, a vastly different view emerges: one that sees the plan, at best, as simply recapturing some of the ground lost due to the "tyranny of the deficit" of the 1990s. At worst, it was a cynical effort to buy time in dealing with future sustainability. For those taking a longer-term view, this may be seen as bringing to a close yet another chapter in the long history of Medicare: one that has seen a gradual diminishment of traditional constituency politics in favor of issue-specific strategic alliances. As we enter into yet another downturn in the economy, the "naked nineties" demonstrates just how defenseless and vulnerable the health system has become in terms of surprise economic and political shocks.

Tyranny of the Deficit

Canada began the last decade with one of the worst economic shocks in the postwar period. Over the early years, we saw real GDP growth decline from 4.9 percent in 1988 to −1.9 percent in 1991 (see Figure 8.1).

This was all the more remarkable due to the fact that, in contrast to the 1981 recession, this was seen generally as a "made in Ontario" recession. While the recession that hit Canada in the early 1980s was more pervasive, hitting every province but our largest, the 1991 economic downturn reminded all Canadians of what happens when the Ontario economic engine goes in for servicing!

The shock to Canadian health care is due to any number of economic linkages, but the most important in terms of its impact on health and social policy planning in this country is the effects of this economic downturn through the redistribution of government purchasing power under the Federal Equalization Program (FEP). Unlike any other federal transfer program, FEP is afforded constitutional protection (Constitution Act, 1982). Its purpose is to ensure that Canadians, irrespective of where they live, have reasonable access to necessary publicly provided services at reasonably comparable levels of taxation. This is achieved through a complicated mechanism of measuring the fiscal effort and fiscal capacity of each province and then adjusting the fiscal capacity upward for so-called have-not provinces to ensure that all provinces in Canada have sufficient revenues to fund a standard set of basic services

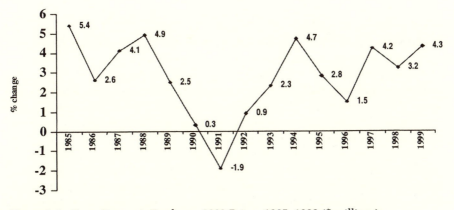

Figure 8.1. Gross Domestic Product—1992 Prices, 1985–1999 ($ millions)
Source: *Canadian Economic Observer,* Historical Statistical Supplement, 2000/2001, Statistics Canada.

(Thomson, 1992; Equalization Program, 2001) The net effect of this and other federal transfer programs is to elevate so-called have-not provinces (all but Ontario, British Columbia, and Alberta) to over 90 percent of the national standard (Thomson).

Beginning in the late 1980s and through to the mid-1990s, governments throughout Canada were forced to face the realities of managing an accumulated debt approaching $1 trillion. This meant, for example, that the federal government was required to use one-third of every federal tax dollar collected to service the national debt. At the provincial level, one of the provinces that hit the so-called debt wall first was none other than the home of Medicare— Saskatchewan. Nothing helps one to better understand the current health policy environment than the nature and extent of the tyranny of the deficit that gripped Canadian governments through the early and mid-1990s. It also helps to understand why those interested in the welfare of health were forced to abandon traditional means of go-it-alone advocacy and representation (a.k.a. "constituency politics") in favor of issue-specific strategic alliances (Tholl & Sanmartin, 1993). The successes and failures of several of these are examined in some detail below.

Politically, the coming of the 1990s also saw a roaring return to power for the Liberal Party of Canada and the virtual decimation of the governing Progressive Conservative Party. The differences in political platforms could not have been more diverse in many respects. In one key area, however, the election brought no change and little comfort; namely, the precipitous slide of federal support for Canada's universal health programs continued. Indeed, the party of Medicare was about to make the Tory "policy by stealth" throughout the 1980s look easy.

Policy by Stealth—Federal-Provincial Health Shares

Throughout the 1980s, the Tory government initiated and successfully sustained what Yale-based Dr. Ted Marmor called a "policy by stealth." Until the spring of 1982, there was an "ironclad" federal government commitment to increasing the annual transfers to the provinces and territories in line with average annual changes in our gross domestic product or GDP. This is essentially a measure of our overall "ability to pay" as a nation for such socially desirable services as health and education. Starting with the 1982 federal budget, the Liberal government started to trim this annual GDP "escalator" by the installment plan—percentage point by percentage point. In successive measures, most of which were the product of arcane fiscal budgetary measures passed late in the night, with little or no public fanfare (hence Marmor's reference to "policy by stealth"), the Tories progressively cut the rate of growth of health and social transfers. This culminated in the 1989–1990 federal budget with a freeze on growth in total provincial transfers or "entitlements"—the effect of which was to reduce year-over-year cash transfers for Medicare programs to the provinces.

With the Liberal landslide victory in the fall 1993 federal election, the health community felt that the never-ending trip to the federal fiscal dental chair under the Tories might just come to an end. Unfortunately, it only got worse as the federal minister of finance realized the extent of what he referred to as the "vicious circle" of federal debt financing. The Tories had been content to see federal cash support for Medicare programs chipped away by the installment plan. In the 1995 federal budget, it was revealed that program-specific grants to the provinces for health, postsecondary education, and social programs would be amalgamated under one transfer program, the Canada Health and Social Transfer (CHST) (*Budget Papers*, 1995), euphemistically referred to in the health community as the "mother-of-all-transfers" or MOAT. The result was to reduce overall federal transfers by a whopping $7 billion.

One of the purported rationales for this move was that it was artificial to separate health and social transfers, since income security and social services are so instrumental in helping achieve overall health goals. In one of the most ironic and perhaps cynical political moves in Canadian history, on the very same day that Parliament passed the CHST amalgamating health- and welfare-program funding, it also passed a bill that formally severed the Department of Health and Welfare! So, while transfers were amalgamated, programs were severed. Desperate times required desperate measures.

Crisis of Accountability

Turning to some of the health-specific policy developments or casualties that helped define the nineties, we also witnessed the massive move to regionalize or decentralize health systems. In every province with the exception of Ontario, the control group, we observed variations on the theme. Various provincial commissions during the period of the 1980s had concluded that Canadians wanted more control over their health services and the way to realize this would be to bring Medicare "closer to home" by decentralizing decision-making responsibility in the system (Canadian Medical Association, 1993).

While Quebec had already decentralized much of its system, it fell again to Saskatchewan to be the first to take the plunge: closing some fifty-two small community/rural hospitals and creating thirty-three regions to serve a population of less than one million people. Other provinces followed suit, with cynics arguing that in times of fiscal feast, responsibility for ribbon cutting tends toward centralized systems while during times of fiscal famine, why not decentralize responsibility for bringing in the wrecking ball?

This political "pull" to downsize and decentralize was aided and abetted by a financial push from health economists suggesting that empowering an individual's control over health decisions also improves the bottom line in terms of health spending. The only way to "internalize" benefit cost decisions is to decentralize resource allocation decisions—or so the theory went.

It also helped that this advice was being tendered at precisely the same time as the then premier of Quebec, Jacques Parizeau, was arguing that "the federal 'snow' was being shoveled onto the provincial driveway" in reference to the substantial cuts in federal transfers. Why not simply decentralize so as to move the federal downloading of costs or "snow" onto the regional or municipal driveway!

Crisis of Financial Sustainability

The 1990s also saw a series of other measures to come to grips with the twin issues of debt reduction and what was perceived as "runaway" health costs. Health care spending had been rising in Canada and, once Canada's GDP took the plunge in 1991, the proportion of our national income going to health soared past the psychological barrier of 10 percent in 1992 (see Table 8.1). We had quickly become the "silver medal" winner in the international health-spending sweepstakes, being outspent only by the United States (Tholl, 1994)! The latest Organization for Economic Cooperation and Development (OECD) data show that Canada has now been "bumped" from the podium into a fourth-place tie with France, trailing the United States, Switzerland, and Germany (OECD Health Data, 2001).

Through the early and mid-1990s, we saw a sea change in public sector support for our cherished health systems. Through this period, we saw provinces roll back a wide range of health programs: dental programs for children, universal and age-specific pharmacare programs, vision care, and, of course, funding for basic hospital and medical care programs.

In terms of real public-sector health spending (i.e., adjusted for inflation), we witnessed seven consecutive years of zero or marginal real growth. Indeed,

Table 8.1.
Total Health Expenditures as a Percent of GDP—Canada/U.S. (1985–1999)

	Canada	United States
1985	8.3	10.0
1986	8.5	10.2
1987	8.4	10.4
1988	8.4	10.8
1989	8.6	11.2
1990	9.0	11.9
1991	9.8	12.6
1992	10.1	13.0
1993	9.9	13.2
1994	9.6	13.2
1995	9.3	13.2
1996	9.1	13.2
1997	9.0	13.0
1998	9.3	12.9
1999	9.3	12.9

Source: OECD Health Data 2001, version 10/08/2001

Table 8.2.
Public Percentage of Total Health Expenditures: Selected OECD Countries

	1990		1998	
	%	Rank	%	Rank
Czech Republic	96.2	1	91.6	2
Luxembourg	93.1	2	92.4	1
Sweden	89.9	4	83.8	5
United Kingdom	84.3	6	83.3	6
Canada	74.6	16	70.1	22
Australia	67.4	21	70.0	23
United States	39.6	26	44.8	30

Source: OECD Health Data 2001, version 10/06/2001

Canada's rankings in terms of public sector spending relative to other industrialized countries went into a precipitous slide.

Table 8.2 illustrates Canada's drop from sixteenth place among twenty-seven OECD countries in 1990 to twenty-second place out of thirty countries by 1998. Turning to Table 8.3, Canada dropped from third place in 1990 to eighth place by 1998.

Table 8.3.
Total Public Expenditures on Health Per Capita,* Selected OECD Countries

	1990			1998	
	$	Rank		$	Rank
Luxembourg	1383	1	Switzerland	2087	1
Sweden	1341	2	Luxembourg	2076	2
Canada	1252	3	United States	1866	3
Denmark	1202	6	Iceland	1773	6
Iceland	1191	7	Denmark	1746	7
United States	1085	10	Canada	1655	8

*Figures in U.S. dollars purchasing power parity.
Source: OECD Health Data 2001, version 10/06/2001

National Forum on Health

Amid rising concerns about the future sustainability of Medicare, the prime minister announced the creation of the National Forum on Health in October 1994. The process that ensued involved an unprecedented effort to reach out to the average Canadian and put every facet of health on the table. The buzzwords included "citizen engagement," "Canada building," and "functional federalism." The outcome was a series of five volumes encompassing some forty-two studies from a variety of health care experts from around the country. Some $12 million was spent, myriad discussion groups were held across Canada, and 2 ½ years went by.

The net result of this expensive and very deliberate process was, in the first instance, the raising of expectations that governments might at long last take the necessary steps to put the system on a sustainable track. This included some very specific recommendations for expanding the scope of Medicare to include both out-of-hospital prescription drugs and home care services. While some recommendations were in fact acted upon, those relating to the need for national leadership on pharmacare and home care remain unfulfilled.

STRATEGIC ALLIANCES IN HEALTH—THE ART OF CARPOOLING

If the foregoing discussion chronicles the tumultuous times for government that were the "naked nineties," then what was the nature of the response from national health organizations? In the early days of shock therapy to the Medicare system, it is probably safe to say that nongovernmental health organizations were caught flat-footed. The federal government(s) had successfully managed to fool most of the people most of the time with its "policy by stealth." Few Canadians understood the manipulations and machinations of federal-provincial fiscal arrangements. Even at the provincial level, only those who actually tried to make the system work understood that the real agenda for regionalization was to download accountability while retaining authority at the provincial levels. The August 1991 report by Dr. Morris Barer and Dr. Greg Stoddart on physician supply, specialty mix, distribution, regulation, recommendation, and training received little attention until its (partial) implementation had all but been finalized. The Prime Minister's Forum exhausted the financial and human resources of virtually every national health organization over three years—only to land with a thunderous "thud" in the laps of a whole new crop of freshly minted health ministers and deputy ministers!

As the pressures on those working in the system became increasingly unbearable and the confidence of Canadians in their treasured Medicare system began to wane, the health sector grudgingly and gradually began to realize the need to join forces. What follows provides two specific examples. The general thesis is that such alliances are formed once and only once. The internal threat of working together—in terms of lost autonomy—is exceeded by the external threat of not working together. Put somewhat differently, if the 1970s and 1980s saw the rise of constituency politics in shaping the national health agenda (e.g., Canada Health Act), then the 1990s witnessed the fall of such politics and the rise of issue-specific strategic alliances.

It is also important to note from the outset that this has not necessarily been seen as a threat to governments or public policy makers, especially at the federal level. Such alliances have been actively and publicly encouraged in some cases while tacitly accepted in others.

The reasons are manifold, but one key precipitating factor that has promoted the importance of NGOs generally and issue-specific alliances particularly in health policy has been the loss of institutional memory among the senior echelons of government, which is all but nonexistent. While the health advocacy community may be somewhat "parochial" when it comes to the affairs of a nation, it has some very distinct advantages when it comes to knowledge of the health sector and how best to address some of the main challenges facing the system. One such advantage of being "advocates" is that nongovernmental organizations (NGOs) tend to be in for the long haul.

But, if strategic alliances have some of the same cost/time-saving advantages of carpooling, you must be sure to share the same destination. Herein lies *the* critical success factor for forming strategic alliances.

Case Study One: Health Action Lobby—Putting the Plug in the CHST Tub

By the early 1990s, it had become abundantly clear that the change in government had not halted the inexorable slide of cash support. Indeed, the new government administered yet another blow to the financial sustainability and national integrity of the system. Without a change in federal policy, federal cash payments for Medicare programs would gradually go to zero—as early as 2002/2003 in some provinces (notably, Alberta) (Bricker & Greenspon, 2001). As was observed by the modern-day mother of Medicare, Monique Begin, and the Canadian Health Coalition, "no cash, no clout!" The national integrity of Medicare programs was clearly in jeopardy as federal cash inexorably marched to zero.

Throughout the late 1980s and very early 1990s, prominent national health groups such as the Canadian Hospital (now Healthcare) Association, the Canadian Medical Association, and the Canadian Nurses Association lobbied—separately and spectacularly unsuccessfully—to call attention to the large and growing problems for the future of health care in Canada. In effect, governments were able to safely ignore representations from any one group by pointing out differences among and between groups. Executive federalism flourished. This sorry chapter for health and social policy culminated with the signing of the Social Union Framework Agreement (Choudhry, 2000), all but shutting out traditional constituency politics at the national level in relation to health and social policy and opening the door to a future dominated by "lowest common denominator" approaches to positioning Canada both nationally and, because of the effects of globalization, internationally. But there was one group that managed to be heard.

Birth of the Health Action Lobby

The February 1991 federal budget was the proverbial "straw" that fractured the financial stability of the Canadian health care system. A series of measures introduced over the previous decade meant that the health system would see some $30 billion cumulatively squeezed from its lifeblood—the Established Programs Financing (EPF) formula (Thomson, 1991). Further, the cash transfers that flowed from EPF to the provinces and territories for health were in peril of disappearing altogether.

Fearing that the integrity of the nation's health system would be threatened if the hemorrhage in federal cash payments was not stopped quickly, a group of Ottawa-based national health care and consumer organizations fashioned themselves in March 1991 into an unprecedented alliance called the Health Action Lobby, or HEAL. Never before had such a diverse collection of health care interests joined forces to tackle a problem that jeopardized not only their members' interests but, more importantly, those of the patients and consumers who relied on the health system on a daily basis.

Balancing the Biases

To be taken seriously, the group realized that it had to be representative of a broad cross section of opinion. At the same time, a cast of thousands would cripple consensus building. In any event, seven organizations formed the inner "cabinet" of HEAL—doctors/nurses, consumers/providers, hospitals/long-term care facilities, health/health care. This marked the first time that an effort was made to "balance our biases" and with the success of HEAL, government divide-and-conquer tactics would no longer prevail.

The challenges of holding together such an alliance were not insignificant. Achieving consensus meant that each organization had to set aside its parochial interests in favor of the overarching and single goal of protecting and pre-serving federal funding for the health care system. The alliance decided the first step was to agree to a "contract" for working together according to a set of prin-ciples that would take an issue-specific approach over a time-limited life span. That part was comparatively easy. The second step, establishing the group's credibility, took longer and required considerably more time, effort, and re-sources to accomplish.

Individual HEAL members had made little headway in drawing the federal government's attention to the sagging financial fortunes of the health care sys-tem because none were able, on their own, to do effectively the detailed analy-sis necessary to make their case. That began to change—slowly at first—as the coalition demonstrated early and often that such an alliance was capable of working as a unit and speaking with one voice. This was important particularly in relation to ministers and department officials within the federal, provincial, and territorial governments. HEAL also proved quickly that it was more than rhetoric and bluster. To be otherwise would have meant running the risk of dis-missal as simply another group with an axe to grind.

Externally contracted research and a rigorous internal process of analysis and debate on potential policy initiatives prior to their release helped solidify HEAL's reputation as a serious and capable coalition. Offering federal officials reasonable and responsible alternatives to the status quo further cemented this position. The alliance also worked to assure these officials that it was prepared to work in a "surprise-free" environment in order to make the exchange of in-formation smoother and less complicated.

Focusing the Issue

HEAL laid the groundwork for its campaign with its seminal piece *Federal Support for Health Care: A Background Paper* (Thomson, 1991). This paper outlined the EPF formula from its inception in 1977 and chronicled the subse-quent changes made up to and including the 1991 federal budget. The conse-quences for the health system were spelled out in glaring detail, beginning with the elimination of "basic cash" in 1982. This change meant that when the value of the tax point transfer (the other half of the EPF formula) exceeded the level of the cash transfer, the provinces and territories could no longer claim the cash payment from the federal government. Changes made to the formula in federal budgets between 1985 and 1991 would further hasten the disappearance of the cash portion of the transfer.

All this meant that, by 1995–1996, the federal government would have withdrawn nearly $30 billion that would have otherwise flowed to the provinces and territories for health. This was too much for the members of HEAL to bear in silence. The ability of its members to provide the types of services and level of care Canadians expected and deserved was clearly threatened and had to be stopped.

Thus began the long, arduous task of convincing ministers and bureaucrats that the Canadian people would soon feel the consequences of the government's actions. The background paper was a direct challenge to the federal government to cease wreaking any further havoc on health system fiscal arrangements. But having thrown down the proverbial gauntlet, HEAL needed to follow through on its commitment to seek reasonable and viable alternatives.

An integral step was to begin focusing the threats to the health care system in the minds of Canadians in the form of HEAL's five-point plan (Figure 8.2), released January 1992 (Health Action Lobby, 1992c). This plan was based on research conducted by three external experts in the areas of finance, administrative and regulatory affairs, and legal issues (Health Action Lobby, 1992a). HEAL's efforts were partially successful. Health was not made part of the Constitution but it did become the motivation for a joint meeting of the federal, provincial, and territorial health and finance ministers held in June 1992. In HEAL's view, it meant recognition of the issue as a national problem requiring immediate action but also the "need to align more closely social and economic policies" (Health Action Lobby, 1992b). On another level, it meant that HEAL had made an important breakthrough with policy makers.

HEAL kept up the pressure through prebudget submissions to the federal government as well as a series of meetings with the health and finance ministers and bureaucrats. The alliance's patient persistence paid off in that no further damage was done to the fiscal health of the system. But just when HEAL thought it had finally clamped off the bleeding, the "mother-of-all-transfers" (or MOAT) became a reality in the February 1995 federal budget. The Canada Health Social Transfer (CHST) came into effect on April 1, 1996, and with it a reduction of over $7 billion in the cash portion of the transfer over two years (plus an additional $1.4 billion cut in the 1996 federal budget) (*Budget Papers*, 1996). HEAL was again forced back into the trenches to fight the reduction and demand restoration of the cash.

By now, the alliance had grown into a much larger group with an even broader collection of health care providers in its membership. More weight had been added to the original construct's message and was reinforced by some of HEAL's larger members such as the Canadian Medical Association, the Canadian Healthcare Association, and the Canadian Nurses Association during individual meetings with government. Aiding the cause was the growing anxiety among Canadians that the health care system was facing serious trouble and the nervous realization that it might not be there for them when they and their families needed it.

---

1. HEAL recommends that illness prevention, the maintenance and promotion of health and the provision of health care based on the five criteria of Medicare be incorporated in the proposed Canada Clause, or equivalent mechanism, in the Canadian Constitution.

2. HEAL recommends that the Government of Canada reaffirm its shared responsibility for the financing of the health care system, as negotiated with the provinces and implemented via the original 1977 EPF arrangements.

3. HEAL recommends that a joint federal-provincial Health and Finance ministers' meeting be convened in the first half of 1992.

4. HEAL recommends that a national arm's-length monitoring process be established around interprovincial agreements and enforced, where necessary, under federal legislation.

5. HEAL recommends a national task force be established under the auspices of the Federal/Provincial/Territorial Conference of Health Ministers.

Figure 8.2.
HEAL's Five-Point Plan—1992

The June 1997 federal election brought the promise, and subsequent implementation, of a CHST cash floor of $12.5 billion. The government tried to claim it as a "reinvestment" in health care when it was simply a cancellation of the $1.4 billion reduction announced in the 1996 budget. Nevertheless, it marked the end of any further reductions in CHST cash transfers. Continued HEAL pressure and public demands that the problems plaguing the system be addressed led to further increases in CHST cash in later federal budgets and to the Social Union Framework Agreement.

HEAL should be given high marks for realizing, in the main, its objective of stabilizing federal financial support for health care. Its adherence to the principle of developing reasoned, responsible, and well-researched alternatives helped establish the alliance as a serious policy player. The alliance's persistence in arguing its case ultimately "won the day" for the system and, more importantly, for the benefit of Canadians. However, there is still unfinished business. The value of the cash is still not protected by any sort of mechanism that accounts for inflation, a growing and aging population, the introduction of more sophisticated technology, and rising patient demands. HEAL can justly celebrate its success.

Case Study Two: Physician Supply—Feast to Famine

As the "tyranny of the deficit" took its toll on public sector spending and the realities of regionalization became more apparent, the Medicare system was subjected to several other serious body blows. The first came out of a well-intentioned, but ultimately overly politicized effort to better manage Canada's human health resources. It would surprise some to know that Canada's health sector employs directly or indirectly some 10 percent of our workforce. It would not surprise many to know, then, that upwards of 80 percent of all health care spending comes in the form of wages, salaries, or fees for those working in the health system. For far too long, public policy efforts had not dealt directly with the need to better manage these resources. The economic pressures of the early 1990s, combined with the rapid realization that Canada's population was aging and that the looming baby-boomer bulge in health demands would have to be addressed, created a need to better manage human health resources. The response of health ministers was to commission two well-regarded and very committed health economists, Dr. Morris Barer (University of British Columbia) and Dr. Greg Stoddart (McMaster University, Hamilton). Their report is undoubtedly the most extensive/exhaustive effort of its kind that any country has undertaken.

At the end of the day, unfortunately, governments did not heed the admonitions of the authors, nor did they listen to the pleas of the various actors in the system. In an infamous meeting held in Banff in the fall of 1991, ministers of health adopted the shortsighted and arbitrary policy of simply freezing the number of physicians relative to population at 1:550. This policy led directly to reducing undergraduate enrollment in Canadian medical schools by 10 percent and the number of post-M.D. training slots for specialists by a similar 10 percent. The authors of the report strongly urged governments to resist the temptation to "cherry-pick" the report, arguing that needs-based planning needed to involve managing the full range of health workers and series of system delivery changes. Every national health advocacy group in the country echoed these concerns. Governments not only did not heed this advice, but also nursing training programs were so decimated across Canada that the 10 percent reduction in MD training paled in comparison.

The CMA and other medical organizations began to seek opportunity for consultation immediately upon the release of the Barer/Stoddart report, by convening a meeting to discuss the feasibility of convening a symposium in the spring of 1992. These overtures were not welcomed by government. The ministers of health subsequently directed deputy ministers to develop action plans for consideration in early 1992 and announced that they would be taking the initiative of holding a national conference on physician resources.

The ministers' aggressive timetable left only a narrow window of opportunity for medical organizations to develop critiques and responses to the Barer/Stoddart report. Of particular significance was the 10 percent enrollment reduction in MD training. In a comprehensive and thoughtful critique published in November 1991, Eva Ryten of the Association of Canadian Medical Colleges pointed out that the enrollment had already been reduced by 7.5 percent following the 1984 report and that, considering future attrition patterns and population growth and aging, if the Barer/Stoddart recommendations were to be implemented, Canada would be facing a significant physician shortage (Ryten, 1991). By early January 1992 the major national medical organizations had made heroic attempts to develop responses to the Barer/Stoddart report. Certainly, in the CMA's case there was not sufficient time to fully consult with the provincial/territorial divisions.

Only after a great deal of behind-the-scenes lobbying did the health ministers agree to receive a delegation from six national medical organizations at their meeting in Banff on January 27, 1992. The so-called Banff 6 presented a consensus position, which focused on a few key messages including the need to develop and implement a mechanism for meaningful and ongoing joint work. As it turned out, while the medical delegation was in the air returning home, the ministers had already reached agreement on and publicly released their twelve-point action plan—"Strategic Directions for Canadian Physician Resource Management"—the most notable point of which was the agreement to reduce undergraduate enrollment by 10 percent in the fall of 1993 (*Strategic Directions*, 1992). Since that time there has been much bemoaning of the fact that the ministers "cherry-picked" the single quantifiable and discrete recommendation, in the Barer/Stoddart report. In retrospect more attention should have been paid to this recommendation, particularly in light of the physician shortage that has developed since that time.

Ten years later, the folly of these shortsighted policies and the failure of constituency politics have just begun to grip Canadians. Canada is facing a significant shortage of physicians, nurses, and other health professionals. To cite just one example, the College of Family Physicians of Canada has suggested that as many as 30 percent of Canadians are currently having difficulty in accessing a family physician (2001). In early 2001 the Canadian Health Services Research Foundation facilitated a national consultation on health services and policy issues on behalf of four other national partners. The consultation identified fifteen research themes and health human resources came out at the top. "Health human resources was seen as the dominant issue for the next two to five years by policy makers, managers and clinical organizations. The concerns of policy makers included regulatory frameworks, mechanisms for avoiding cycles of surplus/shortage and the leadership vacuum within management and policy-making organizations."

During 2001–2002 there have been two federal inquiries under way that are providing opportunities for advocacy on health human resources. The first of these is the Study on the State of the Health Care System in Canada, which was launched in February 2000 by the Standing Senate Committee on Social Affairs, Science and Technology, chaired by the Honorable Michael Kirby (2002). The committee held hearings during 2001 and in their September 2001 Issues and Options report, they noted that "all national organizations representing health care professionals that appeared before the Committee during its Phase Two hearings insisted that what is needed is a country-wide, long-term, made-in-Canada, human resources strategy coordinated by the federal government." The Standing Senate Committee agreed with them on all points, including the need for a federal role, and proposed that a "spectrum approach" be followed, that is, "how to make the best use of the full spectrum of differently qualified health professionals, so that the full range of abilities of each type of professional is productively employed" (2001).

In April 2001, former Saskatchewan premier Roy Romanow was appointed to head the Royal Commission on the Future of Health Care in Canada to offer recommendations on the future sustainability of Canada's publicly funded health care system. In the summer of 2001, Mr. Romanow invited approximately seventy national organizations to submit briefs by year-end on the four themes of values, sustainability, managing change, and cooperative mechanisms (Commission, 2001).

Lessons/Questions for the Future

As of January 2002, we are arguably no closer to having a national collaborative policy capacity between governments and health stakeholders in the area of health human resources than we were ten years ago in January 1992 when health ministers concluded the Banff accord. How then can this be regarded as an example of effective government relations? We believe that the experience of the past ten years offers several lessons that may guide the management of future issues from an interest group perspective.

First, advocacy may be enhanced by bringing together the similar interests that surround a major issue such as physician resources. This helps not only to gain a richer appreciation of all key aspects of an issue, but to align interests along common messages, thus avoiding discordant messages that might tend to cancel each other out.

Second, it is critical to do research homework. For example, the CMA and its divisions/affiliates members have made a major investment in tracking the professional activity of physicians since the early 1980s. These have provided valuable data that have informed the deliberations such as the Canadian Medical Forum Task Force One.

Third, in addressing any commission/inquiry, it is essential to assess the window of opportunity for internal consultation and then make the most of it.

Fourth, in either critiquing government policy recommendations or offering policy recommendations to government, there needs to be a better understanding of the criteria that make them more or less acceptable. For starters, we would propose that the likelihood of adoption of recommendations depends on the degree to which they are:

- evidence-based;
- congruent with the ideology and core values of the parties forming/receiving them;
- practical/concrete/quantifiable;
- likely to result in political credit;
- affordable;
- likely to have payoff/results in a reasonable time frame; and
- acceptable to a range of key stakeholders.

CONCLUSION

Future Directions—Stabilize then Transport the Patient

It has been posited that there are two times when change is possible. One when there is a budget feast; then change can be bought. The other is when there is budget famine, when change becomes inevitable. (Taylor, 1990, p. 206)

The turn of the century brings with it both the best of times and the worst of times for some jurisdictions. Alberta is in the midst of fiscal feast where you can "buy" change but other provinces, such as Saskatchewan and Nova Scotia, are in the midst of a fiscal famine. The clash is likely to intensify because Canada appears headed into a second "made in Ontario" recession, led by high tech. The move to a knowledge-based economy means even more uneven growth over time and more volatility in the economic cycle. In terms of political context, pressure to take the lid off the federal equalization program is likely to intensify. The federal government is unlikely to seriously consider any further enhancements to the CHST—no credit and no earmarking. The idea of tax in support of health policy may garner increasing support but may require a strategic alliance to help advance the notion.

We are also well into the information age where strategic alliances will become even more important not only for the protection of our privacy but also for the determination of what data can be shared in the public interest. The principle of working together means that health is too important to be left just to health ministries. Likewise, privacy is just too important to be left just to the privacy commissioner.

Responding to the Kirby and Romanow reports may also require issue-specific coalitions. It will be a question of timing, predicated around the release of the final reports. The last time a one-man show did this was Mr. Justice Hall in 1981. The direct result? The Canada Health Act. Serious players should take these reports seriously and work together, within any given constituency, and across constituencies.

REFERENCES

Bricker, D., & Greenspon, E. (2001). *Searching for certainty: Inside the new Canadian mindset*. Doubleday, Canada.

Canada. (1995). *Budget papers*. Department of Finance, Ottawa. February 1995.

Canada. (1996). *Budget papers*. Department of Finance, Ottawa. March 1996.

Canada. (2001). Equalization Program, Ottawa. Department of Finance. (Department of Finance Web site: http://www.fin.gc.ca/fedprov/feqe.html. Accessed September 11, 2001).

Canadian Health Services Research Foundation. (2001). *Listening for direction: A national consultation on health services and policy issues*. Ottawa.

Canadian Medical Association. (1993). *The language of health system reform*. Ottawa.

Choudhry, S. (2000). *Bill 11, the Canada Health Act and the social union: The need for institutions*. Osgoode Hall Law Journal. Web site: http://www.law.utoronto.ca/facsites/choudhry/bill_11.pdf. (Accessed September 12, 2001).

College of Family Physicians of Canada. (2001). *Not enough family physicians to meet patient needs*. October 25, 2001. Web site: http://www://cfpc/ca/communications/newsreleases/nr25october2001.asp. Accessed January 5, 2002.

Commission on the Future of Health Care in Canada. (2001). *Romanow outlines four major themes for health care inquiry*. August 10, 2001. Web site: http://healthcarecommission.ca/default.asp?DN=cn=208,cn=15,cn=3,cn=2,ou=Stories,ou=Suite247,o=HC. Accessed December 31, 2001.

Constitution Act 1982.

Health Action Lobby. (1992a). *Exploring options for Canada's health care system: A collection of commissioned background documents*. Ottawa. January 1992.

Health Action Lobby. (1992b). *Health and fiscal policy: Balancing the objectives. A submission by the Health Action Lobby to federal and provincial health and finance ministers*. Ottawa. June 1992.

Health Action Lobby. (1992c). *Medicare: A value worth keeping*. Ottawa. January 1992.

Kennedy, M. (2000). *Complicated deal may need fine-tuning, provinces warn*. Ottawa Citizen, September 12, 2000, A4.

OECD Health Data. (2001). Version 01/08/2001.

Provincial/Territorial Conference of Ministers of Health. (1992). *Strategic directions for Canadian physician resource management*. Banff, Alberta. January 28, 1992.

Rock, A. (2001). *Speech to the members of the Chamber of Commerce et l'industrie Thérèse-De Blainville. Sept. 21, 2000*. Health Canada Web site: http://www.hc-sc.gc.ca/english/archives/speeches/21sept2000mine.htm. Accessed: September 21, 2001.

Ryten, E. (1991). *Should Canadian faculties of medicine reduce the number of places for the study of medicine?* Ottawa: Association of Canadian Medical Colleges.

Standing Senate Committee on Social Affairs, Science and Technology. (2001). *Study on the state of the health care system in Canada*. Workplan. Web site: http://www.parl.gc.ca/37/1/parlbus/commbus/senate/com-e/SOCI-E/press-e/work_plan-e.htm. Accessed January 6, 2002.

Standing Senate Committee on Social Affairs, Science and Technology. (2001). *The health of Canadians: The federal role*. Vol. 4, *Issues and Options*. Ottawa. September 2001.

Taylor, M. (1990). *Insuring national health care: The Canadian experience*. Chapel Hill: University of North Carolina Press.

Tholl, W. (1994). Health care spending in Canada: Skating faster on thinner ice. In A. Blomqvist & D. Brown (Eds.), *Reforming Canada's health system in an age of restraint.* Toronto: C.D. Howe Institute.

Tholl, W.G., & Sanmartin, C. (1993). *The Health Action Lobby: Policy options.* (pp. 18–22). Ottawa. October 1993.

Thomson, A. (1991). *Federal support for health care: A background paper.* Health Action Lobby. Ottawa. June 1991.

Thomson, A. (1992). *Financing health care: A discussion paper.* Health Action Lobby. Ottawa. January 1992.

Chapter 9

Principles, Strategies, and Insights for an Effective Government Relations Program

Darlene Burgess and Gail Warden

Both of us have collectively accumulated more than fifty years in health care and government relations, and have worked together over the past twenty years on health care issues at two unique and remarkable organizations— the Henry Ford Health System (HFHS) in Detroit, Michigan, and Group Health Cooperative of Puget Sound, Seattle, Washington. The high profile of the companies we are affiliated with has allowed us to participate directly in key health policy directions at both state and federal levels. In this chapter, we reflect on our experience in order to encourage others to engage in the influence of public policy. Our focus, therefore, will be on the key capabilities necessary for an effective government affairs program, and, through a discussion of vital elements, recommendations for implementing such a program.

KEY CAPABILITIES

In building a government affairs program, it is essential to understand the core capabilities. In our experience these are:

1. Early Warning Capability. This is the capacity to scan legislation and regulation and successfully identify proposals that may affect the organization.

2. Assessment Capability. The assessment capability will flow from an explicit written business profile and predetermined priorities. This is the capacity to take a bill or new rule or draft proposal and determine exactly how it affects the organization. For example, with each Medicare payment change, the government affairs department needs to assess the extent of financial impact. If your health system is engaged primarily in hospital services, you will pay close attention to payment policies for hos-

pital inpatient services and the new prospective payment system for outpatient services, but you may not need to do more than monitor physician payment, since this is not part of your main business.

3. Policy Development. This is the capability to place a proposed initiative within the context of a more comprehensive policy framework. A proposed Medicare payment change that reduces revenues at your organization by millions of dollars will have to be addressed and defeated or modified, and there is not much policy involved in this decision. However, you will want to place the objections to the proposed change within the context of a policy that explains how this proposed measure hurts the community and harms the public good.

4. Advocacy. There are many forms of advocacy, including the "hired gun" lobbyist, grassroots letter writing, and public forums, as well as the myriad orchestrated public relations campaigns designed to create awareness among voters and encourage public support for solutions. The day-to-day cultivation of good relations with elected officials by inviting them to meet with staff and the executive management, or finding a role for them at various types of celebrations, such as open house receptions or anniversary events, is also an effective advocacy strategy.

A basic government affairs program has some capability related to each of these elements. The exact emphasis and resource investment will vary from organization to organization and will change year to year. The variation is often driven by the personal interest of the CEO or key board members. Extra resources may be brought to bear on an especially critical issue, such as Medicaid restructuring or an exemption from a tax.

The exact structure of the government affairs program does not matter, as long as it meets the needs and expectations of the organization. In some organizations the government affairs program is part of a senior vice president's responsibilities. The execution of these duties, with minimal dedicated staffing, entails occasional visits with a legislator, brief scanning of trade association periodicals, and attending a fund-raiser on occasion. This arrangement can work for organizations such as hospitals that participate in an industry-based trade association, which can handle government affairs for its constituents. Most commonly, a full-time professional is retained to represent the company in legislative matters.

PROGRAM ELEMENTS

Creating a formal government affairs capability involves the establishment of a structure that can be implemented incrementally through a series of steps such as the following:

1. Structure a basic in-house government affairs function that has formal assignment of responsibilities and accountabilities.

2. Establish an overall policy group to address differential government relations needs. The policy group would:

   • Approve government affairs program priorities

   • Provide oversight and resolve conflicts between business units

   • Evaluate capabilities and accomplishments

   • Identify desired future capabilities

3. Produce a business profile (usually consists of a listing of major sources of revenue).

4. Formalize liaison with key special interests.

5. Establish a legislative and congressional Match program.

6. Decide on state, federal, or local focus.

7. Survey and plan for positioning of staff and executives on appointed boards, commissions, and study committees. Secure leadership posts in state and national trade associations.

Structure

Early in Gail Warden's tenure as president and CEO of Henry Ford Health System in 1988, an HFHS task force was organized to review government affairs needs. The task force report proposed that a government affairs department be established. Activities for the department to undertake were specified as follows:

1. Promote image building

2. Advocate health policy decisions favorable to HFHS

3. Form liaisons with special-interest groups

The HFHS government affairs department was established in early 1989 and eventually consisted of four full-time equivalent employees (a vice president, two policy and grassroots associates, and one secretary). State lobbying services were purchased from outside consultants based at the state capitol in Lansing. Federal needs were temporarily postponed, because Medicare had not yet become a target for restructuring or cutbacks, and universal coverage was not a national priority at that time. Direct connections (now available through the Internet) with Congress and the Michigan legislature were installed to provide cost-free access to original source documents and legislation.

The HFHS task force report identified a serious barrier to the ability of HFHS to influence legislative policy—insufficient communication and visibility with elected officials at state, local, and federal levels. Interviews with important community and business leaders revealed a perception of HFHS as an "ivory tower" specialty care institution, with weak connections to the concerns of the state or immediate community.

In establishing the HFHS government affairs program, it was essential to be specific about the purpose for hiring staff and making other resource expenditures, because internal leaders were skeptical about sharing scarce health care dollars with what was viewed then as largely an optional public relations activity. From the beginning, a framework for annual performance evaluation was established. Although performance of individual government affairs staff is important, the focus on performance is on the overall program, a much broader perspective involving many of the company's resources outside the government affairs department. The government affairs staff were hired and trained from the outset as facilitators for the participation of many HFHS executives, managers, and physicians in policy development and effective advocacy.

The HFHS program began small, and added staff as capability and opportunities expanded. Its success continues to be reflected in its ability to produce the following results consistently:

1. timely notification of proposed laws and regulations
2. effective support, opposition, and amendments to legislation proposed by others
3. initiation of legislation to address particular organization-specific problems or concerns
4. significant and measurable leadership and influence in discussions on policy matters that affect the broader community and industry

A variety of organizational structures for government affairs may be considered. Some companies delegate the entire range of government relations responsibilities to an outside private lobbying firm, giving minimal attention as an organization to the political or legislative arena. This works well for companies that have large political action funds (assuring access) and short-range legislative goals (avoiding a tax or getting an exemption). Other organizations will develop a large centralized government affairs department with several full-time lobbyists, analysts, technical experts, and grassroots coordinators. Blue Cross and various union organizations use this model. This structure works well for multistate companies and companies that seek to influence broad policy issues involving multiple jurisdictions over long periods of time.

The more common structure in health care is to recruit or develop a relatively small in-house government affairs professional staff, and use outside consultants to provide direct advocacy (lobbying) and political research services. This structure assumes significant participation across the organization by internal operations departments for analysis and documentation. This structure usually includes an internal senior-level policy committee and some type of a systematic grassroots strategy focused on service-area legislators.

The first step is to survey the company's natural assets. These assets may include (1) the established reputation of the company in areas of special expertise (health care) and (2) the physical location of the company's facilities, customers, and workforce in legislative districts. Building on these assets is an effective way to get started.

The range of regulatory and legislative issues to be addressed determines the extent of resources required. Medicaid and Medicare have grown to become a primary government relations focus for HFHS. In hiring government affairs staff and outside consultants, HFHS learned that legislative budget issues require specialized expertise and personal relationships with a select group of legislators and regulators. In this context, it is particularly helpful to retain a lobbyist specializing in budget issues, who can devote time to a limited range of clients on an almost full-time basis. The lobbying firm is responsible for identifying budget concerns, getting copies of proposals for review, and managing budget advocacy. This is best done by someone who is an insider to government budget discussions in the legislature and the executive departments. The outside purchased services are expensive and must be strengthened and supported with in-house analysis and grassroots contacts in order to be cost effective.

The usual preconception of government affairs is lobbying activities involving private meetings with legislators and other elected officials or testifying at public hearings, including the highly formalized congressional hearings as well as the more informal state legislative hearings. These activities are key elements of the legislative process and exist to fulfill the expectation of transparency in governance for most democratic societies. The government affairs professional will spend significant time in these types of activities.

However, the preparation for each meeting with an elected official or appearance as a witness at a public hearing represents a significant component. Without preparation and continuity, the advocacy effort is handicapped and vulnerable to failure. In most cases, the kind of preparation required for success is the gathering and synthesis of information about the company or the industry the company is part of.

The following background activities are necessary for effective, direct advocacy.

Early Warning System

The intent is to identify new legislation and regulations as they emerge so that timely comments and advocacy can be achieved. Haphazard or complicated state legislative and regulatory systems for public notification of hearings and publishing of proposals can make this very difficult. HFHS outside consultants work "behind closed doors" to assure managers of timely notification of hearings, copies of proposals, and legislative analysis. The consultants can also advise which proposals are significant and which appear to be "trial balloons." Subscriptions and computer ties with the federal and state legislative service bureaus provide other routine advance notification. Most states will have an Administrative Procedures Act (APA) requiring public notice of proposed regulations. The *Federal Register* is part of the federal APA and provides an excellent tool to stay ahead of federal regulatory changes. Unfortunately, the consistency and reliability of public notification varies widely from state to state.

Political Assessments

Prioritizing which issues can be addressed first and which issues can be ignored or postponed requires early accurate judgment. This assessment and prioritization is a joint responsibility of in-house and consultant staff. It involves specialized knowledge about the bill sponsor (is he or she a part of the majority party), the level of interest with committee chairs and caucus leaders, as well as other politically driven factors. Legislative agendas are also affected by deadlines to complete the state budget, the election cycle, and certain overarching events like the September 11 terrorist attack on the World Trade Center or an economic downturn. In some instances, the lobbyists can be called upon to slow down the legislative process to allow for more time and careful strategy on issues important to the company.

Legal Analysis

Legal analysis is critical for assisting affected business units in evaluating the potential impact of proposals and creating a smart legislative strategy. Reliable systems for getting documents to the legal department or outside counsel, and coordinating their input with affected operations departments, need to be established.

Impact Assessment and Documentation

This involves review of legislative proposals by affected departments, with timely feedback to the government affairs staff. The information provided by these departments forms the basis for judging how important the legislation is for the organization and thus indicates how much advocacy effort should be expended.

Written Statements

Positions on key issues must be put in writing. In large organizations, the written statement helps coordinate internal efforts, identify misunderstandings, and standardize the message to allow several people to be involved in outside advocacy. The written statement is an easy vehicle for getting a message (with tailored cover letters) to a broad range of policy makers and special-interest groups. In most cases the written statement can be developed by the government affairs staff with approval of final text by operations managers involved with the issue.

Evaluation

During early development of the government affairs program, evaluation should seek to find a balance between program building and issues advocacy. At the early stages of a government affairs program, evaluation measures should focus on whether the basic functions exist and are able to perform systematically on an ongoing basis. Ultimately, however, evaluation should be based on the ability to effect legislative action. An evaluation should also assess the judgment calls by government affairs professionals regarding how much effort to spend on a bill and the timing of that effort. It does not make sense to do a 100 percent job on all bills, when each has a different priority for the organization and each will come up at a different time for legislative consideration. Also, in many cases it is safe to rely on the efforts of a trade association to adequately address one bill, thus freeing up resources to concentrate on another. The ability to prioritize is a direct result of good program capability and successful performance of the basic functions.

Policy Group

Establishing an in-house policy group of senior executives creates a reliable mechanism to support advocacy and develop legislative policy. This group generally makes decisions from a range of options and recommendations, rather than by analyzing specific legislation. The role of the government relations staff and consultants is to set out the options, identify and thoroughly investigate political ramifications, and minimize risk to the organization.

The deliberations of the policy group usually involve considerations that go beyond the content of any particular bill. For example, the organization's position on an issue frequently involves consideration of the overall mission of the organization (would opposing a bill violate this mission?), possible risks in other areas (such as loss of tax-exempt status), public relations concerns, and how the company's position is viewed by key legislators, traditional allies, board members, and soon. This group is an ideal forum for resolving competing interests of business groups within the company. At HFHS, we often find that the doctors want to support a mandate for coverage of a particular service that is not supported by our health plan. With strong leadership from the policy committee, the government affairs staff and professional lobbyists do not need to and should not be allowed to take responsibility for making policy for the organization.

Policy committee members can provide valuable advocacy and outreach and exert their leadership roles in the company and community, as well as influencing professional associations. The policy committee members can be called upon for personal contacts with legislators.

In some organizations, the CEO or a senior vice president will perform the work of the policy group, or assume responsibility when time frames are very short. In large organizations, the policy committee serves to bring together a wide range of interests from the various business groups in the organization. For example, the HFHS policy committee is chaired by President and CEO Gail Warden. Committee members also include the HFHS Chief Financial Officer, CEO, Senior VPs for Human Resources, Philanthropy, and Strategic Planning, Corporate Board Secretary, Chief Medical Office for the System and Henry Ford Medical Group, and the health plan CEO, Chief Operating Officer, and Chief Medical Officer. Meetings are quarterly or at the call of the chair.

Business Profile

A written business plan is one of the most important tools required to guide the government affairs program for the long term and to help assess the effectiveness of the program periodically. Elements of a business plan are as follows:

1. Environmental assessment (what is going on politically, and in the health care environment).
2. Business profile (inventory) of the major lines of services for the company.
3. Listing of the laws and agencies affecting the organization's major lines of services.
4. Realistic appraisal of the organization's current and future ability to influence legislative, congressional, and agency decisions. This can take the form of an inventory of the organization's strengths and weaknesses as they relate to influencing government policies and decisions, including alliances with other organizations, reputation, memberships and leadership positions in professional and trade associations.
5. Annual appraisal of what might be achieved with additional resources (be specific).
6. Clearly defined structure to keep abreast of broad social policy areas (such as tax reform or redistricting) that will affect decisions of the legislature, Congress, governor, and federal administration. Most state and national trade associations publish weekly or daily e-mail reports on key legislation and regulations. Subscribe and read these bulletins. In addition, the *New York Times, Wall Street Journal,* and weekly *Washington Post* serve as essential sources of information on national trends and political developments. These are "must read" sources for the government affairs staff (and the company's senior executives, as time allows). At HFHS, the public affairs department provides excerpts from these and other periodicals for senior executives on a daily basis.

The core information for most health care systems today is information about Medicare, Medicaid, and the uninsured. For organizations that have an academic mission, basic information about medical education and research activities are also required parts of the business profile. The information should be quantified. For example, what percentage of overall business comes from Medicare and Medicaid? What is the volume and cost for uncompensated care in the current year, and is this number growing or stable year to year?

State legislatures will also address other aspects of health care. These generally include malpractice, professional and facility licensing, and capacity issues through certificate-of-need laws. The government affairs staff needs to understand how these elements of the health care business work and any special problems or interests the company has in these areas. For example, in Michigan, the state health-planning laws have essentially frozen bed capacity at mid-1980 levels. We have been unsuccessful at convincing the legislature to allow hospitals with excess capacity to move beds to communities where population growth justifies new inpatient services. The major barrier has been the hospital industry itself, which views the certificate of need for inpatient beds as a type of franchise.

Unless the information is readily available, it is better to focus on compiling the basic business profile on Medicare and Medicaid first, and then address lower-cost issues as they arise in proposed legislation and regulation. Waiting until a bill is introduced on malpractice liability allows government affairs staff a better opportunity to sit down with legal counsel and get a first-rate education on malpractice liability and the issues facing the company.

Because of the growth in health care expenditures for government-sponsored services at both the state and national level, as well as the overall growth in health care as a percentage of GDP (currently at 13.5 percent), congressional and state government oversight of health care will continue. This makes the government affairs program an integral part of the company's overall business strategy. At Henry Ford Health System, the state and federal legislative issues that take priority are those directly affecting our costs and/or operations. The emphasis on Medicare, Medicaid, and uncompensated care in our business profile reflects this reality.

Although most companies will have finance and legal departments that follow changes in payment, in most cases the focus of these departments will be at the tail end of the legislative process—after the bill has become law and far past the point where there is an opportunity to influence the shape of the new law. In contrast, the government affairs department is almost always engaged with changes early on when a new law can be amended or defeated. What makes the government affairs staff effective with these early opportunities is a basic knowledge of the business and enough understanding of revenue streams to anticipate problems for the organization and make informed judgments on how to shape the proposal favorably.

Over time, the government affairs staff will develop an internal network of experts, which may or may not reflect the formal division of responsibilities in the company. For example, some of the finance people (not necessarily the managers) will carefully read the *Federal Register* or state regulatory bulletins on payment changes and track state and national trends. These people become great sources for assessing proposals. More importantly, they can help structure industrywide solutions that the company may want to promote. Similarly, the legal department will have individuals that work on statewide committees in complex areas involving conflicts between federal and state law, such as privacy and disclosure of medical information, informed consent for medical procedures and research, and medical malpractice liability. Finding these individuals is like striking gold for the government affairs staff. First, these internal experts can review proposals and very quickly find the core issue and suggested solution for the company. Second, they also are a rich source of education for the government affairs professional on these topics, which tend to surface over and over again.

Liaison with Special Interests

The capability to exert influence on legislative issues can be greatly strengthened through good relations with natural allies and a clear understanding of common ground. Placing company representatives on policy panels of natural allies (hospital associations, chambers of commerce, and at medical associations) maximizes the benefit of existing expenditures for corporate memberships and provides a powerful way to steer resources of these larger groups in directions that benefit the company. Personnel to serve as liaison will come from all operations and staff departments, many of whom will view such assignments as valuable professional development. A listing of existing assignments among company managers and executives becomes an important tool for developing a plan to fill in gaps. The government affairs staff should establish an e-mail report or other in-house mechanism to support participants with current legislative and political information.

State and local committee and leadership positions are a good place to focus first, because they are closer to home and are usually easier to secure than the national assignments. The more local focus is also appropriate because decisions by the legislature or state regulatory agencies are more responsive to influence by local companies and state or regional organizations. Their decisions often carry a direct and immediate impact on the company.

Federal efforts should be addressed as resources allow. At the federal level, effective ways to participate are through national trade association efforts to influence Congress (letter writing, congressional visits) and through national grassroots campaigns, including key contact programs for hospital administrators and physicians. Attention should be given to placing company representatives in the state and national groups that focus on the company's business profile priorities such as research, medical education, and group practice issues. These assignments help educate the company's health care managers on legislative policy and expand the government affairs early warning network.

Industry leadership roles by individual executives and professionals should be recognized and encouraged in performance evaluation and in other ways.

The Legislative and Congressional Match Program

The legislative and congressional Match program is a relatively inexpensive and effective strategy to assure that all service-area legislators and members of

Congress get periodic personal contacts from the organization. To the extent that personal relationships can be built over the years, these opportunities should be cultivated. The basic tool for the Match program is a listing of all facilities (clinics, hospitals) by legislative district. The second tool is a mechanism (corporate calendar) to monitor company activities in each legislative district. Begin to organize communications and contacts with elected officials to the extent possible, using special events as opportunities to build relationships. A powerful enhancement to this basic grassroots structure is the ability to tap into personal friendships that executives, managers, and medical staff already have or want to have with local legislators and policy makers. Ways to enhance these relationships should be organized over time, as executives and staff are willing to participate. These may include hosting a legislative briefing at the hospital or clinic and attending fund-raisers.

Relationships should be cultivated with members of the legislature and Congress who serve on committees that decide health policy, especially if you are fortunate enough to have people from your service area in key leadership roles (such as committee or subcommittee chairman). Opportunities to solidify relationships with these members should be the first priority for the state and federal relations efforts.

Positioning (State, Federal, or Local Focus)

Legislative strategy can be compared to "steering an oil tanker." This work consists of a great deal of planning and early effort in order to accomplish any planned change in direction. Relationship building and positioning activities can influence the course of legislative actions early on.

Early identification of emerging issues and early influence on the direction discussions take can be enhanced through placement of people on appointed government boards and commissions, as well as on legislative study committees. Planning for maximizing these types of assignments begins with an inventory of people in the company who currently have these appointments or want some support in securing an assignment and a listing of desired appointments. Outside consulting services can be used for placements (securing appointments from the governor or nominations from professional associations, for example). These appointments usually involve finding a person in the company who fits the profile of the open position (commissions often designate a membership slot for a physician or health care executive, for example), preparing endorsement letters (sometimes a letter from a friendly congressman or legislator will help), and experiencing some degree of pure luck.

Other Considerations

At a very basic level, the ultimate objective of most government affairs activity is to secure legislative time for a special interest. Thousands of ideas in the form of bills are introduced each year and compete with each other for time on the congressional and legislative agendas. Only a small percentage of these ideas are ever addressed. It is important to remember that no legislator or single organization has control over all major variables that affect legislative airtime or outcomes. The more variables an organization can influence, however, the greater the likelihood for success.

Variables that can be influenced by a single organization include relationships, data, information and written policy statements. Failure to do this work becomes a serious impediment to successfully influencing legislative discussions over time. A business profile suitable for sharing with outside audiences and periodic updating of basic numbers for the organization, such as Medicare payment and charity care costs, should be prepared. Numbers should be calculated and presented so that they are consistent year to year. For HFHS, a corporate fact sheet produced annually by the public affairs staff meets these needs.

Another variable within control of a single organization is education and sophistication of senior managers and other employees on legislative policy issues. Recognizing that an informed workforce can effectively multiply the ability of an organization to influence public opinion, attention should also be paid to ways (such as the employee newsletter) for educating employees and keeping them apprised of the organization's government relations and goals.

Administrative Structure

Accountabilities are assured by written job descriptions and specific (written) agreements with contract lobbyists regarding the division of overall responsibilities. These should identify who is responsible for the following:

1. Monitoring the introduction of bills and regulations; internal distribution for comment
2. Political analysis and consultation
3. Impact analyses (numbers, data, or examples)
4. Development of a position (support, oppose, neutral, amend) on an issue-by-issue basis (may be done by a different staffer each time)
5. Documentation (letters, testimony)
6. Advocacy (talking to legislators)
7. Feedback and reporting to executives, medical staff, and employees (monthly or quarterly is good)
8. Grassroots activities and support (usually a full-time job)
9. Staffing internal policy committee

A conscious decision should be made on each major issue regarding who will do what. Leadership for advocacy may be delegated to a trade association, for example, on bills that affect a large industry. Where there is a specific and unique impact on the organization, it may want to "go it alone." What is important is that a decision is made and either adjusted or adhered to, so that responsibilities don't "fall through the cracks" with mistakes occurring due to confusion and conflicting strategy among the players.

Partisan Politics

What experience teaches is that even nonprofit health care organizations must do what they can to support capable elected officials who are willing to devote energy and time to health care policy. Health care organizations today face the same pressures to participate in partisan politics that all other entities seeking to influence public policy encounter. Elections are basic, and some form of participation is expected. Legislators who lose elections can't vote, no matter how much they might want to. For nonprofit, tax-exempt health care organizations, there are two guiding bodies of law that shape what is allowed and not allowed. These are the federal Internal Revenue Code and federal and state electioneering and lobbying disclosure laws.

The statutory provisions for guidance to nonprofit organizations are the IRS rules. Any health care organization engaging in government affairs should consult legal counsel for a thorough understanding of these standards. Very briefly, IRS law permits organizations to spend fairly large amounts of money to support government affairs activities described earlier in this chapter. That is, a tax-exempt company may hire and support costs for lobbying legislators and members of Congress up to a certain threshold amount (will vary depending upon the organization's budget). This lobbying activity must be directly related to the core mission of the organization, in our case, health care. In addition, the organization is permitted to contribute revenue and other resources to ballot initiative campaigns. Again, it is important that the ballot issue be related to the core business of the company, although some latitude is allowed. For example, HFHS found that transportation gaps in our local southeast Michigan community is a huge barrier to patient access to appropriate health care services. Many patients cope with the lack of reliable bus service or inexpensive taxicab service by calling 911. This results in a mandatory ER visit, even if the patient acknowledges the need for urgent, rather than emergency care. In view of these problems, HFHS agreed to contribute to a ballot initiative aimed at consolidating the city of Detroit and Wayne County transportation systems. This was considered within the range of allowable activities under IRS rules.

However, IRS rules contain an absolute prohibition against the expenditure of any of the nonprofit company's resources to in any way help a candidate for public office get elected. At a minimum, this means no corporate money or influence may be contributed in any form to the candidate. Employees and managers may not seek reimbursement for attending a candidate's fund-raising breakfast or luncheon, for example. The corporate mail system or e-mail system may not be used to solicit contributions. The organization may not endorse any candidate for public office, and must avoid promoting candidates through in-house newsletters or other forms of employee or patient communications.

What the organization may do is organize forums during a campaign where all candidates are invited to come and express their views before an audience of employees and/or members of the community at large. This is a very effective way to gain visibility with the candidates and also provide a valuable community service. In Detroit, the three major health systems have had good access to the mayor's office, and the three CEOs hold monthly meetings with the mayor to discuss health care and related community issues. The mayor's Candidate Forum at Henry Ford Hospital during the 2001 campaign provided a way to elevate the importance of health care with the candidates, as well as educate them on which issues would need their attention after the election. Television and newspaper coverage arranged by HFHS helped promote the health care issues with the voting public and gave the candidates welcome free media exposure on a key concern of their voting constituents as well. Everyone benefits from this type of allowable election activity.

HFHS has also hosted senior management and medical staff meetings with the major candidates for governor and will meet with the candidates for county executive. The candidates value this exposure to influential people in the community. As long as all candidates are invited, this is an allowable expenditure of resources.

Understandably, most candidates for office expect contributions as well. For nonprofit hospitals and health systems, participating in a hospital association political action committee (PAC) is one way to address these demands. PAC drives are held each year, with contributions usually divided between the state association and the national association. Usually, the hospital or health system CEO is asked to conduct the PAC drive within his or her own company. Here, again, the IRS rules require caution. The PAC drive must be conducted with volunteers and on volunteer time. Corporate secretaries and other staff may not be used to prepare mailings, and postage must be purchased as an individual contribution. Corporate letterhead and titles of people signing the solicitation may not be used. The in-house mail system or e-mail may not be used.

Federal and state electioneering and lobbying disclosure laws are less restrictive. Any organization wanting to lobby members of Congress or the state legislature or officials in federal or state regulatory agencies should consult legal counsel regarding the applicable requirements for registering individual employees as lobbyists. In general, individuals with a certain threshold number of contacts with elected officials, or amount of expenditures (including travel costs, entertainment, and personal salary for time spent on lobbying activities), must register as a lobbyist. Periodic reports on lobbying activities by individuals and by the organization are also required.

In view of increased pressures to contribute to campaigns for public office, many nonprofit organizations are considering the benefits of setting up special political action committees. It is best to engage legal counsel for guidance on how to do this and whether it is advisable in the first place, taking into consideration the variation in need for, and expected benefits of, having a PAC. The PAC may not be run by the nonprofit organization. The PAC may not be named so as to suggest direct sponsorship by the nonprofit company. Instead, the PAC must be organized separately and is best administered by an outside firm, with costs for administration of the PAC to come from contributions to the PAC. Many lobbying firms can administer the PAC very cost-effectively and provide the arm's-length relationship required by law.

The question of whether mailing lists of employees and executives may be made available for solicitation by PACs should be reviewed and explored on an individual company basis. At HFHS, we determined that a listing of our senior administrative managers and executives would be made available upon request to any group recognized under federal or state law as a legitimate political action committee. We came to this decision based on a legal opinion that we could not give names and addresses to the hospital associations or other affiliated health groups without making the lists available to all groups. Federal electioneering provisions designed to protect employees from undue pressure by the employer to contribute to any political solicitation also come into play. These provisions say that only senior administration personnel may be listed for solicitations. We use the business address for our list, rather than home addresses, and notify everyone on the list annually of our policy.

In spite of the restrictions, leaders of an organization, including the CEO, should feel comfortable helping candidates for office, as long as the support for candidates can be legitimately characterized as support by the individual and not the tax-exempt organization. Many CEOs will be reluctant to permit their name to appear on the list of sponsors for candidate fund-raisers, just to steer clear of any misunderstanding. In special cases, however, the CEO will want to host an event at his or her home. This kind of event will have to be organized entirely with volunteer staffers outside the workplace and is usually done through the candidate's campaign office. Senior executives can host events and permit their name to be used, as long as there is no use of company resources or hint of a corporate endorsement.

Because of the prohibitions and special burdens for nonprofit tax-exempt organizations, health care has never been viewed as a big player in the partisan political arena. Over the past fifty years, this did not matter. Our focus has been, and continues to be, to work with the talented, concerned individuals after they get elected. Increasingly, however, with term limits for legislators and the growth of health care as a significant percentage of GDP, the need to be heard in the partisan political debate has grown for the health care companies. Experience teaches that doing even the little bit of activity allowed for individuals creates a positive working relationship with elected officials who still tend to look to health care for nonmonetary support and approval more than for actual dollars.

Stewardship

Implicit in our comments throughout this chapter is the conviction that government affairs engagement by health care organizations is highly beneficial. At a time when virtually every aspect of health care is subject to government regulation and 50 percent or more of any hospital's or health care system's revenue is directly affected by state and federal government decisions, it would be unwise to ignore the political arena in which such critical decisions are made.

For nonprofit, tax-exempt organizations, the responsibility to educate elected officials becomes part of the organization's stewardship to the community. IRS rules and related regulations specifically require nonprofit, tax-exempt hospitals to serve all segments of the community. Usually this is viewed as a responsibility to keep an open door for people who can not afford to pay for health care services. Advocacy for access for patients who can not pay, as well as advocacy for community-based programs that provide direct services to special and protective populations, should be considered as part of this broad directive. In Detroit, for example, community changes in the last ten years—including the closure of hospitals and clinic sites that have served low-income and uninsured populations and the exodus of primary care physicians to the more affluent suburbs—have produced a massive reduction in primary care access within the city neighborhoods. Detroit's inner-city hospital emergency rooms are crowded with Medicaid and uninsured patients with urgent medical needs.

Our advocacy with Congress and the Michigan State legislature seeks to connect these access issues with the withdrawal of hundreds of millions of dollars from Medicare and the Medicaid program since 1997 and serious flaws in the Michigan Medicaid managed care structure. The Medicaid HMO plans in Detroit are financially troubled and deeply in debt to hospitals and health systems that provide care to their Medicaid enrollees. The HMO accounts receivable to area hospitals is currently more than $70 million. Uncompensated care is an additional $300 million for this community. The hospitals and health systems have collaborated in advocacy for restored funding to the Medicaid program. At the same time, the largest Detroit health systems have banded together to form a program of enrolling uninsured individuals for primary care services at remaining community clinic sites and supporting these sites with inpatient and specialty care. Longer term, our strategy is to bring a comprehensive network of federally qualified health centers into the city, complemented with health centers in most of the city's elementary, middle, and high schools. These community-based legislative initiatives form an important strategy to bring new revenue into the community and fill gaps left by Medicaid and Medicare cutbacks. A new public hospital is also being discussed, with an open debate on how this might be structured, including a virtual public hospital model that consists of designated beds in existing community hospitals.

This kind of government affairs work is beneficial, because it marries the need for health systems and hospitals to address crowded ERs and a growing uncompensated care burden with the enduring need of patients in Detroit to get adequate health care services.

There are really no entities other than health care organizations that can carry out this type of government affairs work. Most elected officials will come to their elected position with very little exposure to health care policy and limited ability to lead on health care solutions. In many states, such as Michigan, term-limit laws that cap out tenure at six or eight years increasingly mean that the state legislators do not have time to learn health care on the job either. They must necessarily focus on the next election and the next step in their political career. Without efforts of the health care community to educate and promote community-based solutions, very little progress can be made in today's environments.

CASE STUDY

In 1987 the Washington State legislature began consideration of a proposal to create an insurance program for the working poor. Many legislators were concerned about the growth of uninsured populations who earn little more than the welfare recipients, but are barred from the Medicaid program because of a slight difference in family income and resources. Legislators from rural and farming communities expressed frustration that Medicaid was not available to many patients served by hospitals and doctors in their communities. Consensus about universal coverage was just beginning to build in the country, although Congress was several years away from deliberating the Clinton Health Plan. The convergence of problems for patients and providers in Washington State, as well as a nationally driven sentiment for universal coverage, produced the Basic Health Plan, which continues today as an important and popular feature of Washington State's health care and social services program.

The original proposal came from a state senator, who was a physician, rather than from an outside commission or group. It was a workable plan, but the early signs were clear. It would not succeed unless the other Washington State legislators heard from their constituents. Unfortunately, the constituents, including many health care organizations, were unfamiliar with the proposed solution. As a result, the first phase of moving this legislation consisted of generating support among the wide range of groups in Washington State that had in the past supported expanded access and universal coverage. The proposal was circulated, and Gail Warden, as CEO of Group Health Cooperative, convened leadership of the key health groups, including the medical society, the hospital association, the nurses association, Blue Cross and the other insurers, business, and the local health-planning agency. This group met at 7:00 A.M. every Friday morning during the legislative session to talk about cost and access issues and the Basic Health Plan proposal. Members of the Friday Breakfast Group sent letters to the legislature and testified at hearings. There was no

opposition. But there continued to be a hesitancy and uncertainty among legislators about how many uninsured people there actually were in the state, what
a benefit package should look like, how much it would cost, and who would run
it. In addition, this was an election year and legislators needed to focus on the
fall campaigns.

In early spring, with the end of the legislative session close at hand, outlook
for the Basic Health Plan bill was uncertain. Each time the bill was brought forward for a vote in committee or on the House or Senate floors, legislators
slowed things down so that there would be time to sound out voters in their
districts and get a handle on some of the technical issues. There was also a distinct desire to be counted as a supporter, if the program turned out to be as good
as it sounded. Rather than risk a narrow victory (and possible repeal in subsequent sessions of the legislature), the lobbyists assigned to getting the bill
passed consulted with the Friday Breakfast Group in Seattle. A decision to post-
pone the final vote was made. Instead, the bill would be turned into a detailed
study resolution, with oversight by a commission composed of equal numbers
of Republicans and Democrats from the House and Senate, plus a highly visible and respected representative of business, who would chair the commission,
and a senior citizen. The technical sections of the Basic Health Plan bill were divided up into work plans for several technical advisory committees, chaired by
and composed of all the special-interest groups involved with the legislation.
Membership on the technical committees was constructed carefully so as to
create opportunities for the special-interest groups to resolve conflicts and
achieve consensus. These technical groups were asked to investigate the benefit
plan, underwriting, eligibility, and other issues critical to predicting costs and
success of the program. The commission was instructed to report back to the
legislature the following January, after a statewide election that would bring
some new legislators to Olympia and return most of the incumbents.

When the bill was brought forward again the following January, it had few
changes from the original proposal. But in the intervening months, large voter
constituencies had accumulated to support the plan and legislators had talked
about it with favorable results during their campaigns. With the Republicans,
the issue of cost arose more importantly in the second round, and almost tabled
the initiative. Democrats (and most of the health care community) felt the
Basic Health Plan should be structured as a new entitlement, like Medicaid. Republicans were dead set against this. The compromise was to make the level of
enrollment subject to appropriation, so that the legislature would have an opportunity to review the program each budget cycle and decide on the relative
priority of the Basic Health Plan with other state programs. The downside was
the built-in limitation on enrollment and vulnerability to changes in priorities
year to year. When the final vote was taken, it was nearly unanimous. The Basic
Health Plan remains today.

The lesson learned is that having a good idea is not sufficient for good legislation. Broad community support and an opportunity for elected officials to be

seen by their constituents as helping with an important community problem is essential. There is a critical role for health care leaders to play in moving an issue to maturity and bridging common ground with the business community. Proponents of legislation will be wise to create a place for all the special interests. This is government affairs at its finest.

Chapter 10

Consumer, Public, and Grassroots Dimensions

Pamela Jeffery

I don't care how many lobbyists you have in Washington, if you are weak
in the streets, you are weak.

Ralph Nader

INTRODUCTION

Health care providers are paying increasing attention to the art of influencing
government for a multitude of reasons. Fiscal pressures that were beginning to
be felt even before September 11 are forcing politicians to rethink how they allocate precious tax dollars to their partners in the broader public sector: municipalities, universities and colleges, schools, and hospitals. The aging population
is putting upward pressure on health spending, so politicians and bureaucrats
are engaged in a tug-of-war over how to spend health care dollars effectively to
improve the quality and delivery of health care. Technology, changing public
attitudes, and globalization are causing governments to "reinvent" themselves;
in turn, governments are looking to their partners to do more with less. In
Canada, the federal government is signaling its interest in making changes to
the Canada Health Act, an act that previously had been untouchable. Against
this backdrop, health care providers are battling to protect their share of government spending through strategic government relations.

This chapter examines how health care providers can work with citizens and
consumers at the grassroots level to influence government. While traditional
lobbying often overlooked these important stakeholders, strategic government
relations often relies on citizen and consumer involvement to enable health
care providers to construct workable solutions to complex issues. In this way,
providers become more knowledgeable and thus better prepared to engage gov-

ernment officials in a dialogue that reflects interests broader than their own narrower interests. Ultimately, this leads to informed discussion and sound policy that reflects an alignment of the public interest with the interest of the provider.

A new approach to finding solutions to meet the changing needs of health care providers is anathema to some institutions because of the new demands it places on those institutions. However, it will ultimately lead to better policy by imposing a discipline that has often been lacking in the development of policy but is necessary today. It mirrors a similar effort underway by governments who too are facing highly complex public policy issues and who are increasingly embracing a move away from traditional policy making that often occurred in a vacuum. Governments today are under pressure to move toward developing legislative, regulatory, and policy change through engaging stakeholders in substantive discussion at the front end. In short, governments are increasingly aware that solutions to health policy issues lie in dialogue with providers as well as with those who have the ultimate stake: citizens and consumers. So too should health care providers engage in dialogue if they want to be part of the solution that government adopts to resolve an issue in which health care providers have a stake.

This chapter will examine the following key questions:

1. What is strategic government relations? What are the key principles?
2. What are the key success factors in creating and executing a successful grassroots campaign to influence government? How can the involvement of stakeholders, including consumer groups and the public, help an organization influence government?

STRATEGIC GOVERNMENT RELATIONS

Strategic government relations is in sharp contrast to traditional lobbying. Traditional lobbying required little more than a stint in government, a good Rolodex, a telephone, and an understanding of the policy-making process. It required little in the way of education.

Strategic government relations demands much more from its practitioners who function in a complex political and policy environment. As a result, most successful government relations practitioners have at least one university degree, if not two. Many have law degrees and M.B.A.'s. They rely heavily on policy analysis, public opinion and survey data, media analysis, and the Internet. They draft policy option documents for review by public sector decision makers. They develop communications strategies to define the issue(s) in the public domain and work with the media to ensure balanced coverage of the issue(s). They work closely with government officials who value their counsel. They undertake stakeholder analysis to identify allies, opponents, and *potential* allies on issues and they develop strategies to engage or neutralize stakeholder groups. They execute grassroots strategies by mobilizing consumers and the public to express support or opposition on any given issue. In short, strategic government relations is about influencing government to embark on a course of action based on sound research, goals and objectives, effective communication, and flawless strategy execution.

Key Principles

Defining the Issue

Often misstated as "spin," how a health care provider defines the issue when embarking on a strategic government relations program is an important factor in the overall success of the program.

In 1998, a pediatric teaching hospital was seeking government funding in order to establish a computer network. The purpose of the network was to allow doctors and staff to transfer health records between the hospital and regional pediatric centers. The hospital had partnered with a leading hardware vendor and together with the vendor wanted to make a case to the government that would deliver them $7.5 million in funding.

In preparing to make the case to government, the hospital felt that the government's health bureaucrats were unlikely to approve the onetime funding at a time of significant tax cuts and mounting pressure on the health budget. It was felt that funding approval would only be given if the bureaucrats were directed to do so by elected officials.

At first glance, the hospital would have defined the issue in its discussions with elected officials as a grant to purchase hardware and software. Instead, the hospital chose to define the issue in a context of the political platform on which the government had been elected in the first place. Their platform had included pledges to bring in the best new management techniques and thinking, to improve services to patients. Knowing the government's political agenda, the hospital defined the computer network as a solution to the problem of outdated information management tools that were adversely affecting young patients. Defining the issue in this way meant political officials saw the network as an opportunity to advance their government's agenda and directed their officials to provide the onetime funding to the hospital.

Defining the issue in this way brought consumers and the public into the issue because of its political nature: the government announced the funding to the applause of patient groups who credited the government for making the right decision and the public who credited the government for keeping a promise it had made. While the hospital had not reached out to these groups when working with elected officials, it paved the way for them to engage in dialogue with them in the future.

Developing Policy Options

One way in which health care providers can work effectively with governments is through the development and analysis of policy options.

In the traditional policy-making process, governments went about developing policy and at some point would canvass a few well-placed individuals they knew to obtain their input. Officials would identify policy options, assess those options in the context of a set of criteria, and recommend to their superiors the policy option that appeared to best satisfy the criteria. Since sound process leads to sound policy, this traditional policy-making process led inevitably to some very bad decisions.

There is growing awareness within governments of the significant value of ideas and expertise from outside the traditional government decision makers. Organizations that are the providers of good ideas are well positioned to be effective advocates on behalf of themselves and their consumer constituents. These same organizations build credibility and are seen by government officials to have integrity because they are engaged in the process. This strengthens the relations between the organization and government since communications are policy-driven, not crisis-driven.

There are several ways for organizations to provide ideas, namely through formal consultation and informal discussions and through their industry associations. Often overlooked is developing and analyzing policy options to address an issue that confronts the organization and which the organization knows is on the government's radar screen. Simply put, this means slipping your own organization's shoes off and stepping into the shoes of government, tackling an issue from this perspective. It means a paradigm shift to strategic government relations, providing solutions instead of only problems to government.

In 1994, members of an industry association were facing a possible new sales tax on their revenue from selling their services to consumers. Another industry association had been pressuring the government to impose the tax in fairness to its members who believed they were now in competition with this industry and it was only fair that the tax be levied on these companies as well. The industry association met with finance officials and proposed to prepare a brief that would identify and assess two options: to impose the tax or to retain the status quo. They consulted with officials on the criteria they would use to assess each option, coming up with seventeen criteria in all. Officials were pleased with the association's effort to engage in the process and were available by phone during the four months it took to prepare the brief. The association set up a steering committee to work with its government relations consultant who wrote the brief.

The thirty-page brief assessed the two options against seventeen criteria. The criteria selected included the impact of the new tax on consumers of the industry's services as well as on the general public. The industry association consulted a consumers group during the drafting of the brief to fully understand the implications of passing along the new tax through increased prices. The brief concluded that the proposed new sales tax would have significant negative impacts on consumers and would give an emerging group of direct competitors not subject to the tax a competitive advantage. This in itself was not viewed to be good public policy since these competitors were located outside of the jurisdiction and therefore did not pay taxes and employ workers as the indigenous industry did. As a direct result of the industry's well-researched brief, finance officials chose not to introduce the new sales tax.

Undertaking Stakeholder Analysis

Identifying all of the stakeholders in any given issue and engaging them wherever possible is another important way in which health care providers can work with governments to bring about constructive legislative, regulatory, and policy change.

The first step is to identify those interest groups who will support your organization and those groups who will oppose your own organization on a specific issue. These are typically groups who are well known to an organization because of historic relationships. As well, those groups who historically have not had an interest in the issue but who are relatively well known and credible in the eyes of the public, media, and/or governments and could be prompted to become involved in the issue should also be identified. Typically, consumer and citizens groups fall into this category since their resources are generally too limited to allow for them to be active on more than one issue at any one time. Stakeholders (who are members of all three of these groups) and their positions on an issue should be closely monitored during a government relations program to ensure a strong base of support and to guard against any erosion.

The second step is to develop ways to engage supportive stakeholders, neutralize opposing stakeholders, and manage potential new stakeholders. By engaging supportive stakeholders, an organization can demonstrate that its position on an issue is more widely supported. If the supportive group of stakeholders includes a good number of stakeholders and is sufficiently diverse, the group's position can be communicated more effectively, and defended more easily, to the public and to governments as a position that is in the public interest. Activities such as coalition building, joint correspondence, and joint communiqués are three ways to actively engage supportive stakeholders. These activities are also appropriate for new stakeholders who have the potential of becoming supportive stakeholders.

Not to be overlooked are those groups who are known opponents. To the extent that an organization can demonstrate that its position is clearly in the public interest through a coalition approach, as described previously, it is more difficult for groups opposing the organization to be successful, since their efforts will not be perceived to be in the public interest. Notwithstanding the suggested coalition approach, activities such as dissecting the opposing groups' positions to identify where interests may align and understanding what aspects of the position public opinion supports are two ways to neutralize opposing stakeholders.

Understanding Public Opinion

It should go without saying that governments are highly attuned to the opinions of voters. Millions of dollars are spent annually by governments of all stripes to gauge public opinion on fiscal issues, health care service delivery, military spending, and any number of government programs. While governments are elected to lead in good times and bad, the reality is that governments often lead only after they have determined when and where voters want to be led.

When embarking on a strategic government relations program, health care providers also need to pay attention to the minds and hearts of voters. Surveying public opinion can be an important step for health care providers to take in order to work with consumers at the grassroots level to influence government. While this may seem a daunting task, a few thoughtful questions posed to patient groups, other stakeholder groups, and the general public through a professional telephone survey can help ensure that the goal of the program is realistic and likely to win government acceptance. In the event that the results suggest that the goal of the program is not supportable as it is currently defined, the goal can be modified and/or arguments can be tested to help increase the likelihood of government acceptance.

A survey of this kind can also be released to the media and used as a tool to more broadly educate voters on a single issue. As part of a government relations program, this can be an important tool to use to help governments prepare the public for change. Sharing this data with government before it is released can be an important part of building strong relationships with government as long as the survey is conducted in a credible fashion.

A drug manufacturers trade association commissioned a public opinion survey on the issue of drug costs. The survey was timed to coincide with a government's review of health care spending in order to bring about savings in the current fiscal year. Survey results demonstrated strong public opinion support for increased use of generic drugs in order to help manage taxpayer dollars more effectively. The association shared the survey results with government officials before releasing them to the media. In this way, officials could review the results and be prepared to offer comments when contacted by the media. The survey generated significant media coverage that included the government's carefully calibrated response expressing support for the importance of managing health care spending wisely. The survey was remarkably successful in that it educated the public about potential savings to the health care system through the use of generic drugs.

Engaging the Public Through Grassroots Activities and Media Relations

While technical issues that confront health care providers are of little interest to citizens and consumers, there are many more "strategic" issues of significant interest to providers and to the public. It is these issues that demand government action and require input from myriad stakeholder groups. Examples of these issues include hospital bed funding, emergency room overcrowding, nursing care levels in publicly funded long-term care facilities, and physician compensation. Since these issues are politically sensitive because they affect large numbers of people (and help sell newspapers through attention-grabbing headlines), elected officials tend to work at resolving them quickly and in a way that mirrors public opinion. It is these types of issues that give health care providers the ideal opportunity to work with citizens and consumers at the grassroots level to influence government.

In the mid-1990s, a group of physicians broke away from their provincial association and formed their own lobby group over a disagreement involving physician compensation. The group quickly settled on a name and engaged our firm to advise them on how to achieve their compensation goals. We developed and helped them execute a grassroots lobbying strategy that saw them become recognized as a bona fide physicians group with legitimate concerns and a solution to the compensation dilemma plaguing the entire profession that was in the public interest.

Each physician was encouraged to meet with his or her local elected representative to brief him/her on the broader issue of physician compensation in the context of the ongoing negotiations with the government. In order to ensure each meeting went according to plan, each physician was given background on his or her individual elected representative, issue materials, and meeting "guidelines" to help facilitate constructive dialogue. At the same time, the group began to issue carefully crafted press releases designed to position them as a credible voice for the profession and to advance their arguments in a reasoned tone. Coincident with these activities was the distribution of issue backgrounders to consumers through the physicians' individual offices. Elected representatives were given copies of the backgrounders so they could be prepared to discuss the issue with constituents if asked. Simultaneously, a large meeting was held at an airport hotel that drew over 200 physicians and several television news crews.

Over the course of six months, the group was highly successful in tackling the issue of physician compensation. They were asked to join the negotiations with a seat at the table next to their former association. This helped them win a major concession from the government and gain recognition from the media and the public as a bona fide group, including a front-page appearance in a national newspaper and appearances on national television news.

At the consumer level, they succeeded in educating hundreds of patients about the issue in a nonthreatening way. Elected representatives saw the physicians' group as a legitimate voice for the profession and a community resource to them on the complex issue of physician compensation. Importantly, elected representatives saw how the physicians had become credible spokespeople on the issue to their constituents, increasing their political risk of not supporting the physician group's solution.

GRASSROOTS CAMPAIGNS: KEY SUCCESS FACTORS

Building the Case

An organization or a coalition of organizations that wants to lobby government on a strategic issue through a grassroots campaign needs to bring forward a defensible set of arguments as to why the public should support its position. This reflects the political reality that strategic issues are subject to public debate and scrutiny. Ideally, an organization needs to be proactive in constructing the arguments in order to help shape the ensuing debate as well as the ultimate decision. These arguments are integral in defining the issue, a key principle of strategic government relations as discussed earlier in this chapter.

In order to develop this set of arguments that will move public opinion in the right direction, it is important for the organization to undertake research and analysis in order to reach conclusions on a specific policy option. This entails a thorough examination of the consequences for the public of the government supporting the organization's position or the government opposing its position. This will accomplish three things: (1) enable an organization to become more knowledgeable (and often more knowledgeable than the government itself, which is key since knowledge is power); (2) position the organization as a resource to government on the issue, helping the organization to build credibility and goodwill; and (3) help advance the issue by developing research-based arguments that withstand public scrutiny, thereby laying the groundwork for a favorable government decision.

A case that illustrates the effectiveness of "doing one's homework" involves an industry association whose member companies were being threatened by a newly elected government's campaign pledge to take the industry out of private hands, making the sector publicly owned and run. The association developed a comprehensive, strategic government relations plan that included research into the economic consequences for the government and for voters should the government proceed with its plans. The research, undertaken by a high-profile, reputable international accounting firm, quantified the job losses (in the thousands), lost direct investment dollars, forgone tax revenue, and several other key economic consequences.

The research led to the firm's conclusion that the government's plans were not of net economic benefit to taxpayers. Once the research was completed, the industry association found itself in the enviable position of having significantly more knowledge of the economic consequences of the government's plans than did the government itself. The association chose wisely to share the information with government officials at both the bureaucratic and political levels. This marked the beginning of a greatly improved relationship between the industry and political officials. A few days later, the association then held a press conference at which it released the research along with a carefully prepared analysis of other options that the government could assess as alternatives to its planned industry takeover.

As a result of the industry association's examination of the consequences of the government proceeding with its plans along with an analysis of policy alternatives, the industry gained significant credibility not only with the government but also with the public. The association had wisely chosen to have a third party conduct the economic analysis, so that its conclusion would not be judged by either the government or the public as having been predetermined by the industry itself. The association had strategically brought consumers and the public into the debate by providing them through the media with indisputable data that they could assimilate in order to form an opinion on the issue. The following month, public opinion polling done by the association showed that the industry association had overtaken the government as the most credible source of information on the issue of the government's planned takeover. Six months later, the government announced it was not proceeding with its plans on the basis of the very arguments made by the industry as backed up by its research.

Educating Elected Officials

Once the case has been built, it needs to be taken to the men and women on the front lines: the politicians themselves. An organization needs to educate state/provincial and federal politicians about an issue from a community perspective during a grassroots campaign in the hopes of winning their support and their assistance in lobbying government from the inside. Keeping in mind the oft-repeated "all politics is local" truism is helpful in order to ensure that the grassroots campaign focuses sufficient resources at the community level. Politicians need to have their proverbial finger on the community pulse; effective grassroots campaigns give them the opportunity to demonstrate to their constituents that they are listening. This means that a successful grassroots campaign educates politicians on the issue broadly as well as on how a favorable decision will benefit the politician's constituents.

The first step for an organization to undertake is to identify people within the organization who reside in the various constituencies and to select from among them a set of individuals who will then be matched one-on-one with their elected representatives. The next step is to brief these individuals and to provide them with information and material that is tailored specifically to meet the needs of elected representatives. The third step is for these individuals to begin meeting with their elected representatives on a regular basis in order to educate them on the issue and obtain their support.

In these meetings, the individual will want to be positioning himself/herself as a resource on the issue to the elected representative and his or her aides so that the elected representative can go directly to the individual when faced with a constituent's question or concern. It is important to provide concise material that describes the issue in succinct terms. While the ideal outcome is for the elected representative to not only support the position but also lobby inside government, it can also be extremely helpful to the campaign if the meeting(s) raise questions in the politician's mind that he/she can explore with political colleagues at the appropriate time.

If an organization has been proactive in its government relations, it will already have operationalized its "grassroots network." The individuals who make up the network will have already developed relationships with their elected representatives in anticipation of an issue arising for which they will need the support of their elected representatives. Most organizations however are not proactive and as a result only contact elected representatives when a problem arises. This is a far less effective approach because there is no history with the individual. The nature of human relationships is such that in these situations, elected representatives are not inclined to do anything other than listen. They are also less likely to accept as gospel the information they are being provided. This differs when an individual has taken the time to establish and nurture a relationship. In this situation, an elected representative is much more likely to provide real assistance and to accept the information being communicated as truthful and of value.

The physician group's lobbying efforts with their elected representatives, described earlier in this chapter, were a key success factor in the group's ultimate success. In their initial round of meetings, they provided their elected representatives with a thorough briefing on the issue of physician compensation. The physicians then provided them with the issue backgrounders in advance of their distribution to patients in their waiting rooms so that the elected representatives could be prepared to respond to phone calls from constituents. The physicians also provided copies of press releases to their elected representatives so that they could be prepared for media calls.

By working to educate their elected representatives in this way and by providing them with the information they needed in order to respond to constituents and the media, the physicians gained credibility in the politicians' eyes in a short period of time. As a result of the physicians working with the media to get their side of the story out, the public became better informed. As the physicians moved public opinion in their favor, they kept their elected representatives informed of their progress with the government and the favorable feedback they were receiving from patients.

All these activities in turn enabled the politicians to keep their finger on the pulse of the issue and to be on the right side of public opinion in their discussions with the media and constituents. To their constituents who were increasingly supporting the physician group's position, the politicians were able to articulate their support knowledgeably and position themselves as in tune with the views of their constituents.

Creating a Strong Base of Support

Making the case to the public and consumers can be easier and more effective if a strong base of support exists beyond the organization itself. This allows an organization to show to government and the public that its concerns go far beyond its own narrow self-interest and helps position the organization as acting in the public interest.

In order to begin building a base of support, the organization needs to start with those other organizations who also have a stake in the outcome and who are its natural allies. Traditionally, employees, suppliers, customers, and shareholders are four stakeholder groups who, depending on the circumstances and the relationships, can be approached and asked to support the organization on an issue. Other stakeholders who may support the organization include the media, interest groups, its industry association, other levels of government, and the public.

The industry association described earlier in the chapter embarked on an aggressive strategy to create a broad-based coalition of support on the issue of the government's planned takeover. Its success in mobilizing and compelling a multitude of stakeholders to become actively involved in the campaign illustrates the importance to grassroots campaigns of creating a strong base of support.

Individual companies that were members of the association contacted a large number of customers by including information on the issue in their billings. The information explained the consequences of a takeover, focusing on an expected decline in customer service through a government-run monopoly. Customers were asked to write key political officials directly to express their concerns. Customers responded in no small part due to the credibility the industry had following its well-publicized report on the economic implications of the government's plans. In this way, the industry was able to mobilize its customers.

After the press conference at which the job-loss data was released, management at individual companies encouraged their employees to become involved in the campaign in a productive fashion. Employees who were fearful of losing their jobs responded in a vigorous fashion. The employees who were already involved in the grassroots network on the issue emerged as the leaders in their respective workplaces and counseled their fellow employees about the issue and how they could become involved. These employees in turn began to write their elected representatives, stage small demonstrations in front of their elected representatives' constituency offices, and visit with their elected representatives.

The public was also mobilized through newspaper advertising and editorials that ran in the weeks preceding an expected decision. The advocacy advertising went beyond the traditional to include specific job-loss figures for each community. In this way, the public understood instantly the consequences for their communities.

Media relations was another key component of creating a strong base of support. Meetings took place between the industry association and editorial boards of every major newspaper following the release of the report at the press conference. Follow-up calls were made in the weeks leading up to the decision with the result being that editorial positions began to be published supporting the industry. In this way, the industry was able to continue to build broad public support and understanding that was essential to persuading the government it was no longer in their interest to proceed with its plans.

In addition to the editorial board meetings, individual reporters were also briefed about the expected job losses in their communities at the time the advertisements ran. Stories appeared about the job losses, again reinforcing the government's perception that the political risk to proceed was far higher than expected.

CONCLUSION

Strategic government relations is about influencing government to embark on a course of action based on sound research, goals and objectives, effective communication, and flawless strategy execution. Grassroots campaigns have an important role to play in strategic government relations when the issue itself is of public importance. Well-run campaigns based on the key success factors identified previously are extremely effective in persuading a government to take a particular course of action because good campaigns mobilize consumers and other important stakeholder groups.

All of us who are governed by democratically elected governments have the choice to become involved in the political process as active citizens—grassroots campaigns give us the opportunity to do this. Health care providers who give consumers the opportunity to become involved in an issue through a well-executed grassroots campaign can benefit from the public policy solutions that are achieved.

Chapter 11

Influencing Governmental Decision Making: The Role of Corporate Leadership

Ginger L. Graham

INFLUENCING GOVERNMENTAL DECISION MAKING

As part of a highly regulated health care industry, my company, Guidant Corporation, is continually impacted by governmental decision making at all levels. Regulatory bodies around the globe, such as the Food and Drug Administration and the Centers for Medicare and Medicaid Services in the United States, decide whether products will be made available for patient use, and whether providers will be adequately reimbursed. Policy structures and regulatory actions can virtually destroy a business by stifling, or even obliterating, its ability to innovate. At every turn, governments affect our market opportunities—and our ability to meet the needs of the patient, who is our primary concern.

Because the impact of government is so enormous, I'm continually amazed that so many otherwise proactive business leaders react like the proverbial deer in the headlights when it comes to public policy. Some choose to abdicate any personal responsibility by delegating the entire government affairs function to an often overworked and understaffed corporate department or to outside consultants and paid lobbyists. Some rely exclusively on their trade associations to do the heavy lifting, and others simply bury their heads ostrich-style, cross their fingers, and hope for the best.

There is an old business adage that identifies three kinds of people in any given industry: those who make things happen; those who watch what happens; and the vast majority who don't have a clue. We in the health care industry can't afford to be clueless, nor can we afford to sit on the sidelines and watch. If our companies are to grow and prosper—and if we are to meet our objectives in serving patients—senior management has no choice but to step up to the plate as corporate and industry leaders in influencing the governmental decision-making process.

Many of us in the health care industry are doing just that, and my company is no exception. Influencing health policy is Guidant's number one strategic issue and has been a high priority since our formation in 1995. In our initial planning process, we identified ten strategic tasks that would be pivotal in making us an exceptional company, and one of the most important was our ability to influence public policy in the health care arena. Since then, that issue has risen to the top of our list, and I believe it should be at the top of yours.

It simply isn't enough to do everything else well: product development, operations, quality assurance, sales and marketing, customer service, and the like. It's not enough to understand how to manage our cost structure and how to drive profitable growth for our shareholders. Even if our markets allow us to create value, and even if there are numerous opportunities for new therapies and new product concepts to fuel our growth, we could still come up short. Why? Because there is one issue that can prevent growth from happening. That issue is health policy. We believe that informed and educated policy decisions are crucial to the continued success and long-term viability of our company, and to the success of every company operating in health care, particularly those—like ours—that depend on innovation and invention as their competitive advantage.

Guidant is a $2.7-billion manufacturer of cardiac and vascular devices, with more than 10,000 employees worldwide. Our products integrate the technologies of the computer industry with the most significant advances in material sciences, and apply them to medical needs. Our research and development investment over the past five years has been $2.4 billion. New therapies, enabled by those technologies, have saved or improved millions of lives, and we believe that's only the beginning.

Like so many of us in the health care sector, we are working hard to help find solutions to the challenges of an aging population, longer life spans, increased incidence of disease, and higher demand by consumers to be healthy longer. Our goal, quite literally, is to provide better health for all of us at a more cost-effective value proposition for society. In order to reach that goal, we must shape a public policy environment where medical technology is valued, where patients have timely access to innovative therapies, and where investment in medical innovation is supported and ongoing.

CHALLENGES TO INNOVATION

The medical technology industry is made up of thousands of relatively small, highly entrepreneurial companies, and new products are its lifeblood. Pressure for new ideas and superior therapies is intense and, throughout the entire sector, the level of spending on research and development (R&D) has steadily increased over the past decade. In the year 2000, Guidant, for example, spent more than 14 percent of its sales revenue on R&D. This is not surprising when we consider that more than 60 percent of our corporate revenue comes from products that are less than one year old. That's one of the realities of the medical technology industry.

Another reality is the ongoing need for a steady supply of private investment capital to fund state-of-the-art experimentation and research. Our industry is made up primarily of companies with fewer than fifty employees, and much of our innovation comes from early-stage start-ups that are absolutely dependent on investment and venture capital, and from academic centers. To attract potential investors, we must demonstrate a reasonable likelihood of acceptable return, despite our long development times, intensive capital needs, and complex regulatory structures. If we can not make that case, we lose on two counts: we do not attract the investment capital we need and we do not attract the intellectual capital that follows it, which is where all creativity resides. When intellectual capital becomes an endangered species, innovation rapidly declines and the patients of today and tomorrow are the ultimate losers.

Public policy has a major impact on the medical technology industry's ability to innovate and policy issues continue to challenge companies eager to develop new products for enhanced health care. Broadly speaking, these fall into three categories.

First, government policies can determine whether the research that results in innovation is conducted at all. Innovation requires access to skilled technical workers and a steady flow of intellectual and monetary capital. It follows that education, training, immigration, and tax policies can help or hinder the ability to innovate.

Second, government policies determine how new products are reviewed, approved, and brought to market. As medical technologies become increasingly more complex, regulators around the globe must have the resources and technical expertise to keep pace with the rate and scope of innovation.

Finally, there is the issue of reimbursement, a major concern to medical technology companies, as well as to providers, clinicians, and patients. Government reimbursement policies and processes can impose major hurdles—and sometimes become an outright barrier—to the introduction of vital medical technologies.

We in the industry, however, believe that if policy makers truly understand the value of medical technology, they will want to ensure its availability to patients now and in the future. But to foster that kind of understanding, we must do a much better job of bringing hard data, credible information, and unassailable logic to the forefront. That is where Guidant has made some very significant investments. Early in 2000, we funded an independent research project to assess general knowledge about medical technology, to identify alternative methodologies for evaluating innovation, and to determine the impact of public policies on capital flows. Our findings were made available to policy makers, the media, and other influential individuals through a series of policy forums held in major U.S. metropolitan centers. These provided a prime opportunity to illustrate clearly that technology is a vital part of the solution in extending life and the quality of life, as is doing it cost effectively. It's good for the patient and good for our society.

If we do not accelerate these kinds of efforts to influence the policy environment, public policies will seriously impede our ability to rapidly develop products and to make those products accessible to all patients. In a very real example, as a bioterrorism bill was drafted in the United States, key members of the House of Representatives inadvertently included language that would have severely restricted the value of the FDA Export-Import Act to medical technology firms. But it is not just one government we have to reckon with, because these are truly global issues. Regulators around the world increasingly share information, both informally and formally. With the rise of global media—whether it be CNN, BBC World, global newspapers, or the Internet—news now travels around the world in a nanosecond. If France decides not to reimburse a technology, it may mean that neither will Hong Kong, nor Singapore, nor Japan, nor Brazil. Advocacy has become a global proposition and, for U.S. companies that have worldwide markets, an exclusively U.S.-centric approach is a recipe for disaster. That is the reason we make such an effort, not only to address specific issues wherever they might exist, but also to shape the policy environment on the global playing field.

Ron Dollens, president and CEO of Guidant Corporation, has clearly stated that "Government can be a cost center or an opportunity center, and it's our responsibility as a company to shape policy so it becomes an opportunity" (2001)—a fact of life that all of us in the industry should take to heart. For just Guidant last year, we had more than sixty inspections by various regulatory groups from around the world. Valuable time and manpower is expended for each, by the company and by the regulators. Mutually acceptable criteria would be cost effective for all involved and present an opportunity for industry and regulators to work together to find a better way.

At Guidant, we invest our time and energy where we can be most effective in influencing the adoption of health care policies that reward innovation, and in pushing toward meaningful cost reductions in health care delivery. The active involvement of our senior management is part of our strategy. We communicate on a corporate and personal level and we partner closely with others in our industry—with hospitals, insurance companies, and pharmaceutical firms, and with academic institutions as well—because the medical technology segment can't do it alone.

When we in the industry assume a leadership position in influencing government decision making on all levels—from local to global—we are helping to create a worldwide policy climate where the health care sector can thrive. Also, by focusing much of our effort on educational initiatives, we are safeguarding against unintended consequences of uninformed or misguided legislation or regulations that could severely damage a small, innovative industry and severely hamper its efforts to meet the health care needs of patients and providers.

SHAPING PUBLIC POLICY

Corporate initiatives designed to help shape public policy must begin in the strategic planning process. At Guidant, we have adopted this approach, and it is one that seems to be gaining momentum across a broad spectrum of businesses. According to the *1999–2000 State of Corporate Public Affairs Survey*, released by the Foundation for Public Affairs, corporate initiatives have become increasingly more strategic, and nearly 75 percent of the 223 surveyed companies reported that their public affairs departments now have a "review and comment" role in corporate and business unit planning. For many companies, that is a quantum leap forward, but the relegation of the public affairs function to a circumscribed role of review and comment—after the fact—may be a classic case of too little, too late. Public policy and government affairs issues need to be on the table before strategic business decisions are actually made. Otherwise, companies may find themselves in a constantly defensive position, often blindsided by legislation and regulation they did not foresee, but should have.

Not surprisingly, I am recommending the strategic planning model we use at Guidant, and that begins with a broad assessment of all external factors that could affect our business. Along with macrotrends, major demographics, and incidence of disease, we also take a hard and careful look at geographic trends in public policy, legislation, and regulation. We ask our Asia, Europe, and U.S. leadership teams, and our global network of government affairs and policy professionals, to share their views on the regulatory environment, the reimbursement environment, and their own key priorities. From this compilation of all relevant data, we build our business and strategic plans for the year ahead and beyond. This involves aligning our government affairs objectives with our business goals, prioritizing our agendas, and providing adequate resources worldwide—people, time, and funding—to tackle the policy issues we need to address. It also means developing individual programs to support our objectives, and delineating specific activities, tactics, and measurement techniques, so that we can monitor our success along the way. These programs are primarily designed to open new communications channels between our industry and its regulators; engage customers, partners, and policy makers in ongoing dialogues; improve governmental and media understanding of our industry and its concerns; and support a health care advocacy agenda.

In June 2000, for example, Representative Jim Ramstad (R-MN-3), a member of the Health Subcommittee of the powerful Ways & Means Committee, spent a half day at Guidant's cardiac rhythm management operation in St. Paul, Minnesota. Organized by our government affairs office and planned in conjunction with the Healthcare Leadership Council Congressional Outreach program, this visit provided the congressman with an opportunity to learn more about the value of medical technology to patients, and the role that medical technology companies play in the economy of the state of Minnesota. It also provided us with an opportunity to showcase our corporate commitment to shaping policy, and to bring "official Washington" to our employees.

Dressed in a sterile gown, Representative Ramstad visited our "clean room" for an in-depth briefing on the manufacturing process. He then toured other parts of our operation, meeting many Guidant employees who are also his constituents. He also participated in a roundtable discussion of health care policy with Guidant senior management, who provided firsthand accounts of the impact of specific policies on research, manufacturing, and clinical trials.

These kinds of events, held at all of our business units, inform members of Congress about the critical role medical technology plays in advancing the quality of care and, at the same time, provide them with a broader understanding of the policy environment essential to continued medical innovation. By establishing these platforms, we are able to solidify our message—echoing in a congressional member's own backyard the messages he or she has heard from our lobbyists on Capitol Hill.

Guidant also sponsors programs in Washington, D.C., that underscore our commitment to good public policy and to patients. Recently, we partnered with a leading medical institution, the Washington Hospital Center, as well as with the Congressional Black and Hispanic Caucuses, to host a special briefing on the impact of heart disease on women and minorities. I was very pleased to moderate this briefing, which included presentations by leading members of Congress as well as other leaders in the Washington political community. It raised our corporate visibility with congressional caucuses, and highlighted our commitment to improving women's health through increased patient and public awareness of disease symptoms and care options. It also provided a prime opportunity to inform women of the possibilities offered by new medical technologies, and to engage policy makers in a discussion of the importance of cardiovascular research.

To deepen our own understanding of emerging policy and regulatory issues in major offshore markets, we have established advisory boards in Europe and Japan, composed of senior professionals with long and distinguished careers in health care or related fields. Our advisory board members, ranging from practicing cardiologists to seasoned business executives and former government officials, meet with us at least twice a year to discuss the political dynamics in their corners of the world, changes in their environment, and factors that are driving those changes. They are a valuable touchstone and sounding board, while we continually update and fine-tune our government affairs strategies on a global scale.

Internally, we encourage all of our employees to become active participants in the political process, through educational programs and periodic grassroots calls to action when issues that significantly impact our business are looming on the horizon. Many of our people are also involved from time to time in providing what we call "proof points," which are real-life examples of the probable consequences of uninformed legislation. Armed with this data, we can approach our legislators on very solid evidentiary ground.

To illustrate, a recent biomaterials legislation posed a very serious threat to our business. Not an obvious connection, to be sure, until we considered our raw-material supply. We purchase plastic pellets from major chemical producers, who sell these products primarily to large-volume industrial users. As a small-quantity buyer, we're not even on their radar screen as a customer. They have absolutely no impact on what happens to their plastic once it is in our hands, but, nonetheless, legislation—as it existed for a while—held them responsible, and this is how it was supposed to work: If we took their plastic and made a very sophisticated medical device with it, and if that device were used in a human being, and if that person were harmed, their family could sue the plastic pellet manufacturer. This was not a very happy prospect for our suppliers, so they refused to supply our industry with pelletized plastic. This move could have literally ended medical-device manufacturing, which was an unacceptable scenario for us.

In collaboration with one of our trade associations, we responded by gathering the proof points we needed to make our case. We were able to take examples of products we had to pull off the market, associated job and revenue loss, and the cost accrued in identifying a substitute raw material and redesigning our bench testing and all of our animal and human testing, and we calculated exactly what it would take—in terms of time, money, and people—to get back into the marketplace. Because of that approach, we were able to successfully make our case and come away with a legislative answer that provides a sturdy firewall between the liability issue and our raw-material suppliers.

THE POWER OF ONE

When we talk about our strategies in influencing government decision making at Guidant, we talk about grassroots and "grass tops." "Grass tops" programs, involving our senior managers and their personal commitment, are a vital part of our strategy. We encourage their participation in attending local political events and town meetings, in maintaining close and active relationships with their own legislators, and in making their positions known to the community through op-eds, letters to the editor, and other forums.

At least once a year, when our management committee meets in Washington, D.C., we expand our agenda to include special meetings on Capitol Hill, with invitations to key policy and decision makers. We regularly invite congressional staff to visit our business units, tour our research and manufacturing facilities, and meet with senior executives to discuss our business, our public policy concerns, and other key issues.

Our senior managers are no strangers to Capitol Hill offices, where they spend many a grueling day, going door to door, from one appointment to the next. Because I'm one of those managers, I know all too well the barrage of questions that I ask myself on the long flight home: "Did I really do anything worthwhile today?" "Did I really make a difference?"

For many of us in the private sector, government relations is not a natural fit. Senior management expects to have a fair amount of control, to set directions, declare objectives, and measure results. We put a challenge on the table, and we expect a solution within a given time frame. We might ask: "Where will we be on this project by the third quarter?" and we'll get a definite answer. Not quite so in the political arena. To be effective and realistic there, we must first translate the political culture to the business environment. To do this, we must recognize that the calendars we use in government relations are based on congressional calendars and presidential terms, and not on our quarterly earnings reports or annual shareholder meetings; that our concerns are not the only ones under consideration; and that we cannot control the results of our debate. We must always remember that there is more than one way to get from here to there. Also, it is not always a direct road from the start to the finish line, and sometimes there are more than a few bumps along the way.

A lot of our activities in government affairs just don't fit a standard business model. The reasons are that much of what we do is to provide education and much of the time we are trying to influence people with very different agendas than our own. Sometimes we are doing our best to protect our company and our industry from the worst possible outcome, and we may not always get a highly desired result. Nevertheless, because public policy has such a huge impact on our businesses, we simply have to try. It is part of our responsibility and accountability as senior managers, and no one should understand that better than the chief executive officer. At many companies, however, that understanding is unfortunately lacking, and here is a case in point.

At a recent gathering of executives, I found myself in conversation with the CEO of a Fortune 500 company. When I told him that I spent a significant amount of my time making the case for my company and industry before members of Congress, he was surprised. "Why on earth would you do that?" he asked. "I can't imagine a greater waste of my time."

His attitude is fairly common among the senior executives I meet, who have little or no interest in sitting down with their elected representatives. These same executives can instantly describe the more traditional risks and opportunities their businesses face. They can name their top customers, key employees, market vulnerabilities, and significant investments. But to many, government is like the weather—an inescapable, often unpleasant fact of life best left to its own mysterious devices. "I need to stay focused on running my business," these executives tell me. "I'll leave lobbying to the professionals."

With this approach, two major opportunities fall by the wayside. First, because public policy can affect shareholder value, a CEO must work to inform and educate the people who can change the rules that drive value, and many of those people are members of Congress. Second, sole reliance on professional lobbyists and corporate government affairs professionals to get the job done fails to fully capitalize on the strengths of a senior executive. Such executives, who are already practiced in translating the details of business operations to Wall Street, industry analysts, and journalists, are uniquely prepared to deliver their most important messages, and more effectively than any lobbyist ever could.

A well-placed call from a CEO, representing thousands of employees who buy homes, raise families, pay taxes, and vote in an official's state, can provide meaningful input into important decisions. I have found that placing such a call is not all that different from making a sales call to a major customer. In presenting my case to an elected official, I highlight the value of my "product"— that is, the importance of my business as an economic engine in the politician's district. I try to understand the official's positions and biases, address any objections, and speak his or her own language. When the meeting is nearing its end, I ask for the politician's business, so to speak.

The next time a CEO suggests that I'm wasting valuable time in flying to D.C., I intend to respond with the questions I once heard former House Speaker Newt Gingrich pose to a group of health care leaders: "What are the things that can significantly affect the value of your firm? Not getting paid? Not getting access to new markets? Not getting regulatory approval? Not having enough skilled workers?" Guess what? The government is at work right now making decisions on such questions—with you or without you. I think it would be a whole lot better if you were there.

THE POWER OF MANY

Educating elected and regulatory officials does not have to be a solo act—and, in fact, it should not be. Partnering with like-minded constituencies should be part of our strategy, not only because it brings us all closer to our mutual goals, but also because a partnering approach with trade associations or academic institutions offers some distinct advantages. Dr. David Gollaher, president and CEO of California Healthcare Institute, makes the point exceedingly well. "The effectiveness of any one company is limited to a serious degree not only by its resources, but also by a perception of self-interest," he says. "A broader coalition of stakeholders adds credibility, appeals to a wider spectrum of legislative interests, and provides a lot of leverage to an individual company or a senior manager who would otherwise be seen as just speaking from his or her own perspective" (2001).

At Guidant, we take a "tiered" approach, participating in public policy issues on the local, national, regional, and global levels—and on every one of those, we've seen real benefits from collaboration. In working with industry associations in Europe, for instance, our senior management was deeply involved in the development of legislation that changed the approach to medical-device regulation in the European Economic Area (nineteen countries of Western Europe) in the early 1990s. This legislation established one single process for the review and approval of medical devices so that when a device is approved in one of those nineteen countries, it can be sold in the other eighteen without any further evaluation or review by national authorities.

Guidant was also actively involved in the negotiation of the Mutual Recognition Agreement between the European Union and the United States, so that a recognized conformity assessment body in either location could assess a medical device for both European and U.S. requirements. Based on their findings, the product could be sold in both places simultaneously, significantly improving efficiencies on the manufacturer's end and substantially reducing the time involved in getting life-saving and life-enhancing medical devices to patients in Europe and in the United States.

More recently, we have taken an active role in working closely with the Global Harmonization Task Force (GHTF), an informal group of industry regulators and representatives in the medical-devices sector. The GHTF is attempting to reduce or eliminate technical differences in the regulatory requirements of Australia, Canada, Europe, Japan, and the United States, which, when taken together, account for approximately 85 percent of global trade in medical technology. The GHTF not only is focused on those five countries and regions, however, but also is designed to create models for other countries or economies, which are developing their own regulatory approaches, many in consultation with the World Health Organization. Through its own collaborative efforts among regulators and industry, the GHTF intends to protect public health, share best regulatory practices, and facilitate trade around the world. Guidant senior management is supporting that effort through active participation in the premarket approval and regulatory systems and event-reporting study groups, as well as the twenty-four-member steering committee.

Participation on the national level in individual countries where we do business also brings significant rewards. In the United Kingdom, for instance, by working both independently and through industry associations, Guidant senior management was able to help shape the charter, procedures, and modes of operation of the National Institute for Clinical Excellence (NICE). To ensure maximum value in medical technologies and therapies, NICE provides guidance to the United Kingdom's National Health Service, and many of its findings are based on information submitted by the medical technology industry, including Guidant.

In Japan, our senior managers work with the Japanese offices of AdvaMed (Advanced Medical Technology Association), the American Chamber of Commerce Japan (ACCJ), and the Japan Federation of Medical Devices Association to help create a positive public policy environment for health care. Also, one of our managers, working directly and through a local industry association, is one of the few outside experts assisting the Japanese government in framing new legislation on medical devices.

Close involvement with industry associations is a major strategy in the United States as well, and membership is encouraged throughout our company. At the same time, we have never joined an organization just to add our name to the membership list. We expect to lead, to contribute, and to get something back. One of many examples is AdvaMed, an industry association of more than 800 manufacturers of medical devices, diagnostic products, and health information systems. AdvaMed operates on the state, federal, and international levels to promote legal, regulatory, and economic climates that advance health care by assuring worldwide patient access to the benefits of medical technology. Our policy, technical, regulatory, and clinical professionals serve on a host of its committees that help shape government regulations. Our president and CEO, Ron Dollens, is a past chairman and currently a director. During his chairmanship, AdvaMed shifted its traditional emphasis from manufacturing to technology, expanded its focus to include not only the regulatory approval process but also payment issues, and adopted a more global approach.

In January 2001, Ron became chairman-elect of the Washington, D.C.–based Healthcare Leadership Council, a coalition of chief executives from diverse disciplines within the health care industry. Their goal is to jointly develop policies, plans, and programs to advance a market-based health care system that values innovation and provides affordable, high-quality health care.

Through collaborations like these, we can increase our effectiveness in influencing governmental decision making, to help shape a public policy environment that is favorable to the health care industry and the patients it serves. These kinds of partnerships are also invaluable in addressing specific policy or political issues that may adversely affect our entire industry.

DEALING WITH ISSUES

In 1996, a ballot initiative called Proposition 211 threatened the entire medical research sector in California, home to more than one-third of the nation's biotechnology and medical-device firms. Because of the volatility of their stock prices, high-tech companies had been the prime targets of abusive class-action shareholder lawsuits until 1995, when the U.S. Congress passed new laws to limit securities lawsuits with no merit. Prop. 211—the Attorney-Client Fee Arrangements Act, written by securities lawyers specializing in shareholder class-action lawsuits—would have negated these federal reforms and, from the perspective of California's biomedical research community, created the most hostile legal environment in the United States.

The high-tech industries banded together to oppose this initiative and the California Healthcare Institute (CHI), which I recently chaired, played a vital role. Representing more than 200 of California's leading biomedical firms, universities, and private research institutions, CHI commissioned independent research to predict the probable consequences if Prop. 211 became law. These included a major cutback on medical research and development; a delay of 384 new medicines and treatments for disorders like AIDS, Alzheimer's, cancer, and heart disease; the loss of as many as 63,000 jobs; and a direct wage loss to the California economy exceeding $3 billion.

Armed with these findings and more, CHI took its case to the voting public with a very focused message that Prop. 211 would be bad for jobs, bad for the high-tech community in general, and ultimately bad for patients if companies were spending millions of dollars fighting lawsuits rather than on research. The message was heard, the voters made their decision, and Prop. 211 was soundly defeated. Could its demise have been brought about by just one company acting alone? Highly unlikely. But by acting in unison—through one powerful industry association—the initiative was defeated.

Industry associations can also facilitate ongoing dialogues among all stakeholders when wide-reaching issues are on the health care agenda—issues like conflict of interest, for example. Focused on financial relationships within the research process, the conflict-of-interest issue arises when people in the academic community develop an invention that is subsequently commercialized, and the affiliated university owns part of the patent or will receive other remuneration. Or, in another possible scenario, the inventor is a physician who not only treats patients with this invention, but also owns part of the company that will commercialize it, or receives payment from that company. Many are concerned that potential financial gain for investigators or institutions could bias the research and/or harm the patient, and the increasing collaboration between physician/inventors and innovative companies is presenting new and challenging public policy issues.

To explore this issue from a range of relevant perspectives, CHI cosponsored with the Medical Technology Leadership Forum and Stanford University a summit meeting in July 2001. Five expert panels were assembled, including innovator/physicians, government officials, patient and research advocates, and innovator/industry representatives, with a university perspective provided by the deans of four major medical schools.

As Dr. Gollaher, CHI president and CEO, explained, "We are trying to facilitate a dialogue among people in government who may write laws or enforce regulations in this area, people in commercial research and the academic community where most of this actually takes place." "We see our role in two ways," he said. "One is ensuring that research in the long-term interest of patients continues because, without it, medical progress will come to a halt. But because we have a moral, ethical and practical interest in protecting patients, we're simultaneously committed to appropriate levels of research oversight and supervision, to make certain that what's done is ethical and conforms to both legal and moral guidelines" (2001).

Dr. Gollaher's statement also sums up our position at Guidant, and we are working with our industry associations on both of these fronts. We are also working independently. One example is my own personal involvement with the Association of American Medical Colleges (AAMC) Task Force on Financial Conflicts of Interest in Clinical Research. Formed early in 2001, the panel is charged with assessing current AAMC guidelines on conflict of interest, and with formulating new principles that address financial interests in research held by both individual investigators and institutions.

As one of three industry representatives on the twenty-eight-member panel, which includes academicians, attorneys, ethicists, journalists, public/patient advocates, and researchers, I am striving to voice the collective opinion of the medical technology industry, and at the same time help move us all toward a consensus that will protect today's patients, while still ensuring the continued research necessary for the patients of tomorrow.

WIDENING THE CIRCLE

Partnering with industry associations is an obvious step in reaching out to like-minded constituencies and building strong coalitions that can impact public policy and foster the kind of innovation necessary for both continuously improving health care and reducing cost. However, it is certainly not the only step. There are broader constituent sets out there, and it is in everyone's best interest to bring them into our circle.

To better reach consumers—the current and future patients we all serve—and to meet their ever increasing demand for timely information, we should take a very hard look at our utilization of the Internet and the state of our own Web sites. Guidant redesigned its Web site early in 2001, tailoring its content to both physicians and patients, and providing them with an easily navigated cardiovascular and vascular disease site with accurate and comprehensive information on those diseases and on the newest advances in treatment options. In addition, we helped form eHealth Initiatives, an advocacy organization working to ensure that electronic-based technologies are used effectively to promote quality health care. We also joined the Alliance for Aging, another advocacy organization, this one for seniors, and our president and CEO now sits on its board. The Alliance supports continued research in medical technology—one of Guidant's highest priorities—as a means of ensuring that new advancements are readily available, as the baby boomers join the "senior class."

Another major constituency in the drive to improve health care through research and innovation is the academic community. Our colleges and universities play a leading role in fostering an ongoing innovation cycle, which, together with their policy voice and community leadership, makes them ideal partners. Guidant actively pursues these kinds of relationships, and, if you are not already partnering with academia, you should find a way.

At Guidant, we are currently working with Stanford University to help support—and encourage our peers to support—the creation of a biomedical school of engineering, where the best of Stanford science and medicine can come together to create new solutions for better health. Guidant has funded a chair in support of this program and I and other industry leaders are on the faculty for this biomedical program.

We also have a long-standing relationship with the Keck Institute in southern California, not only through board representation, but also through funding support for advanced-degree biomedical students, helping them prepare for a future leadership role in medical technology.

IT'S ALL ABOUT HEALTH

Improving world health care policy is not just about our industry. It is about health. A favorable public policy environment is indispensable in supporting the ongoing innovation cycle so necessary in improving health care, reducing health care costs, and making a meaningful difference in the lives and longevity of millions of people around the globe suffering from life-threatening diseases.

Shaping that policy environment requires a concerted effort from each of us, not only in our own fields, but also in the broadest possible definition of those fields. To have a real impact on health, the whole wheel must be touched, and that means medical technology firms, biotech and pharmaceutical companies, physicians and hospitals, insurance companies and other payers, academic institutions, and, perhaps most importantly, the patient/consumer.

As an industry, it is our responsibility to help find solutions to the challenges facing health care. But our ability to find those solutions can be seriously curtailed or virtually eliminated by uninformed public policies that stifle innovation. Preventing that erosion and ensuring our continued effectiveness demands an active leadership role for each of us in influencing governmental decision making. For many of us, unfortunately, government affairs is not as fulfilling as running a business, but if we are to succeed in meeting the world's current and future health care needs, policy work simply must be accepted as part of our job descriptions.

When it comes to health policy, we cannot just watch what happens; we have to make it happen. If we are dependent on someone else doing the job for us— or if we are closing our eyes to the issues at hand—we should not be sleeping very well at night. We have to wake up, and step up. We have to be engaged. What better deserves our engagement than improved health, enhanced quality of life, and longer lives for us all?

REFERENCES

Dollens, R.W. (2001, July). Senior Management Leadership Conference. Northland Inn, St. Paul, MN

Gollaher, D. (2001, January). California Healthcare Institute Chairman's Dinner. Pelican Hill, Newport Beach, CA.

Conclusion: Synthesis and Insights

Peggy Leatt and Joseph Mapa

In this book we have defined government relationships in health care as the interaction between two or more individuals or organizations in order to influence health policy formation and implementation. Throughout the book we have stressed that harmonious relationships between governments and health care organizations are necessary if all parties are to meet their objectives of maintaining and improving the health of the population. In our introduction and commentary, we proposed that the development of a sound government relations strategy is vital for health care organizations in today's society. In the chapters that follow, the author-colleagues have focused on a variety of perspectives and their own experiences with relationships between governments and health care organizations. Three aspects of government relationships have been emphasized: first, the legal and regulatory stage that the country's political system sets for government relations with health care organizations and its impact on health policy decisions; second, the need to clarify accountability relationships; and third, the applicability of principles of strategic planning and management for developing effective government relations. Building on this framework, the value and limitations of advocacy and negotiation processes were outlined followed by several "case examples" of strategies for promoting effective relationships in different contexts. These case examples reflect the similarities and differences in health policy processes in the United States and Canada.

In this conclusion we bring together some of the key ideas and experiences from the previous chapters. We attempt to synthesize the main points and advance the debate about creating and maintaining effective government relationships in health care. The conclusion is divided into five parts. First, we argue for government relations with health care organizations as the core element of health policy making. Second, we stress the importance of public opinion in

shaping health policy and describe some possible strategies to enable public
opinions to be heard. Third, the role of leadership as a vital component to government relations is addressed. Fourth, a plea is made for a plan to promote effective government relationships as an essential component of any group or
organization's strategic plan. Fifth, we outline strategies for sustaining effective
government relationships and raise issues that must be addressed for the future
if win-win scenarios are to be achieved.

GOVERNMENT RELATIONSHIPS AS THE CORE
ELEMENT OF POLICY MAKING

In theory, it might be debated whether health policy making should be
driven by logic or political means. In reality, policy making is a mixture of both
approaches: a strong evidence-based foundation is essential as a starting point
to make sure everyone has the facts; and then, complex political exchanges take
place that influence the policy outcome. In short, policy making and the appropriation of funds are intricate processes involving both science and art. In order
for acceptable health policies to evolve it is the quality and depth of government relationships that count. The dynamic interplay that takes place between
politicians, civic servants, health care providers, consumers, and the public is
continuously changing and must do so if effective relationships are to be sustained. In this book, the authors have tried to balance different perspectives on
government relationships without the implication that one side of the relationship is more appropriate or more just than another. As Owen Adams and Kevin
Doucette suggested in Chapter 8, effective government relations are perhaps so
complex and intriguing that when they are not in full view they become conspicuous by their absence—in other words, they may be some of those things
that you recognize best only when you don't have them!

Several authors have explicitly or implicitly made the point that government
relationships are best understood from a system's perspective on health policy
as *inputs, processes,* and *outcomes.* The systems approach articulated in detail
by Beaufort Longest in Chapter 2 captures the dynamic and cyclical nature of
health policy processes. If we view government relationships as *inputs* to policy
making, effective relationships require input from individuals or organizations
outside governments for policies to emerge and be implemented. Without
input through government relationships, politicians and civil servants would
develop policies in a vacuum and would have no way to predict whether a policy would be acceptable to the public at a later time. Government relations are
also *processes* of continuous interaction between external organizations and
governments providing a wide range of opportunities and stages for policy to
be influenced and validated. As *outcomes,* government relations emerge as
shared commitments to common goals for effective policy making by govern-

ments and external bodies. A system's approach to government relationships provides opportunities for *feedback* at every possible point of the policy-making life cycle.

THE IMPORTANCE OF PUBLIC OPINION

Democratic processes in the United States and Canada are designed so that citizens have the opportunity to express their views and preferences. In democratic societies it is important that the public both feels it has the government's ear, especially regarding social services such as health care, and is assured that actions will be taken as and when necessary. Raisa B. Deber and A. Paul Williams in Chapter 1 outlined the parliamentary and balance-of-power systems that characterize the Canadian and U.S. political arenas and described how the different systems channel the public's influence on policies.

Recent public opinion surveys have shown there is growing discontent with health services internationally and the public's confidence in health systems is being shaken. Reports from Australia, Canada, New Zealand, the United Kingdom, and the United States (Donelan et al., 1999) have shown a steady increase in dissatisfaction with health services over the past decade and the perception that major health system change is needed. While the United States leads the world in terms of expenditures on health services, the public is still concerned about access to services for those who do not have health insurance. In Canada, expenditures on health services are lower than in the United States but the public is still anxious about restrictions to access imposed by long waiting lists for nonurgent services. In addition, Canadians are more likely to rate hospitals as fair or poor and complain that their length of stay in hospitals was too short than citizens in other countries. This research also showed that health services continue to be vitally important to the general public and that individual citizens are very sensitive to any perceived change in the level of service. Most citizens expect basic health services to be free at the point of delivery because of their payments to tax systems and/or health insurance. Consumers are willing to bear additional out-of-pocket payments for higher quality or improved access to services, although somewhat reluctantly (Donelan et al., 1999).

The American public is proud of its innovative role at the forefront of medical science. Compared with hospitals in most European countries and Canada, the United States allows greater access, for example, to cardiac procedures such as cardiac catheterizations, angioplasties, and by-pass surgery. The United States, compared with the rest of the world, has more technical equipment such as magnetic resonance imaging (MRI) and computer tomography (CT) scanners and other new technologies that drive up the costs of health care (Kim, Blendon, & Benson, 2001). The public in both the United States and Canada now expects advanced medical technologies to be readily available to them despite the increasing costs. If access is denied or delayed, individual consumers or the public as a whole is likely to voice their complaints and expect speedy responses from politicians, governments, health care providers, and so on, to rectify services.

Public opinion cannot be ignored. However, governments cannot possibly meet all health care expectations and still keep costs under control. Politicians are, therefore, in the unenviable position of trying to maintain costs while satisfying consumers for high-quality services. The United States has used "managed care" to try to improve efficiencies and to restrict choice (Starr, 2000). Canada has used a myriad of incremental changes to contain costs through limiting access (Naylor, 1999), but neither country has escaped the public criticism of the quality of health services. The challenge is to ensure effective government relationships between the politicians, the bureaucracy, and members of the public that will facilitate an open exchange for making choices between health policy options.

OPPORTUNITIES FOR PUBLIC AND STAKEHOLDER VOICE

Gary Filerman and D. David Persaud in Chapter 4 emphasized the role of advocacy as a means for the public and other stakeholders to express their opinions. They outlined government relationships as processes of persuasion where one party pits its views against those of others; the goal of government relationships, therefore, is to persuade and the means is advocacy. Advocacy can take on many forms. For example, it can be as simple as one individual member of the public expressing his/her views to politicians in a local town hall meeting or as complex as a submission from a consortium of health care providers that proposes major changes in health care delivery.

Colleen Flood in Chapter 3 described several strategies to enhance opportunities for the public to voice their opinions, such as devolution of authority, election of officers, and consultation processes. Devolution or decentralization of decision making to regional or local authorities opens up possibilities for individual citizens to speak up. Local authorities focus on issues of relevance to people who live or work in the region and may provide convenient ways for people to bring their concerns to the attention of local decision makers. A disadvantage of speaking out at a community level could be that individuals' views may not reach higher or more centralized levels where policies are being designed. Election of officers and representatives of the public goes hand in hand with devolution. In many countries, local citizens actively participate in regional decision making by their participation on governing boards of hospitals or other health care organizations. In the western provinces of Canada, there is a trend away from appointed board members to election of individuals as representatives of the local community. From their positions as board members, local residents have access to information about new or pending policies and are more likely to have their opinions heard. Some health care organizations choose to employ the assistance of "expert" consultants to prepare statements or briefs to help them lay the foundation for their position on a particular issue. In several of the chapters, our authors suggested consultants can be very helpful but cautioned that it is important to be clear in advance on the specific issue and on tasks expected from them.

Lobbying

Although often thought of in a negative way, lobbying is quite simply a way of getting those perceived to be in powerful positions to pay attention to others' points of view. Longest (2002) has told an interesting story about where the term "lobbying" originated. Apparently, lobbying arose in reference to the place or location where it first occurred. In the early days of policy making in Washington, D.C., before members of Congress had either offices or telephones, individuals who wanted to influence the thinking of legislators waited for them and engaged them in conversations in the lobbies of the buildings they frequented. The activities of lobbying are central to relationships between governments and health care organizations. Formal approaches to lobbying usually focus on the legitimate concerns of interest groups who wish to change or modify health policies. The results are often unpredictable. There is always the danger that the goals of lobbying may be distorted away from the genuinely interested group and focus only on the self-interests of a handful of individuals. Lobbying activities may also be pursued too aggressively and have a negative impact (for examples see McDonough, 2000).

In Chapter 10, Pamela Jeffery provided us with her experiences in engaging the public in grassroots activities. While provider groups tend to focus on technical issues in health care, the general public and consumers are more interested in issues that have an immediate impact on their daily lives. For example, issues about access to health care such as lack of hospital beds, overcrowding of emergency rooms, funding for home care, and so on, are politically sensitive issues that can be overwhelming to members of the public. Consumers who can effectively voice the public's opinions on these issues can pressure elected officials to act quickly and in a way that mirrors what the public wants. Through this type of lobbying activity, health care providers can forge partnerships with consumers in their quest to influence the government policies that are important to them.

Negotiating

The processes of creating, modifying, and implementing health policy involve different parties coming together to air their views. In almost all instances there will be extensive debate as well as major areas of conflict as different interest groups expand on their positions. Mary Jane Mastorovich, in Chapter 5, emphasized the need for adequate preparation by organizations when they enter negotiation processes with governments. In most instances, she explained, organizational leaders are insufficiently prepared and greater attention is necessary to identify who should represent the organization and the type of technical expertise that is required.

Interest Groups

Another effective way to influence health policy is through the formation of interest groups that can add more clout to individual opinions. Interest groups can be made up of a variety of stakeholders but have collective interests in the outcomes of specific policies. Provider associations such as the American Hospital Association, the Canadian Healthcare Association, and medical and nursing associations exist at federal, state/provincial, and local levels to represent the collective interests of provider groups. Similar interest groups may be formed around consumer groups such as cancer societies or heart and stroke associations who ensure that their interests are heard at the political level. Interest groups have many goals in common with other provider and community groups who aim to develop and maintain relationships with governments so that changes in policy will not be detrimental to the health and wellness of their members. These groups spend a large portion of their time and resources scanning policy proposals to assess the potential impact on their group. In some instances, interest groups may join forces with other groups to enhance their abilities to have an even stronger influence on policies. Interest groups have been surprisingly successful in communicating key messages when they have been able to find out, in early discussions, which other groups are prepared to collaborate in joint submissions or presentations.

Government Perspectives

While we frequently think about government relationships from the perspectives of provider groups such as hospitals, physicians, and nurses, as well as from the viewpoints of consumers, it is also important to examine the responsibilities and needs of governments. Politicians and civil servants have a responsibility to ensure that open communications exist between the public, consumers, and provider organizations. Indeed, governments cannot fulfill their mandate of accountability to the public without appropriate channels of communications. As noted in Chapter 10 by Jeffery, the public must have opportunities to speak to their elected politicians and have sufficient reassurance that their opinions are being heard. From time to time, governments may organize town hall meetings as one way of opening a dialogue with the public about pressing health care issues. Government employees may use similar approaches to obtain input to policies and to test out options for policy changes.

It is in the interests of governments to ensure that they understand the opinions of key stakeholders. For example, Adams and Doucette, in Chapter 8, describe the variety of strategies federal and provincial governments engage in to ensure they solicit the collective voice of physicians. Focus groups are one method frequently used by governments to seek external opinions on various policy options. Policy development and implementation will simply not work if governments do not consult with the public. Experience has shown that major health system change cannot be achieved without public and/or medical profession support (Shalala and Reinhardt, 1999).

Structural Approaches

Formal authority structures can be designed to facilitate communication, coordination and common commitment for effective government relationships. Formal structures have the advantage of "forcing" different groups to sit around the table and share their views. A variety of task forces, committees, working groups, and commissions may be organized on a temporary or semipermanent basis to facilitate input from various stakeholder groups. Thomas Ricketts and Melissa Fruhbeis, in Chapter 6, described the experiences of federal and state governments in creating a coalition to raise the profile of rural hospitals and other health care services. As part of this initiative, several states received grants to develop networks that could bring together small limited-service hospitals with an acute referral hospital in rural communities. The coalition had essentially an advocacy role to press for policy changes so that access to health care in rural communities could be improved. The coalition functioned as a lobbying group with representatives from several levels of governments, constituents, and beneficiaries. Initial evaluation of the coalitions has shown some positive results but additional work is necessary to further enhance coordination of activities. In Canada, G.H. Pink and P. Leatt (2002) described the experiences in Ontario of the creation of three different arm's-length coordinating bodies to link stakeholders to governments for policy development purposes. The membership of these committees included providers, technical experts, and consumers, who provided directions to government on needs for cardiac care services, health services reform, and hospital funding. Although the committees appeared to be successful in the provision of policy advice, which allowed governments to test whether stakeholders would be receptive to their ideas for change, they were not immune to political interference.

The Media

What better way to attract the attention of people with power to make or change health policy than to speak out to the media? Headlines proclaiming shortcomings of health services, such as overcrowded emergency departments or an unfortunate death, are a guaranteed way to get responses from politicians and to sell a lot of newspapers! However, as noted by Bruce MacLellan in Chapter 7, relationships with the media require careful planning and scrupulous execution and an understanding of risk to government relations. Media experts stress that interviews with the media can provide timely opportunities to speak out but interchanges should be designed to present well-reasoned arguments in a credible voice. Editorials in newspapers can be particularly helpful in educating readers about different issues and creating a healthy dialogue about the implication of specific policy options.

Leadership Roles

Effective government relationships are about influencing policy-making processes and, therefore, about the power of leaders to affect change. When individuals are hired for senior management or leadership positions in health care organizations, it is usually because of their leadership abilities or potential. Leadership is the ability of individuals to influence situations and to make things happen for the good of their organization. Leadership, then, is a key component of successful interactions between all levels of government and health care organizations. Leaders are expected to speak up and articulate the views of the groups they represent. Influence or power of leaders may be exercised through formal hierarchical relationships or through informal means. Opportunity to exercise power may be easier in situations that are ambiguous, where roles and relationships are unclear, and where goals are conflicting. These situations are common in relationships with governments where politics may be rampant. In developing effective government relationships, leaders need to use a combination of rational and political approaches. Effective leaders must demonstrate a rational approach by accumulating data and collecting evidence to support their case. They must also be prepared to be political and take on advocacy roles, lobbying, collaborating with interest groups, and so on, as the situation demands.

Some of the outstanding characteristics of effective leaders include being able to generate ideas, to think the unthinkable, and to give vast amounts of energy to the success of their enterprise (Tichy and Cohen, 1997). Leaders are usually focused, determined to achieve their goals and enjoy the challenges of complex and difficult work. An outstanding leader is able to turn negative energy into positive uses on behalf of the organization. Winning leaders have strong values of their own that become the fabric of their organization's culture. Most times, leaders can bring a sense of urgency to the organization's mission, inspire followers, and define goals that require everyone in the organization to stretch and grow. In short, this type of leadership behavior frequently stimulates an organization to change or transform from status quo. Winning leaders are able to create winning organizations. They know that games are won on the playing fields and the team with the greatest number of excellent players wins (Tichy, 1997).

In discussing leadership at Guidant, Ginger Graham in Chapter 11 talks about "grassroots" and "grass tops." The grass-tops initiatives involve senior managers, a vital part of Guidant's government relations strategy. Senior managers, as leaders, participate in local political events and town hall meetings. They assist in maintaining close and active relationships with their own legislators, as well as making Guidant's positions known to the community. Graham described how at Guidant's annual management meetings in Washington, D.C., the agenda includes special meetings on Capitol Hill with key policy and decision makers. Guidant regularly invites congressional staff to visit their business units, tour research and manufacturing facilities, and meet with senior executives. At Guidant, the leadership gives priority to nurturing government relationships even though it may not seem like a natural fit for leaders in the private sector.

STRATEGIC PLANNING AND MANAGEMENT

Since the 1970s, health care leaders and managers have used strategic planning as a tool for thinking about future directions for their organizations (see, for example, Zuckerman, 1998). It has become the norm for a new CEO or person hired into a leadership position to initiate a strategic planning process early in his or her mandate. Lack of such an action automatically places the individual under suspicion! Strategy is the most important road map to the future.

While health care leaders and managers are accustomed to carrying out strategic planning exercises for their own organizations or group, applying the same set of principles to strategic government relationships is often overlooked or neglected. As Longest described in Chapter 2, even though governments are critical components of the external environments of all health care organizations, a deliberate planning process does not seem to occur to identify strategies for influencing governments and health policy. Several of the authors have advocated that individuals and groups with a commitment to health policy should adopt a strategic management philosophy (Coddington, Fischer, & Moore, 2001; Ginter, Swayne, & Duncan, 2002). Strategic management asks broader questions than planning issues and addresses the validity of the basic goals, objectives, and niche of the organization as well as ongoing implementation. Strategic management, then, takes a long-term view of government relationships and can help individual organizations predict and respond to state and federal policy and planning efforts.

While there are several variations on methodologies, strategic management typically involves a set of logical steps to help leaders understand the current environment of the organization and to develop decision-making guidelines for the future. The steps involve external environment analysis (the general environment as well as the specific health care environment); competitor analysis—assessing the strengths and weaknesses of competitors and identifying the niche for the organization; internal environment analysis—defining the values and strengths and weaknesses; specifying the vision, mission, and goals; and strategy formation—developing and weighing strategic alternatives.

Chapter 9 by Darlene Burgess and Gail Warden provided a vivid example of how the Henry Ford Health System has used a strategic management approach to government relationships. While the details provided in this chapter are specific to one very large health services system, the strategies outlined are equally valid for a wide variety of health services organizations. Henry Ford's hands-on experience with effective government relations shows not only that a strategic, long-term approach is essential, but also that the plan for enhancing this relationship must be built into the organization's strategic management approach. Burgess and Warden emphasize that the development of a business plan for government relationships is critical and requires commitment from everyone in the organization, especially the CEO and senior managers.

EFFECTIVE GOVERNMENT RELATIONSHIPS

The term "effectiveness" has a universal appeal but it is an elusive term. It is often interpreted broadly to mean "not only doing things right but also doing the right things." With this definition, effectiveness becomes a basic value of an organization. Organizational effectiveness is frequently translated into goals and measured by the extent to which an organization or group is able to meet specified targets. Let us assume that the strategic goal of effective government relations is to have demonstrable influence on the policy capacity of governments and consequently on health policy. This statement reflects the goals of health care provider organizations. But each organization might have a more specific goal; for example, members of the medical profession might have a goal to ensure that fee negotiations between governments and the medical profession result in optimal fee settlements for physicians. Nurses might have a goal of ensuring that politicians understand the expanding roles they would be able to assume if appropriate legislation were in place. An academic health science center might have the goal of influencing governments' funding arrangements to obtain increased funding in recognition of the complex types of care they provide and their additional roles of teaching and research. The public or consumers' goal in interacting with governments might be more focused, for example, ensuring public policies reflect the needs of specific communities and interest groups for access to high-quality health promotion services. From the perspective of governments, politicians may have the goal of demonstrating to the public that "their" party has been successful in improving quality or starting an innovative health service—but the superordinate goal here might be to be reelected. Civil servants, on the other hand, might have the goal of maintaining the health programs of greatest interest to them. Depending on the perspective of interest for evaluating effectiveness, then, a variety of goals for government relationships exist and it is unlikely that there is much agreement on which goals are most important to stakeholders.

Part of the problem surrounding organizational effectiveness is deciding how it should be measured. In health care, measurement is particularly problematic because there are no gold standards or well-defined benchmarks. There are a host of other challenges in evaluating health services effectiveness, such as defining the unit of analysis, specifying performance indicators, and choosing time periods and comparative groups for evaluation. As MacLellan pointed out in Chapter 7, government relationships cannot be evaluated by the scientific measurement associated with medicine or other basic science disciplines. One approach to assessing organizational performance that is gaining popularity in health care is the use of the balanced scorecard. The idea of a balanced scorecard to monitor performance was introduced by R.S. Kaplan and D.P. Norton as a way of persuading managers to use a broader range of performance indicators beyond financial data (Kaplan & Norton, 2001). A balanced scorecard examines performance from four perspectives: financial, customer, internal business processes, and learning and growth. Indicators of the four dimensions can be used to monitor performance through time as well as to compare the performance of several organizations or groups. The advantage of the scorecard framework is that it starts with the vision, mission, and strategies of an organization and can be built into the organization's strategic management approach. A scorecard for government relationships in health care could focus attention on exactly what is being done by an organization to facilitate relationships and then compare this to what is being achieved. It can be built into the existing performance management program of the organization and provides regular opportunities to examine government relationships and make adjustments as necessary. A major challenge, however, still remains in identifying and validating the most appropriate indicators of success of a government relations program.

THE FUTURE

The conclusions from the experiences of our authors would suggest that there are two levels or types of government relationships and both are essential. First, interactions with governments are essential when an individual, a group, or an organization wishes to make their position known and to influence government thinking about a particular health policy. Second, a longer-term program for government relationships must be in place so that when specific issues arise the channels of communication are open.

Influencing Specific Issues or Policies

When individuals or organizations are alerted to health policies that may impact them, it is critical that they be prepared with background information to get the attention of politicians and civil servants.

We suggest the following guidelines:

- Clearly define the issue of importance and why it is of interest.
- Set goals for what is to be achieved and begin defining a strategy to initiate government contact about your goals.

- Conduct background research on the history and evolution of the issue.
- Analyze the external environment to identify, for example, the social, political, cultural, economic, and legal factors of importance.
- Identify the public's views on the issue and which interest groups might be impacted by the policy.
- Narrow in on key contacts in government, including politicians and members of the bureaucracy, and begin interacting with them.
- Identify the interests of other organizations in the issue, including "competitors."
- Explore different scenarios and options.
- Explore which options the government is likely to favor and for what reasons.
- Understand which option(s) the public and key stakeholders are likely to favor and how to bring them onside.
- Mobilize support from within the organization—communicate about the issue, build knowledge, identify employees and volunteers who might have political contacts or knowledge and skill to add to the position.
- Mobilize support from outside, including interest groups, coalitions, and other groups of high influence and credibility—identify win-win strategies.
- Seize any window of opportunity that presents itself to interact with others about the issue.
- Keep in mind that simple solutions are the best. Make sure your proposals are: evidence based; congruent with the ideology and core values of the parties forming/receiving them; practical/concrete/quantifiable; likely to result in political credit; affordable; likely to have payoff/results in a reasonable timeframe; and acceptable to a range of key stakeholders.

Ongoing Relationships

While the preceding guidelines are necessary for interacting with governments about specific policies, it is critical that ongoing relationships be established so that when issues arise, building blocks of a relationship are in place. In this way, discussion of specific issues can be couched in a broader strategic framework that has been developed specifically for the organization and is part of the organization's strategic plan.

A government relationships program for health care organizations should include the following:

1. Begin by introducing and promoting the idea of a government relationships program in the organization. Assess and establish priority ranking for the organization's needs from government in order to achieve excellence in the health services the organization provides.
2. Ensure government relations are overseen by the leaders and/or governing board and include members of the senior executive and the board as part of the ongoing process.

3. Incorporate a program into the organization's strategic plan and management approach. Lead the organization through a process to delineate a vision, mission, goals, and strategies for accomplishing the government relations plan.

4. Set goals, target audiences, allocate resources, assign roles, and develop performance measures.

5. Establish priorities for which strategies will be addressed, and in which order, recognizing that priorities can change quickly.

6. Work with the public and special-interest groups. Establish dialogue with provider organizations and consumer groups to understand and reflect the broader needs of the community.

7. Develop a communication network and maintain ongoing contact with key individuals representing the groups with common interest to you; for example, politicians, civil servants, and CEOs of public and private health care organizations. Be prepared to lobby and negotiate.

8. Understand the position of the government of the day on key policies that could impact your organization or group. Get to know their processes and criteria.

9. Understand the political and bureaucratic goals of the government of the day, as well as the political environment that prevails, and find opportunities where you can support the government.

10. Build contacts and relations at every level of government, including regional staff, senior civil servants, and politicians.

11. Establish a team that can represent the organization at these various levels, ranging from operational administrators, chief of staff, CEO, and select board members.

12. Be open and accessible when government calls in crisis situations. Call to congratulate or bring good news.

13. Understand the problems and issues that are of highest priority to governments. Explore with them the kinds of options they are considering as possible policy solutions.

14. Be sure local, state, provincial, and federal representatives know what the organization does and what services or products are provided.

15. Build in a system for monitoring the government relations program, including assessment of key strategies such as lobbying, negotiating, developing interest groups, encouraging media relationships, and other performance indicators.

So what is the last word on government relationships in health care? Historically, the approaches have been reactive. This can no longer continue. It is time for these relationships to become an essential component of all health care groups or organizations' strategic planning and management efforts. Management of effective government relationships must become part of the mainstream for senior leaders. It is time for managers and clinicians to join forces with the consumers and the public.

REFERENCES

Coddington, D.C., Fischer, E.A., & Moore, K.D. (2001). *Strategies for the new health care marketplace: Managing the convergence of consumerism and technology.* San Francisco: Jossey-Bass.

Donelan, K., Blendon, R.J., Schoen, C., Davis, K., & Binns, K. (1999). The cost of health system change: Public discontent in five nations. *Health Affairs 18* (3): 206–216.

Ginter, P.M., Swayne, L.E., & Duncan, W.J. (2002). *Strategic management of health care organizations.* Oxford: Blackwell Publishers.

Kaplan, R.S., & Norton, D.P. (2001). *The strategy-focused organization: How balanced scorecard companies thrive in the new business environment.* Boston, MA: Harvard Business School Press.

Kim, M., Blendon, R.J., & Benson, J. (2001). How interested are Americans in new medical technologies? A multicountry comparison. *Health Affairs 20* (5): 194–201.

Longest, B.B., Jr. *Health policy in the United States* (3rd ed.). (2002). Chicago: Health Administration Press.

McDonough, J.E. (2000). *Experiencing politics: A legislator's stories of government and health care.* Berkeley: University of California Press.

Naylor, C.D. (1999). Health care in Canada: Incrementalism under fiscal distress. *Health Affairs 18* (3): 9–26.

Pink, G.H., & Leatt, P. (2002). The use of arms length organizations for health systems change: Some observations by insiders. *Health Policy.* Accepted for publication.

Raffel, M.W. (Ed.). (1997). *Health care and reform in industrialized countries.* University Park, PA: Pennsylvania State University Press.

Shalala, D.E., & Reinhardt, U.E. (1999). Viewing the U.S. health care system from within: Candid talk from HHS. *Health Affairs 18* (3): 47–55.

Starr, P. (2000). Health care reform and the new economy, *Health Affairs 19* (6): 23–32.

Tichy, N.M., & Cohen, E. (1997). *The leadership edge: How winning companies build leaders at every level.* New York: HarperCollins.

Tuohy, C.H. (1999). Dynamics of a changing health sphere: The United States, Britain and Canada. *Health Affairs 18* (3): 114–143.

Zuckerman, A.M. (1998). *Healthcare strategic planning: Approaches for the twenty-first century.* Chicago: Health Administration Press.

Index

AAMC (Association of American Medical Colleges), conflict of interest guidelines, 192–193

ACCJ (American Chamber of Commerce Japan), 190

Accountability: agency costs and, 51; costs of care and treatments, 68–70; definition of, 51; enhancement of mechanisms for, 49–50; for government health care decisions, 50–53; market discipline and, 59, 66–68, 71, 86; monitoring performance and, 57–58, 69, 205; need for explicit goals, 55; political incentives, 57–66; and political voice, 58–59, 70–71; private health insurance and, 66; responsibility for procurement, 53–58. *See also* health care purchasers

ADA (American Dental Association), 89

AdvaMed (Advanced Medical Technology Association), 190–191

Advocacy: civil service and, 11, 12, 79; consumer groups, 171, 173, 174, 177, 179, 199; evaluation of new legislation and regulations, 153–154, 186–187; grassroots campaigns and, 169–170, 175–180, 186, 199, 202; guidelines for government relationships, 206–207; and hospitals, 123–130; impact assessment, 38–39, 154; individual agents of, 77–78; in-house policy advisory groups, 155–156, 186–187, 198–199; international regulations and, 184; media relations and, 80, 126–127, 201–202; and NGOs, 138; proof points, 186–187; public forums and, 183–184; senior management and, 188–189; specific issues, 145–146, 205–206; strategic government relations, 170–176; Web sites, 193; written policy positions, 154, 160, 186–187. *See also* interest groups; lobbyists; public opinion; trade associations; voice, political

Advocacy coalitions, 80, 111–113, 201; Friday Breakfast Group, 165–166. *See also* strategic alliances

AFL-CIO (American Federation of Labor-Congress of Industrial Organizations), 87

AHA (American Hospital Association), 90

Alberta, health boards in, 62

Alliance for Aging, 193

AMA (American Medical Association): and Medicare, 87, 88

About the Editors and Contributors

Peggy Leatt is Professor and Chair of the Department of Health Policy and Administration, in the School of Public Health, University of North Carolina, Chapel Hill. She teaches courses in organizational theory and behavior, and strategic management and marketing. Her research interests are in health services research, organizational culture, design, and behavior in health care organizations. She has published widely in research and professional journals in these areas. She is founding editor and Editor in Chief of *Hospital Quarterly* and *Healthcare Papers*, two prominent Canadian publications.

Peggy Leatt was Professor and Chair of the Department of Health Administration, Faculty of Medicine, at the University of Toronto from 1987 to 1998. She was principal investigator for the Hospital Management Research Unit funded by the Ontario Ministry of Health from 1989 to 1998. She served as a board member (1984–1989) and chair of the board of the Association of University Programs in Health Administration (1987–1988) and a board member (1989–1995) and chair of the board of the Accrediting Commission on Education for Health Services Administration (1993–1994).

From 1998 to 2000 she was seconded from her position at the University of Toronto and appointed as Chief Executive Officer of the Ontario Health Services Restructuring Commission, an independent organization at arm's length from government with the mandate to direct health reform in the province of Ontario, Canada.

Joseph Mapa is President and Chief Executive Officer of Mount Sinai Hospital, Toronto, and Assistant Professor of Health Policy, Management, and Evaluation, Faculty of Medicine, University of Toronto, from which he graduated. He also obtained his M.B.A. from the Joseph L. Rotman School of Management, University of Toronto. He is a Fellow of the Canadian College of Health Service Executives, as well as a Fellow of the American College of Healthcare Executives.

He is the coauthor of three books focusing on the topic of humanistic health care and has written numerous articles on health care management issues. In 1997, Joe was honored to receive the Ontario Regent's Award from the American College of Healthcare Executives for distinguished leadership in the field of health care. In 1998, he received a Literary Award from the Society of Graduates in Health Administration, of which he was formerly President, for his publication on organizational ethics. In 2000, he received the Leadership Achievement Award from the Society of Graduates in Health Administration in recognition of his academic contributions and his leadership in role modeling, lifelong education, and professional redevelopment as a form of adapting to change and environmental trends.

Owen Adams is Assistant Secretary General, Research Policy and Planning, Canadian Medical Association, Ottawa, Canada. He is also Assistant Professor, Adjunct, Department of Community Health and Epidemiology, at Queen's University in Kingston, Ontario. Mr. Adams is a member of the Editorial Panel of *Global Healthcare 2002*, the official publication of the World Medical Association.

Darlene Burgess is Vice President of Corporate Government Affairs for the Henry Ford Health System in Detroit, Michigan. She has had more than twenty years of experience in legislative and regulatory initiatives, and has helped shape federal and state health policy. Ms. Burgess serves on committees of the American Medical Group Association, American Hospital Association, American Medical Association, Premier Institute, and the American Association of Medical Colleges.

Raisa B. Deber is Professor of Health Policy, Department of Health Policy Management and Evaluation, Faculty of Medicine, University of Toronto, Canada. She received her Ph.D. in political science from the Massachusetts Institute of Technology. Professor Deber has lectured and published extensively on Canadian health policy; advised numerous local, provincial, national, and international bodies; and served on editorial boards and review panels.

Kevin Doucette is Program Manager, Strategic Information and Analysis, Research Directorate, Canadian Medical Association, Ottawa, Canada.

Gary L. Filerman is Professor and Director, Health Systems, School of Nursing and Health Studies, Georgetown University, Washington, D.C. His fields of interest are leadership development for health services, health workforce policy, and global health. The Filerman Prize for educational leadership was established in 1996 by the Association of University Programs in Health Administration to honor Dr. Filerman for his many years of service.

Colleen M. Flood is presently Assistant Professor and a member of the Health Law Group in the Faculty of Law, University of Toronto. She practiced law for three years prior to beginning her graduate work. Her primary area of scholarship is in comparative health care policy, public/private financing of health care systems, health care reform, and accountability and governance issues. She is the author of numerous health law articles and book chapters, and has consulted nationally.

Melissa Fruhbeis is Social Research Associate at the Cecil G. Sheps Center for Health Services Research, University of North Carolina at Chapel Hill. Ms. Fruhbeis obtained her M.S.P.H. in health policy analysis at the University of North Carolina at Chapel Hill.

Ginger L. Graham is Group Chairman, Office of the President, Guidant Corporation, in Indianapolis, Indiana. She has responsibility for the activities of Guidant's geographic operations in the United States, Europe, Japan, the Middle East, Africa, and Canada. A native of Springdale, Arkansas, Ms. Graham received a Bachelor of Science in agricultural economics from the University of Arkansas and a Master of Business Administration degree from Harvard University.

Pamela Jeffery is President of the Pamela Jeffery Group, and the founder of the Women's Executive Network, a national speaker series. She has been involved in politics for many years, both provincially and nationally. Ms. Jeffery holds an M.B.A. from the Richard Ivey School of Business at the University of Western Ontario. She is also an Adjunct Professor at the Rotman School of Management, University of Toronto, Canada.

Beaufort B. Longest, Jr. is the M. Allen Pond Professor of Health Policy and Management and Director, Health Policy Institute, Graduate School of Public Health, University of Pittsburgh, Pennsylvania. He is also Professor of Health Services Administration, Joseph M. Katz Graduate School of Business, University of Pittsburgh. Dr. Longest has both published and presented widely and has engaged in major research.

Bruce MacLellan is President of Environics Communications, a North American public affairs consultancy with offices in Toronto, Montreal, Stamford, and Washington, D.C. He has also worked in the provincial and federal levels of government, including time as Chief of Staff to the Minister of National Health in Ottawa.

Mary Jane Mastorovich is Assistant Professor and Graduate Program Coordinator, Health Systems Administration, Georgetown University School of Nursing and Health Studies, Washington, D.C. She has over twenty-five years of experience in the health care field and is a Wharton Fellow in the Program in Management for Nurses.

D. David Persaud is Assistant Professor at the School of Health Services Administration, Dalhousie University, Halifax, Canada. He is a graduate of the doctoral program in health administration from the University of Toronto, Canada. His research interests are in the areas of health services integration, organizational change, and performance measurement.

Thomas C. Ricketts is Professor of Health Policy and Administration and Deputy Director of the Cecil G. Sheps Center for Health Services Research, University of North Carolina at Chapel Hill, where he is Director of the Programs in Health Policy Analysis and Rural Health. He also holds an appointment as Professor in the Program in Public Health Leadership in the UNC-CH School of Public Health and as an Adjunct Professor in the Department of Social Medicine in the UNC School of Medicine.

Gail Warden is President and Chief Executive Officer of Henry Ford Health System in Detroit, Michigan, one of the nation's leading vertically integrated health care systems. Mr. Warden is an elected member of the Institute of Medicine of the National Academy of Sciences, and among his many prestigious appointments, he is Chairman of both the National Forum on Health Care Quality Measurement and Reporting, and the Healthcare Research and Development Institute.

A. Paul Williams is Associate Professor, Department of Health Policy, Management, and Evaluation, Faculty of Medicine, University of Toronto, Canada. He is also affiliated with other academic programs both in Canada and in the United Kingdom. Dr. Williams teaches graduate courses on Canada's health system, and he is a lead investigator on a series of major research projects.